'Challenging current practice models in social work and social care, Payne explores the concepts of citizenship, social work and participative interdependence and skilfully demonstrates how these could – and should – be applied to practice with older people at the end of life. This groundbreaking work is essential reading for practitioners and academics alike.'

– *Sue Taplin, University of Suffolk, UK*

# OLDER CITIZENS AND END-OF-LIFE CARE

Older people are, like younger people, citizens in the communities of the nations in which they live. This book sees ageing as a life journey that incorporates a process of citizening, in which people build their identity as part of their family and community. But the social experience of illness, frailty, disability and reaching the end of life may de-citizen older people by devaluing the social identity that comes from continuing social engagement. We de-citizen older people by emphasizing dependence on services and their cost to public expenditure instead of valuing the interdependence of participation and mutual respect. This book argues that older people retain full citizenship for the whole of their lives, up to the moment of death; but what does this mean for health and social care?

In this groundbreaking book, Malcolm Payne argues that social work with older people must build re-citizening practice strategies in order to value both the common and the special aspects of the citizenship of older people. Current models of social care and social work create dependency, rather than relying on values of participative interdependence. The failure to recognize the end of life as a crucial element in all social care and social work for older people means that the lessons learned in providing palliative and end-of-life care in healthcare have not been transferred to social care, and the priorities of end-of-life care have not been adequately encompassed in social work with older people.

**Malcolm Payne** is Emeritus Professor, Manchester Metropolitan University and Honorary Professor, Kingston University; formerly Director of Psychosocial and Spiritual Care, St Christopher's Hospice, London.

# ROUTLEDGE KEY THEMES IN HEALTH AND SOCIETY

Available titles include:

**Turning Troubles into Problems**
Clientization in human services
*Edited by Jaber F. Gubrium and Margaretha Järvinen*

**Compassionate Communities**
Case studies from Britain and Europe
*Edited by Klaus Wegleitner, Katharina Heimerl & Allan Kellehear*

**Exploring Evidence-based Practice**
Debates and challenges in nursing
*Edited by Martin Lipscomb*

**On the Politics of Ignorance in Nursing and Healthcare**
Knowing ignorance
*Amélie Perron and Trudy Rudge*

Forthcoming titles include:

**Social Theory and Nursing**
*Edited by Martin Lipscomb*

**Identity, Ageing and Cultural Adaptation**
Understanding longevity in crossdisciplinary perspective
*Simon Biggs*

**Empowerment**
A critique
*Kenneth McLaughlin*

**The Story of Nursing in British Mental Hospitals**
Echoes from the corridors
*Niall McCrae and Peter Nolan*

**Living with Mental Disorder**
Insights from qualitative research
*Jacqueline Corcoran*

**A New Ethic of 'Older'**
Subjectivity, surgery and self-stylization
*Bridget Garnham*

**Older Citizens and End-of-Life Care**
Social Work Practice Strategies for Adults in Later Life
*Malcolm Payne*

# OLDER CITIZENS AND END-OF-LIFE CARE

Social Work Practice Strategies for Adults in Later Life

*Malcolm Payne*

LONDON AND NEW YORK

First published 2017
by Routledge
2 Park Square, Milton Park, Abingdon, Oxon OX14 4RN

and by Routledge
711 Third Avenue, New York, NY 10017

*Routledge is an imprint of the Taylor & Francis Group, an informa business*

© 2017 Malcolm Payne

The right of Malcolm Payne to be identified as author of this work has been asserted by him in accordance with sections 77 and 78 of the Copyright, Designs and Patents Act 1988.

All rights reserved. No part of this book may be reprinted or reproduced or utilised in any form or by any electronic, mechanical, or other means, now known or hereafter invented, including photocopying and recording, or in any information storage or retrieval system, without permission in writing from the publishers.

*Trademark notice*: Product or corporate names may be trademarks or registered trademarks, and are used only for identification and explanation without intent to infringe.

*British Library Cataloguing-in-Publication Data*
A catalogue record for this book is available from the British Library

*Library of Congress Cataloging-in-Publication Data*
Names: Payne, Malcolm, 1947- author.
Title: Older citizens and end-of-life care : social work practice strategies for adults in later life / Malcolm Payne.
Description: 1 Edition. | New York : Routledge, 2017. | Includes bibliographical references and index.
Identifiers: LCCN 2016043822 | ISBN 9781409440840 (hardback) | ISBN 9781138288720 (pbk.) | ISBN 9781315572161 (ebook)
Subjects: LCSH: Social work with older people. | Social work with the terminally ill. | Bereavement in old age.
Classification: LCC HV1451 .P396 2017 | DDC 362.17/5--dc23
LC record available at https://lccn.loc.gov/2016043822

ISBN: 978-1-4094-4084-0 (hbk)
ISBN: 978-1-138-28872-0 (pbk)
ISBN: 978-1-315-57216-1 (ebk)

Typeset in Bembo
by Taylor & Francis Books

# CONTENTS

*List of figures* *viii*
*List of tables* *ix*
*Acknowledgements* *x*

Introduction 1

**PART I**
**The role of social work in end-of-life care with older people** **9**

1  The ageing journey and the end of life 11
2  Citizenship processes: Citizening, de-citizening and re-citizening 26
3  Social work and palliative care: Contributions to end-of-life care 42
4  Partnership practice strategies 63
5  Advance care planning 79

**PART II**
**Practice strategies for end-of-life social work with older citizens** **95**

6  Preparing for later life: Adulthood and the third age 97
7  Direct social work with older citizens in the fourth age 117
8  Ageing, end-of-life and bereavement care 140
9  Conclusion: Practice strategies for older people's citizenship 165

*Bibliography* *172*
*Index* *185*

# FIGURES

| | | |
|---|---|---|
| 1.1 | The life journey through ageing towards the end of life | 16 |
| 3.1 | Social work and palliative care contributions to end-of-life care | 43 |
| 4.1 | Social work and palliative care contributions to multiprofessional care | 64 |
| 5.1 | Social work and palliative care contributions to advance care planning | 80 |

# TABLES

| | | |
|---|---|---|
| 1.1 | Transitions in later life | 14 |
| 6.1 | Supported housing | 102 |
| 6.2 | Social and related care provision | 106 |
| 7.1 | Types of abuse of adults at risk | 131 |
| 7.2 | The main types of dementia affecting older people | 135 |
| 8.1 | Euthanasia, assisted dying and related terms | 151 |
| 9.1 | Practice strategies summary | 169 |

# ACKNOWLEDGEMENTS

I acknowledge material derived from previously published papers included in this book, as follows:

Chapter 2: Payne, M. (2013) Applying citizenship social work with older people and people at the end of life. *Azarbe: Revista Internacional de Trabajo Social y Bienestar* 2: 69–79.

Chapter 3: Payne, M. (2014) Exploring meaning in end-of-life care practice. *European Journal of Palliative Care*. 21(5): 240–244.

Payne, M. (2013) Psychological, social and spiritual meaning in palliative care. In Krzyżanowski, D. M., Payne, M. and Fal, A. M. *Ból I Cierpienie – ujęcie interdyscyplinarne. [Pain and Suffering – an interdisciplinary approach.]* Wrocław: Presscom: 165–194.

Chapter 5: Payne, M. (2013) Extending advance care planning over the care career. *European Journal of Palliative Care*. 20(1): 34–37.

Payne, M. (2010) Advance care planning in participative social work practice. *Revista Portugueasa de Pedagogia/Psychologica*. Numero Conjunto Comemorativo 30 Anos, 2010: 105–119.

Chapter 8: Payne, M. (2015) Assisted dying: Moral panic or moral issue? In Smith, M. (ed.) *Moral Regulation*. Bristol: Policy Press: 57–68.

# INTRODUCTION

How long are you going to live? Another way of asking this question is: when are you going to die? None of us can know the answer to these questions, however you ask them; but for many of us statistics suggest that it will be longer than our parents' generation and perhaps longer than we expected when we were children. What are we going to do with that longer life? How are we going to live it? Perhaps we will live longer than we want: in many societies across the world, people are talking more about assisted suicide when they become old and ill. So there are important questions to ask about how we are going to live with ageing and death in societies across the world, and social workers are going to be part of people rethinking social assumptions about ageing and death. We have to equip ourselves and the social care services to be part of this job of rethinking.

The UK Office for National Statistics (2015) summarized the average length of lives in the UK with statistics covering the years 2012–2014 as follows:

- A newborn baby boy could expect to live 79.1 years and a newborn baby girl 82.8 years if mortality rates remain the same as they were in the United Kingdom in 2012–2014 throughout their lives.
- In 2012–2014, a man in the UK aged 65 had an average further 18.4 years of life remaining and a woman had an average further 20.9 years of life remaining.
- The most common age at death for men was 86 and for women was 89.
- Life expectancy at birth in the UK has increased since 1980–1982 by 13.5 weeks per year on average for men and 9.8 weeks per year on average for women (Office for National Statistics, 2015).

Factual statements like this do not tell us anything about how people live these lives at any stage of the ageing process. These particular statistics tell us nothing about the changes that have taken place in ageing over the lives of people who are currently reaching later life or the changes that they will see in the future. People's perceptions of ageing, either in society in general or among people in later life, are relevant to how older people see themselves and how they live in society. Such generalized information also tells us nothing about inequalities between different groups of older people. Inequalities among people in later life are particularly important to health and social care services. This is because preventive services may need to do more to improve the factors that contribute to ill-health and social difficulties in later life. Also, services for older people adversely affected by unequal life outcomes may need to do more, although work to improve everyone's health and social care is important too.

What these simple statistics do tell us, however, is something about the extent of the task, and alongside that the importance of consistency of our concern and our provision over quite a long slice of people's lives. If you take 65 years of age as a marker of the starting point of older age groups, as pension policies and public services in many countries do, social workers with older people can expect to be working with people over about 20 years or more of their lives, and that period is likely to rise over the next years and decades. Looking at these figures the other way, social workers with older people can expect to be helping people at the end of their lives from around their mid-80s onwards. This book asks: what is the implication for the way in which they organize their practice of these realities about dying in old age?

This book aims to help social work practitioners and students who work with older people take responsibility for and work with the personal and social significance of the end of life in later life. It also presents an approach to social work with older people that integrates end-of-life care throughout their care career; this is not yet commonplace in social care services. Instead, we are still concentrating on operating person-centred care planning systems, when it is also important to help with the human and family consequences of ageing and the end of life.

Integrating social care with healthcare is an important policy objective in the UK and relevant to practice anywhere. Part of this is an aim to develop social care involvement in end-of-life care (National End of Life Care Programme, 2010). Again, this is relevant to social work and healthcare practice everywhere, since end-of-life care is important for many healthcare systems across the world; it is also a firm objective of the World Health Organization (World Health Organization, 1998). So a book about social work practice with older people that incorporates end-of-life care connects with and emphasizes current trends.

I also advocate a citizenship social work with older people. Marshall and Tibbs's (2006) analysis of citizenship social work with older people is well established in social work. It emphasizes the importance of their participation in every aspect of human living in their society including, but not limited to, decision-making about their care. But we need to go further than that, recognizing the complex ways in which citizenship is both lost and also built up in social processes. Our practice is part of the process that can help to develop rights towards fuller citizenship for older people. In Chapter 2, I argue for a practice to:

- oppose de-citizening older people by taking away their human rights;
- re-citizen their lives by building on their human rights to a successful later life leading to their dying well.

My account of social work with older people (Payne, 2012) took up citizenship ideas because they implement my analysis of social work as a humanistic enterprise (Payne, 2011). This puts our recognition of the humanity and human rights of all the people that social work serves at the centre of our practice.

It is no longer possible to practise social work with older people adequately within the professional roles allocated to social workers by community social care services, hospitals and hospices. Instead, social workers must return to their profession's historic aims to be a part of a community that responds to and cares for older fellow citizens. To do the best job for people as they age, we have to help everyone, no matter how young, grapple with thinking about and planning for ageing and the end of life. We certainly have to help older citizens move with grace and forethought towards their death. You lose rights if you do not plan to retain and build them. Social workers must also act as citizens to be part of the citizenry. It is not enough to do the jobs of assessing older people and their carers to decide what public services are to be allotted them. It is not enough just to pick up social needs generated by ill-health or by the need for safeguarding older people against abuse and neglect. These established professional service roles are valuable, but social workers also need to bring their understanding of people's experiences in later life into the community. We all make our own journey through ageing, and social workers can help everyone plan to age well as they travel their path through life. And ageing well also means dying well, because dying is an important part of the journey in old age, and therefore an important part of the journey of the family and community around the person who dies.

We need major change to provide a good quality of life for all older people that enables them to die well. People sometimes talk about 'a good death' but dying is a process that goes on for some time, not an event that takes a few hours, so I prefer to talk about 'dying well'. Such changes in services are needed across the world, because most societies are experiencing an increase in the proportion of older people in their populations. It is welcome that many people live a longer and more valuable life; part of that life is dying well. Dying well means having lived your life well.

On the other side of the equation, people worry about current assumptions about care for older people. Can we live a working life, finance our later life and make a place in our lives to care for older people in our family and community? Is it impossible to age and die well and to find the care that we might need to do so? Pickard (2015) estimates that the demand in the UK for help by unpaid carers who are adult children of older people with disabilities will exceed supply in 2017, and by 2032 that there will be a shortfall of 160,000 carers. New technology that enables surveillance for older people's security and provides support for their needs in their own homes will bridge some of that gap. But responding to care needs disclosed by new technology will still rest on families and communities. It is not clear that improvements in technology are the full answer the older people's care needs, and it is clear that human caring is still going to be in the front line.

Governments are concerned about how the state should respond to the social pressures that the demographic turn to longer life will create. It may render traditional patterns of the life course and care within it inadequate, because a 'care deficit' (Hochschild, 1995) means that we can never provide enough care. One reason is that care for older people requires significant state provision. Paying for care in the market is impossible for people who are unfortunate enough to be among the minority who need the most extensive services. Current social policy relying on neo-liberal economic thinking denies this reality, and consequently accepts inadequate policy and services which, in turn, makes relying on present care practices insecure.

But that is not the most important reason why there will always be a deficit in the provision of care. To understand this, we must think about how most people would like to live in their old age, and how they would like to die. A UK study of older people's views about the services they receive when they have 'high support needs' (Katz *et al.*, 2011) makes it clear that we can do more to maintain people's citizenship by promoting good relationships in their families and communities and helping them remain in control of as much as possible of their life experience. Most people would prefer to live a generous period of healthy old age in a familiar home in the community where they have emotional ties in longstanding relationships, and they hope to die fairly quickly in reasonable comfort, preferably in the security of their own home, surrounded and cared for by people whom they love and who value and respect them. The reality is that many people experience a long period of declining health and fitness, cared for 24/7 by a spouse or partner. Other family members may be unable to provide much care either because they are themselves ageing or because of family and work commitments, which may also mean they live at a distance. Many people die after a health problem during which they are admitted to hospital in an emergency and they die in a busy ward without the serenity that we might wish to have in our last hours. Alternatively, they are discharged without much planning to a care or nursing home that they would not have chosen and where they die shortly afterwards.

## Building end-of-life care into social work with older people: Practice strategies

Part I of this book shows how social workers have important social roles and valuable practice skills to offer older people who are approaching the end of life. Social work has made a big contribution to the specialist areas of end-of-life and palliative care, which have several decades of experience in working with dying and bereaved people, their families and carers. Social workers working with older people can learn from that specialist experience.

You may feel inhibited in building up end-of-life care by the workload of the main social work role in services for older people. Good assessment for person-centred care planning is important for the justice and quality of social care for older people. But practitioners feel the constant slog of targets for completing the bureaucratic requirements for providing and organizing services within the seriously underfunded social care systems. It seems like a constant struggle to do something meaningful to help carers where older people are struggling themselves with physical frailty and encroaching psychological, social and spiritual problems. A few years ago I was involved in a number of projects where teams of social workers in UK social care services for older people were encouraged to work on end-of-life care issues with their existing caseloads. Many practitioners were extremely cautious: how could they possibly take on these difficult issues as well as meet their targets for completing assessments, and difficult safeguarding issues? Some were fearful of being unable to deal with powerful emotions of grief and anxiety that might go with working with people who are dying. Some were also ambitious. This was what they had come into social work to do: not just care planning and service delivery, important though it is to do these tasks well, but helping people make the best of living well, even in poverty and struggle. And making the best of dying well, in spite of the hindrances to it.

Three important aspects of making those projects work were, first, a commitment from senior management downwards to supporting their staff in taking on that additional burden; second, additional training from experienced practitioners in end-of-life care to help them feel confident in doing this work; and, third, the end-of-life pathway introduced by the National End of Life Care programme, which helped them conceptualize their role in the range of services available for people as they approach the end of life. Many of these points are discussed in detail in the programme's guide on social work at the end of life (National End of Life Care Programme, 2012).

Special projects may help to introduce new services, but can seem out of reach to practitioners struggling with everyday pressures. So I emphasize the idea of developing practice strategies to manage your work, while taking end-of-life care into your practice with older people. *A practice strategy is a plan for implementing social work practice tasks so as to meet additional valued aims in social work.* Not just any old aim set by an agency following some government policy, then, but aims that incorporate important human objectives in social work.

Going about your normal business as a practitioner working with older people, you can help them have a better quality of life if you are alert to end-of-life issues, aware of situations in which end-of-life issues are often raised, and prepared to be active in responding to end-of-life issues. This helps citizening, because planning for the end of life is a crucial part of a high quality of life. If an older person misses out on it, they are not achieving their full potential as fellow citizens. This is true of many aspects of social work practice which are not in the centre of our formal responsibilities, but are present in many people's lives. It is easy to forget about them, or miss what you *might* do in the pressure of what you *must* do. But if you are alert, aware and active about an issue, such as end-of-life care, that can be very important personally to older people, their carers and families. You will often help them think through and improve upon their own management of the life-stage that they are negotiating.

In this book, therefore, I don't aim to give you a picture of or guidelines for practice with older people in general. Rather, I want to help you form strategies for yourself in your existing practice so that you can take on end-of-life care issues without that adding a burden to your main responsibilities. You are probably confident you can do the basic professional job well, and there are many useful books, journals and websites that will help you – see the 'Additional resources' at the end of this and every chapter. You will certainly be pressed and perhaps helped by colleagues and managers to carry out your responsibilities for person-centred, self-directed care competently. It can seem a difficult extra to take on end-of-life care. Partly, this is because end-of-life care is an area that many people, including many social workers, find thinking and talking about emotionally demanding. The emotional responses, hopelessness, tears, grief, depression and fear of confronting the unknown, make us all shy away from dying and bereavement. Yet often it is only social workers who are prepared to do the emotional labour, and ask the hard questions about feelings that people find difficult to struggle with. Only social workers have the skills and confidence to help people work their way through these struggles. It is a strong aspect of what social work can offer older people, their families, carers and the community around them. That is, it can be if you develop the confidence to use those skills in end-of-life care and to wind yourself up to use them when you see it as necessary. So my aim in this book is to help you create a strategy to include end-of-life care into your practice with older people.

My primary experience of social work with older people and in end-of-life care is in the UK, but I have taught about both in many countries, including Canada, the Czech Republic, Finland, Italy, Korea, Poland, Slovakia and the US. I am conscious that the national systems of social care services, and the settings in which we practise, affects how we practise. Research and professional development, though, is international, and we must try to present ideas and information so that colleagues everywhere can translate them to use in their own cultural, legal and professional setting (Payne and Askeland, 2008). When I describe UK or English policy and practice on social care with older people and in end-of-life care, I have taken care to emphasize those elements that chime with policy in most developed countries and that are relevant to less developed countries, following the World Health Organization policy that end-of-life care should be an element of health and social care everywhere. Harding (2008) argues that although end-of-life care may seem a low priority when compared with curing acute illness or preventing accident and injury, it is a moral responsibility to provide it where needed. How could we not make the social care contribution, if it is of value? Social work can make a valid and important contribution to end-of-life care everywhere, even if services have poor resources and work pressures to face.

The pressures and underfunding of our current social care systems and the care deficit mean that the social work professional practitioner needs to go out into the community and accept the additional role of helping everyone prepare and plan for ageing and the end of life. Only that will put older people, their families, carers and communities in the position to age and die well. That must be the ultimate citizening aim of any social work service for older people, their carers, families and communities.

## Plan of the book

This book is divided into two parts. The Introduction and Chapters 1–5 analyse the contribution that social work can make to end-of-life care for older people, and discuss what they can draw from the experience of specialist end-of-life and palliative care services. Chapter 1 introduces the idea of the 'ageing journey', to help provide a structure for our thinking about our role and contribution in every stage of ageing. Subsequent chapters explore each of my themes: citizenship and shared human care as an essential part of it (Chapter 2), the contribution of social work and end-of-life care services (Chapter 3), the importance of multiprofessional and multiagency service provision (Chapter 4) and the value of advance care planning (Chapter 5). These chapters set out the principles of citizenship social work with older people approaching the end of life.

The second part of the book, Chapters 6–8, looks at what provision and practice resemble if they focus on full citizenship for older people throughout their lives. These chapters draw out practice strategies for incorporating end-of-life care into social work with older people in ways that promote citizening. Chapter 6 brings together social action that is needed in the childhood and adulthood phases of life to enhance the citizenship of older people as they approach the end of life. I look at social education for young people in ageing, death and dying and preparation for ageing in adulthood. Chapter 7 examines the third and fourth ages and how social work can contribute to successful citizenship in ageing and in the approach to the end of life. Chapter 8 looks at social care and social work practice in end-of-life care services and in bereavement care.

Chapter 9 brings together the themes and practice strategies, looking forward to creating the policy, services and professional practice we will need for older people to age and die well.

## Conclusion

Thinking about the citizenship of our sisters and brothers who are living their later lives means valuing their life and their end-of-life experiences, enabling them to live well and to die well. It is easy to see older people and the social reality of the growing population as a burden on the economy, on our social relationships and on our public services. But they are citizens alongside us, so we must find ways of organizing our society, providing our public services and offering support and care where necessary for everyone to live their lives and their deaths well.

## ADDITIONAL RESOURCES

### Books

Payne, M. (2012) *Citizenship Social Work with Older People*. Chicago, IL: Lyceum; Opole, Poland: Opole University Press; Bristol: Policy Press.
A general text presenting my humanistic citizenship approach to working with older people. This current book is a follow-up incorporating end-of-life care more prominently into that approach.

Reith, M. and Payne, M. (2009) *Social Work in End-of-life and Palliative Care*. Chicago, IL: Lyceum; Bristol: Policy Press.
A general text introducing social work in a range of end-of-life care roles and settings. This current book develops ideas presented there by focusing on the needs of older people at the end of life.

Other general social work texts on social work with older people that may be helpful are presented in alphabetical order of first author, as follows:

Crawford, K. and Walker, J. (2008) *Social Work with Older People*, 2nd edn. Exeter: Learning Matters.
Greene, R. R. (2008) *Social Work with the Aged and Their Families*. New York: Aldine.
Greene, R. R., Cohen, H. L. and Galambus, C. M. (2007) *Foundations of Social Work in the Field of Aging: A competency-based approach*. Washington, DC: NASW Press.
Hall, D. and Scragg, T. (2012) *Social Work with Older People: Approaches to person-centred practice*. Maidenhead: Open University Press.
Harris, J. and Tanner, D. (2007) *Working with Older People*. London: Routledge.
Kaplan, D. and Berkman, B. (eds) (2015) *Oxford Handbook of Social Work in Health and Aging*, 2nd edn. New York: Oxford University Press.
Lymbery, M. (2005) *Social Work with Older People: Context, policy and practice*. London: Sage.
Lynch, R. (2014) *Social Work Practice with Older People: A positive person-centred approach*. London: Sage.
McDonald, A. (2010) *Social Work with Older People*. Cambridge: Polity Press.
McInniss-Dittrich, K. (2013) *Social Work with Older Adults*, 4th edn. New York: Pearson.
Ray, M., Bernard, M. and Phillips, J. (2009) *Critical Issues in Social Work with Older People*. Basingstoke: Palgrave Macmillan.
Ray, M. and Phillips, J. (2012) *Social Work with Older People*, 5th edn. Basingstoke: Palgrave Macmillan.
Richardson, V. E. and Barusch, A. S. (2010) *Gerontological Practice for the Twenty-first Century: A social work perspective*. New York: Columbia University Press.

Youdin, R. (2014) *Clinical Gerontological Social Work Practice.* New York: Springer.

In addition, for more critical analysis of changes in the adult social care system for older people in the UK, offering policy analysis from the practitioner perspective:

Lymbery, M. and Postle, K. (2015) *Social Work and the Transformation of Adult Social Care: Perpetuating a distorted vision?* Bristol: Policy Press.

## Websites

The Organisation for Economic Co-operation and Development (OECD) has an extensive programme of work in social issues, with many interesting publications available on this website, including work on pensions and on the future of families, which includes family support for each other:
http://www.oecd.org/social/

Official statistics websites, where you can find out about population and population changes are as follows, comparing different countries with your own:
UK (Office for National Statistics): http://www.ons.gov.uk/ons/index.html.

Eurostat (for information about European issues): http://ec.europa.eu/eurostat/ and click on 'Regional and social conditions'.
US: http://www.infoplease.com/ipa/A0004920.html.
Australia: http://www.abs.gov.au/websitedbs/c311215.nsf/web/People+@+a+Glance (this takes you to the 'people at a glance' pages).
Statistics Canada: http://www.statcan.gc.ca/start-debut-eng.html (click on 'browse by subject').
New Zealand: http://www.stats.govt.nz/browse_for_stats.aspx (this takes you to the 'browse for stats' pages).

# PART I
# The role of social work in end-of-life care with older people

# 1

# THE AGEING JOURNEY AND THE END OF LIFE

In this chapter, I set out the main themes of the book:

- Seeing ageing as a journey through life which we all follow.
- Understanding that the end of life is part of that journey, even a culmination of it.
- Identifying practice strategies for social work with older people in later life as they move towards the end of life.
- How the idea of citizenship social work encapsulates those strategies.

## Main themes

Over the first half of the 21st century, rethinking services for older people is going to be an important priority in many countries. Why? Because during that period the number and proportion of older people in the world population will increase naturally as a result of people living longer. This will affect most countries, although the patterns of change vary. As we saw in the Introduction, population data and projections for the future can offer an idea of the changes that we can expect, but do not tell us about their social and personal consequences. It is useful to build on that with information specifically about ageing. We can put information about our own country in context by using international variations to compare the impact of population structures in different countries. I have listed some accessible sources to help you do this at the end of this chapter.

One often-mentioned statistic is the ratio of older people dependent on younger people who can support them economically. This indicates the pressures on a society better than information about simple increases in the proportion of older people in the population. This is because it indicates the ease with which a national economy can support its older people. For example, the UK is likely to have a higher proportion of adults of younger working age to support its rising number of older people than many other European countries and Japan because of immigration in recent decades. Migrants are more likely to be younger and have larger families than more established populations, and so are more likely to contribute to the ability of an economy to support older people in its population. Some unwarranted assumptions lie behind statistics like this, however. For example, focusing on this 'dependency ratio' could wrongly imply that people in later life are dependent economically and in other ways on younger people or that economic factors are the main things we should be thinking about when we consider older people's lives or services for them.

As a result of population changes, a fairly settled view (a 'political and social settlement') of the role and social position of older people in many societies is inevitably changing. This book proposes that social work practice in social care services needs to change by including older people's approach to the end of life.

In doing so, I address a failing in social care policy for older people. Social care policy often sees them as part of the administrative category 'adults'. As a result, we do not focus on particular needs and interests of people who are in later life. Most policy on ageing emphasizes their social and healthcare needs, rather than broader aspects of their role in social life. The result is that older people are in a policy ghetto focused on problems they present to state social and healthcare services. I argue that policy should aim to enhance their lives in the same way that policies for children aim to enhance their development, or promote employment for young people, or good housing for families. Policies for older people should start from enhancing the experience of ageing and older age groups and increase the opportunities available for a positive lifestyle and well-being for older people. We should not start with the problems they present to our services.

Why does policy fail older people? We used to see old age as a 'threshold' category, but this is now inappropriate. To explain: people reached the threshold of becoming a pensioner or a 'senior'. In their early 60s, they stepped over thresholds from working life and from being in the centre of their family. Soon, they would step over another threshold: decline towards death, in their mid to late 60s. For a while, when Western market economies required it, some people retired from work in their 50s or even earlier, either willingly, accepting generous retirement packages to free opportunities for younger people or reduce employment costs, or unwillingly, as industrial change and decline wiped out their work. They also began, with medical advance and healthier lifestyles, to live longer. Retirement stretched into many people's 80s. Some older people experienced a long period of poor health before reaching death at an advanced age. Medicine became better at keeping people alive and maintaining their independence even though they suffered from long-term disabilities or health conditions. Well-off people could enjoy a life of leisure pursuits. Others, perhaps less publicized but more common, found that they scraped a less exciting existence.

How we see the end of life thus becomes more important to people in later life, because the thresholds between work and family life to a later life and then from old age into death have become separated and we have created a new stage of life. The early stages of old age are now an extension of normal living. It becomes clearer that later old age is about the process of coming to the point of dying. Without the opportunities that a happy retirement on a reasonable income can offer, this extended end-of-life process can seem interminable to poorer people who are frail and ill. Longer periods of ill-health and increasing disability and longer periods of an existence with little worthwhile achievement both suggested that it would be worth being able to make the choice to decide to end life; hence, the rise of concern with assisted dying, helping people to take their lives if they seemed worthless. Later life seemed an increasingly long prelude to end of life.

Reflecting the change in the political and social settlement for older people, the first part of this book identifies and builds upon five main themes in services for older people at the end of life that are relevant to social work practice. They are:

1. *Ageing and the end of life are positive parts of our journey through a total life experience.* Provision for older people must enhance their journey through their whole life, not be a separate service 'delivered' to meet 'needs' defined by other people's assumptions about, and focused on, their health and social care needs.
2. *Older people are citizens.* Therefore, services for them must emerge from their citizenship, starting from valuing older people as participants in their communities. If we devalue ageing and older people, we de-citizen them and take away some of their citizenship. As a result, we should aim to be positive about the value of older people in our society and of positive opportunities for them. If they have lost value we must re-citizen them.
3. *Care is part of a wider positive policy for older people, including social care and end-of-life care.* Care is not an optional add-on. It is a natural part of human relationships. We see care as central to children's development and essential between husbands and wives and life partners. It must therefore be a significant element of provision for older people. We should not see care through a 'provision of services' lens, but recognize it as a valuable aspect of relationships in later life in the same way as it is for all other age groups. This means focusing on care as part of essential social and community relations, not as a substitute service to deal with social and health problems. Incorporating dying well into later life is part of mutual care in our social relationships, not something to be denied and avoided. This reflects the reality that dying is closer to older people than most of us, and caring in later life must be included in our citizening and in services for older people.
4. *Health and social care services should be multiprofessional and community focused.* Although I focus in this book on social work practice, it can only exist as part of wider services, connected with other professionals and the services they work in and with the needs of the community of older people and their families.
5. *Advance care planning is crucial in end-of-life care and social care for ageing people.* Because planning for social relationships and end-of-life care in older age groups enhances choice, opportunity and well-being, it is integral to citizening. Older people benefit from planning for their social relationships as they age and so that they can die well.

Each of these positives suggests services for and professional work with older people must be as life enhancing as services and professional help for children, families and all the other people social and healthcare provide for. We are too often stuck in the assumption that old age is a less important phase of life: vitality comes from work and family responsibilities in adult life, but in later life death will not long be postponed. Instead we must provide for a valued and valid later life, leading to opportunities to die well. In this chapter, I want to explain my reasons for emphasizing these themes. If we think of older people as citizens, they must be able to contribute to society, not just take from it, and the important characteristics of their stage of life must be provided for. Among those important characteristics is appropriate provision for the end of life. I start from the idea of ageing towards the end of life as a journey, and in subsequent chapters in the first part of the book, I look at the other themes.

## The concept of 'journey'

Most people are ambivalent about ageing and they may see death as a final end to life. This is so even if they believe – for example, through commitment to the Christian, Hindu and Islamic faiths and other religions – that some aspect of their continuing identity such as a spirit or a soul continues beyond death. Ageing is not a good thing in many people's eyes; they resist it or see it as bringing them problems. Western culture values youth; becoming older is not valued. Neo-liberal and capitalist societies see the working life, personal independence and individualistic competition in markets as natural forms of human society, devaluing non-work time and cooperative and mutual forms of support in life. This neglects the role of care for others in human relationships as also a natural form of human relationships. Most people see living as an individual and personal journey through society. Death is not-life, the opposite of living, the end of the journey.

All of this means we do not value ageing and dying well as part of the journey that defines our humanity and identity. Yet, we all age and we all die, so old age and dying are parts of life like our childhood, our teenage period, our adulthood, our work life and our midlife. All of these phases of human experience contribute to the happiness or dissatisfaction that we experience as we live. Until we have died, we continue to have experiences, and that includes the process of dying. By seeing old age and dying as part of everyone's human journey, we are saying that it is possible as human beings to make the best of this part of our lives. Robertson (2014) emphasizes how by identifying important transitions in later life, we can see this as a positive journey like the earlier stages of our lives. By thinking about the transitions we may make in later life, we can also avoid thinking of later life as marked by chronological age – the number of years we have lived. In the past, we have thought of the retirement age as marking the beginning of old age; but this marker is shifting upwards and in any case does not reflect physical changes that affect older people. And the physical changes do not reflect changes in expectations, or the social life that we lead. When people call 70 the new 50, comparing the physical and psychological experience now with the experience a couple of generations ago, they are identifying changes in the cultural experience of ageing.

While Robertson's (2014) focus on transitions is useful, therefore, in not seeing these changes too negatively, he reflects common social attitudes about later life. In Table 1.1,

**TABLE 1.1** Transitions in later life

| *Robertson's transitions in later life* | *Ways of living through transitions in later life* |
| --- | --- |
| Retirement | Creating and achieving new personal development and education goals |
| Moving home | Creating a secure and positive environment for living, even if there are limitations |
| Becoming a grandparent | Building respectful relationships with your children as parents and maintaining new contact with young people |
| Relationship breakdown | Making new relationships and social connections |
| Becoming a carer | Valuing caring and helping roles |
| Bereavement | Memorializing important aspects of past relationships and incorporating them into a new lifestyle |
| Acquiring a long-term health condition | Managing health conditions successfully |
| Entering a care environment | Creating a new lifestyle in care |
| Preparing for the end of life | Completing life tasks and relationships |

*Source*: adapted from Robertson (2014)

therefore, I list important transitions that he identifies, and attach some of the positive aspects of living that can emerge from them.

Just as we experienced caring in childhood, between adult partners, friends and relatives throughout that life journey, so we should value care when it appears as part of ageing and completing that journey in dying. Helping professions, such as social work, and informal carers among family and friends should aim to contribute to the best age and dying experiences. This is important because their care is an integral part of the society and the community caring within these aspects as well as throughout our life journey. Social care and social work should avoid dealing only with the problems of ageing and end-of-life care. Instead, they should contribute to a society that cares about providing for ageing and dying well.

In Figure 1.1, I have set out 'ages' of the life journey, picking up a commonly used concept. Here, later life is divided into a third and fourth age.

Although Shakespeare and many other writers have talked about the phases that people go through in life as 'ages', there are problems with doing so. As our cultural experience of chronological age has changed, so too has our experience of phases of ageing. 'Phases' can become too prescriptive. We might come to think that everybody lives their life according to these phases. We might even come to act on the assumption that they *should* live their life in this way and there is something wrong with them if they don't. A general problem with calling such phases of life 'ages' is that they become attached to people's chronological age. Consequently, we might not only assume that people do or should live their lives in the same order, but they do or should reach each phase at a particular age or stage of life.

To take these general criticisms further, recent conceptualizations of later life, particularly the idea of the 'third age', are contested. Laslett (1996) formulated the idea of a 'third age' of life in which older people developed active and fulfilling lifestyles unconnected with their employment. This idea originally comes from the French 'universities of the third age' in which older people come together to share their learning and experience and renew their education, not focusing on preparation for work, but taking up education as a fulfilling experience. These have grown into a worldwide movement. There is also a connection with Pifer and Bronte's (1986) 'third quarter' of life, which includes changing attitudes to work in the chronological age period of 50–75 years. Another connection is with Neugarten's (1974) distinction between the 'young-old', who remain active, and the 'old-old', who become more dependent on health and social care.

The 'third age' idea proposes that retirement or other changes in middle age, such as children leaving home to begin independent lives, offered people opportunities and 'agency' – that is, psychological and social control – to put new ideas about how they wanted to live their lives into action. Many people receiving health and social care services feel that maintaining control of their life experience as they aged was important, even when they had 'high support needs' requiring a lot of health and social care provision (Katz et al., 2011). The opportunity to fulfil personal aspirations fits with ideas about having a positive later life, and has similarly been very attractive in public and policy debate. Seeing this phase of life positively, however, raises an immediate problem because it pushes dependency, difficulties, illness and disability into a 'fourth age' which can then be seen negatively, containing all the stereotypes of a decrepit old age (Baltes, 1998). In reality, people often move into and out of temporary incapacity. Also, dependence should not inevitably be seen negatively. It might be better to see dependence in later life as a growth of interdependence through enhanced

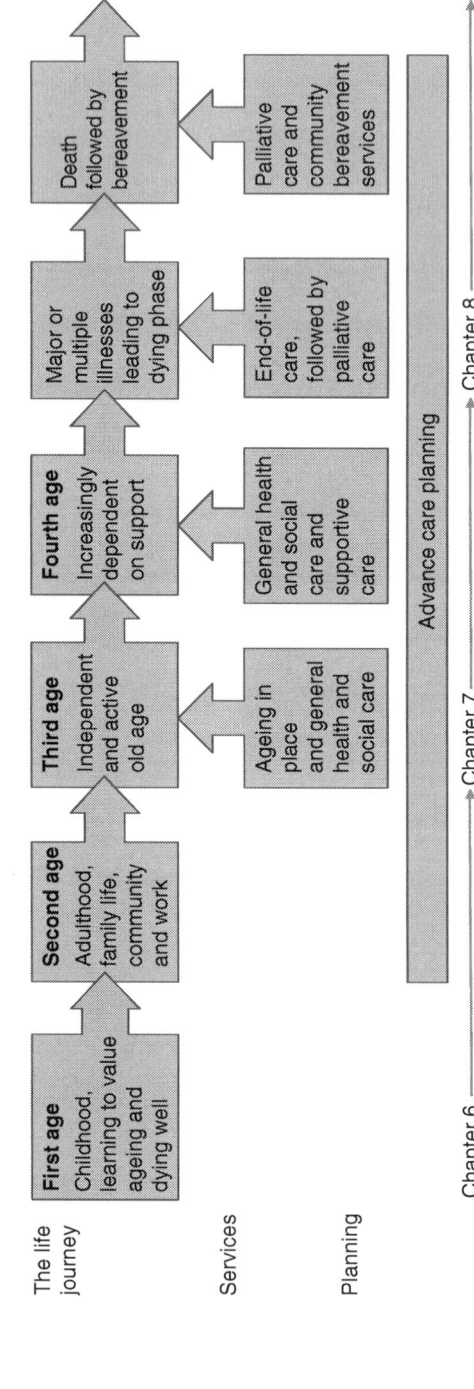

**FIGURE 1.1** The life journey through ageing towards the end of life

relationships in marriage or with children and grandchildren, and it may be a positive experience for everyone involved.

Thinking about a third age as a positive period of active old age also raises sociological issues. Phases such as the 'young-old' and the 'third age' arise because they are relevant to discourses in society about issues that are in public or at least academic debate. One debate has been about whether people's lives have been extended by medical and social advance at the expense of longer phases of illness and disability. Laslett (1996) was concerned about social responses to the changes in demography that have led to longer life. Gilleard and Higgs (2002) note that experiencing a third age may be a characteristic of 'well-off ageing' lived only by middle-class people with good incomes and pensions, and not by working-class and poorer people. It may also refer only to a cohort of ageing people in Western societies, born after World War II, who experienced a childhood of economic growth and a life protected by generous social provision without the social disruption of war and social conflict. This cohort is comparing its experience of ageing with previous more troubled and poorer generations. Political debate about intergenerational conflict also connects with these ideas, in particular the sense that the present generation of 'baby boomers' has benefited from the economic and political stability of the latter part of the 20th century, to the disadvantage of younger generations (Bristow, 2015). Such debates lead us to understand analyses about images of ageing and later life as a cultural construct (Featherstone and Wernick, 1995; Gilleard and Higgs, 2000). Later life and old age are created by political debate, marketing, and deeper stereotypes and fears of social relationships such as personal independence and dependence on others. Social values such as the value of youth and the youthful body, and fear of the ageing body are also relevant and affect how others see us and how we see ourselves (Blaikie, 2008; Ylänne, 2012; Gilleard and Higgs, 2013).

In spite of the difficulties, understanding the third and fourth ages as cultural interpretations through which we develop images of later lives is useful. This is because it helps us to see ageing as containing positive social experience. That is what I want to concentrate on in this book; and in particular I want to say that rather than see the fourth age as one of increasing decline, I formulate it as a period of opportunity to pursue a successful phase in the end of life. Another advantage of employing the ages concept is the possibility of using our cultural understanding of ageing as a positive basis for successfully dealing with the disadvantages and difficulties of ageing.

In Figure 1.1, therefore, I start with childhood, the first age. Our policy aims in this phase of the development of our personality and cultural understanding should include young people learning to appreciate people in their later life and to value ageing and dying well. Citizening involves educating fellow citizens to appreciate and value others' citizenship, so young people should learn about and value ageing and dying as phases of life. Fear and avoidance should be reduced through young people experiencing contact with people in these phases of life. We can achieve this through their family lives, by enabling children to encounter older people and build successful relationships with grandparents and older relatives and members of their communities. They also need to encounter death and learn to participate in dying and bereavement processes.

In adulthood, their second age, people live as part of families and communities and often they also work. No services concerned with ageing are required; but during this stage it is helpful to their older self if people think and plan for ageing and the end of life. They may be helped in doing so by engagement with an older generation in their families and communities who are experiencing the later stages of ageing and approaching the end of life. This enables them to plan to avoid de-citizening loss of opportunities and devaluation in later life. In the third age, they are in old age and living active and independent lives. Social provision at this stage is mainly focused on facilitating their ageing in a positive pattern of social relations and in their place in a community, maintaining their citizenship. They may also increasingly be calling on health and social care services. Social work contributions concerned with ageing and the end of life during the first three ages is dealt with in Chapter 6 of this book.

It is useful in their third age, a period of active life in retirement, if people's engagement during the first and second ages with ageing and the end of life moves even more strongly towards active planning and preparation for the fourth age. In the fourth age, people become increasingly dependent on help and support from outside their immediate family. This is mainly provided by ordinary health and social care services; but where they have identifiable serious illnesses, they may be receiving 'supportive care', which helps them to deal with the psychological and social consequences of their condition. This avoids de-citizening that comes about when illness and disability cuts people off from community social relations. Social work practice concerned with ageing and the end-of-life third and fourth ages is dealt with in Chapter 7.

After this phase of their lives, people develop either a major life-threatening illness or several minor illnesses whose combined effect is to limit their lifestyle. They may eventually come to be regarded as having 'high support needs', often combining social care needs with multiple long-term health conditions and an increasing range and intensity of services (Katz *et al.*, 2011; National Institute for Health and Care Excellence, 2015). Providers of health and social care become aware that they are likely to die within the next 12 months and shift their support to providing end-of-life care. Our aim here should be citizening – that is, maintaining social rights and participation in community and family. A 'dying phase' follows, in which their social relations are seriously affected by their health conditions, and they and those close to them are aware of the likelihood that they will die within a period of days or weeks. Intense health and social care support may be required at this time. Finally, their death occurs, followed, for some people close to them, by experiences of grief and bereavement. Information and some bereavement care support may be required. Citizening is equally important in all of these aspects of the end of life. Social work practice concerned with ageing and the end of life during this period of increasing ill-health and disability and with the dying phase, death and bereavement care is dealt with in Chapter 8.

Building on their early planning in childhood and adulthood, advance care planning is required at every stage of this journey because it maintains and enhances citizenship to plan for your future life, and because this increases the possibility of maintaining control over what happens to you.

The phases of this journey form the structure of the second part of this book, as we look successively at social work practice within a wider policy on ageing in each phase. The idea of ageing as a journey complements the National End of Life Care Programme pathway approach to integrating services and professional practice in end-of-life care. One of the important reasons for focusing on the ageing journey is that the pathway approach focuses on services, professionals and organization, while the concept of journey focuses on the changing needs of the older person and their carers. I think this puts the emphasis where it ought to be. It also broadens the focus from the end-of-life care phase to ageing and dying well as a part of life, and I think that's where the emphasis ought to be as well.

## The idea of practice strategies

In each of these chapters, I identify 'practice strategies' for developing social work contributions to the ageing and later life, and I bring these together in Chapter 9.

What is a practice strategy? How is it different from an approach or a procedure or a method or a theory? And why use a practice strategy in preference to those other things? Let me explain. I am writing this book for practitioners working with older people, part of agencies and organizations that already give them a big job to do. You have expertise in doing that job, procedures to follow, theories you have learned and practice skills you have developed.

Throughout Part I, I argue that you can, and should, also take on board the experience, knowledge, skills and processes that come from end-of-life and palliative care services. This benefits the service and older people because it puts into your work a growing issue in their journey through life and enables them to deal better with it. Bringing end-of-life care skills into social work with older people creates a strategy for doing the work that you already do and know how to do. I don't ask you to do many more things, fill in more forms, follow more procedures. I ask you to look at your work through a lens tinged with the reality that older people are coming towards the end of their lives, and they, their carers, families and communities will be helped by your inclusion of that reality in your work with them.

The older person may be aware of the end of their life, but find it difficult to discuss it with others. Others may avoid it or fail to pick it up in time. Your colleagues in healthcare may be working with an end-of-life care focus particularly if they have identified the reality that an older person's life is coming towards its close. If you are not involved in that, you are operating in separate zones of the older person's life, perhaps not connecting with or supporting one another. And if you are not thinking 'end-of-life care', you are not bringing the social into healthcare.

So a practice strategy is a focus on your service responsibilities that shifts how you take on those responsibilities. A practice strategy in end-of-life care for older people includes planning and action that will help an older person, their carers, family and community to respond to the reality for them of the end of life. For each individual and those around them, it will, of course, be a different personal and social reality.

## Humanistic social work practice and the older person as 'other'

If life is a journey and later life and dying a valued part of it, we must see these experiences as integral to all human experience, and therefore to the life journey of all people who are citizens in our society. That includes ourselves, the professionals working in this field, as well as the older people who are our clients. But we fail to do this: instead we often see older and dying people as 'other' than people who are living their lives. I think we often see older people as 'other' at least partly *because* they are closer than us to death. Another reason may be that they often require care, and our neo-liberal individualistic societies see people who need special provision for care outside their everyday relationships as 'other', because they are dependent on care and the idea of care as integral to human existence is rejected by capitalist political and social thought. My view is that social work relies on humanistic philosophies (Payne, 2011, 2012). These propose that human beings are capable of overcoming personal and social problems through their collective endeavours, using our human reasoning and capacity for emotional connection with others.

'Older people' is a current professional term referring to an administrative category of people who were previously called 'the old' or 'old people' or 'elderly people'. Social workers or nurses specializing in working with older people might identify themselves as 'one of the older persons team' or something similar. In doing this, practitioners are naming and thinking about a category of people who are other than themselves. An older person, a dying person or a bereaved person is other to the professional working with them.

There are three points to make about facing otherness. The first is that otherness is never complete. We all share something – physical limitations, spirituality, use of language and speaking voice, many ways of being and living – with the other person. We will be older in the future; they were younger in the past. The second point is that because we share something with the other, as we engage with them we accept an ethical responsibility for how we act in our behaviour towards them (Levinas, 1985). Third, because of what we share, accepting our human responsibility for the other means using our human capacity to turn our uncertainty round. Humanistic social work ideas say that what makes us all human is the capacity to use our mind to develop understanding and change our immediate response to otherness.

Therefore, we have a professional responsibility not merely to deal with older people in a service-providing, efficient-delivery sort of way. That is essential. But, in addition, we must accept the ethical and social responsibility to use our intellectual capacity to turn round our 'not-us' attitude to the otherness of older people, including those who are approaching the end of life. Part of that is to turn round social attitudes that say: 'when you are an older person, when you are at the end of life, there cannot be any more high points'. We, professionals working with older people at the end of life, should be seeking, up to the moment of death, opportunities for further high points.

## Implications of the ageing journey for citizenship practice

Seeing end-of-life and palliative care as part of the life journey through ageing raises important implications for social policy and citizenship for older people, and also for social work practice. As people progress through the journey, their shift into greater dependence may mean that:

- They increasingly lose the physical and mental capacity to exercise their citizenship.
- Their dependence means that others begin to question their contribution to society in exchange for citizenship rights. Perhaps they also do so themselves.

Citizenship social work argues, first, that loss of any kind, including the loss of capacity, does not mean the loss of the right to age in the place that you want to be and to make the most of the social environment in which an older person lives. It is the responsibility of formal and informal support services to combat de-citizening. Second, seeing dependence as an inability to make economic and social contributions to society is a conservative communitarian position. Citizenship social work takes the radical communitarian position that dependence lays responsibility on services and practitioners to enable older people to continue their involvement in active citizenship. Dependence is not a mark of decline or lack of responsibility to the community; it is a signal that a community response is required to the needs of one of its members, so that the community's solidarity is enhanced. In turn, the radical communitarian position incorporates an 'ethics of care' view, which says that connections and care between human beings is a natural part of life and relationships, and that assuming individualistic independence is a neo-liberal, conservative position (Barnes, 2012). These ideas connect with accepted public policy, such as, for example, the World Health Organization (2002) and European Union policies on 'active ageing' defined by the EU as 'helping people stay in charge of their own lives for as long as possible as they age and, where possible, to contribute to the economy and society' (European Union, 2016).

Among the implications of this approach in social work with older people is the need for a strong awareness of the pathway through ageing towards death. Citizenship social work requires practitioners to be alert to the need to help people understand and react to the transitions along the pathway, so that older people can be prepared for the changes in their lives and can have the opportunity to complete social tasks that are important to them at each stage. Otherwise, they are de-citizened, losing some of those rights and opportunities. Since, as we have seen, every social worker will deal with the consequences of death, dying and bereavement in the lives of their clients, so all social work, not just in practice concerned with older people, from time to time requires alertness to raise awareness of and engagement with death, dying and bereavement.

---

**CASE EXAMPLE: HELPING EDWINA WITH HER MOTHER'S DEATH**

Edwina, a 47-year-old woman with learning disabilities, was supported in specialized housing by a social worker, Georgiana, who learned that Edwina's mother, now in her late 70s, had terminal cancer and was expected to die soon. Care workers at the housing scheme had decided that Edwina would be distressed by seeing her mother's illness, and decided not to arrange any visits to her mother until after the death. Georgiana knew that people with learning disabilities often need repeated information-giving and opportunities to discuss what is happening to understand and manage important events in their lives. She decided that it would be better for Edwina to have increased contact with her mother, so that she could see and understand how ill her mother was, and begin to accept the reality that she was dying. To make the communication easier for Edwina and her mother during this period of increased contact, she helped them to create a scrapbook together of important events that they had shared during Edwina's life. This gave them a topic of conversation, and a practical and creative task to share. Georgiana was helping both mother and daughter take up their right as citizens to engage creatively with the ageing and dying processes, rather than exclude them from this opportunity to have an important dying experience in their lives.

---

## The importance of social work and end-of-life care

This book argues that social work is crucial to working with and providing services for older people, even though healthcare is often the organizational base for provision. End-of-life care is also equally important. The distinctive characteristics of social work give it an important role in working with ageing and the end of life, although many social workers struggle to find and maintain a strong distinctive position as part of 'health and social care', as official jargon today refers to it. The claim that service users among older people and their families will benefit from undifferentiated 'healthnsocialcare' because it will be more integrated and continuous is a misunderstanding. By claiming that social care is an adjunct or assistance to healthcare, it homogenizes distinctive traditions and knowledge bases in health and social care. It devalues the social as an important part of human life and of healthcare. Services benefit from practitioners being aware of and clarifying the role of the characteristic contributions made by both traditions and knowledge bases to care for older people and at the end of life.

I make three main points arguing for this emphasis on social work. First, the journey through life into ageing and the end of life will always be a social one, involving an older person's social relations in their family and community. Second, to avoid seeing older people as 'other' and helping to citizen or re-citizen them can only be done by promoting their integration within community, family and social relations. Third, working with the social, developing social cohesion and social relations are defining roles of the social work profession. These roles have always had a place in serving older people. The focus of healthcare professions, including medicine, nursing and psychology, is primarily on the older person and the physical or psychological consequences of their ageing. This does not exclude concern for their social role and relations, but it does not emphasize it. Only social work among health and social care professions places the social in the foreground of its objectives. This makes social workers crucial contributors to healthcare because their involvement makes healthcare services more holistic. Social workers help their colleagues balance their appropriate professional focus on health and medical care with a contribution that allows an understanding of the social to influence the whole service.

Even though we all die, dying, and the approach to it, is unique to each individual. Nobody else can experience this death or the totality of the life that leads to it. This death is a mystery that the dying person faces alone, and can never describe; everyone else is an outsider to it. The life that led to this death has only been experienced by the one person who lived it; nobody else can experience it in the same way. Death is, nevertheless, always a social experience, because it removes a person from their relationships and their social position in society. Even if they are living a completely isolated life, their absence has an impact upon others. Most people have a network of relationships in their family and community which is interrupted by death and by the needs of someone who is approaching the end of life. We are presented with this person and must respond to whatever their needs may be as a human being, and as an older person, and as someone approaching the end of life and as a dying person. Those needs will reflect their whole life experience, and we must respond to that. Consequently, social workers are also crucial participants in end-of-life care, because they bring that social and whole-life perspective into provision for healthcare.

One final point about the role of social care services in overall provision for older people at the end of life is an organizational matter. Social care services for older people in most countries, and this is also true of the UK, are part of 'adult services'. This very clearly aligns them with treating people as adults, with the rights, responsibilities and concerns of adult citizens in our community. It also allows us to draw on several decades of learning in services for disabled people and people with learning disabilities and mental illness. This tells us that care requires improving citizens' human rights, independence, participation and planning in their services, and increasing people's control of their lives is a positive aspect of social and healthcare services. Community care of this kind both enhances people's well-being and satisfaction and usually reduces demands on expensive services. Fostering self-care and independence does not mean, however, stepping away from situations where help is required. People cannot avoid dependence and develop the capacity for self-care unless we actively seek to develop it.

The concern of social care and social work for the social also emphasizes the importance of carers, family members, neighbours and strangers, paid and unpaid, who help older people moving towards the end of life meet the needs of living which they cannot meet themselves. Adult services have increasingly been concerned to protect carers from the damaging effects that caring often has on their lives and enhance the experience of caring so that carers are valued by those they care for, by professionals involved and by society. This expertise is another important contribution of social work to end-of-life care.

The main points arguing for my emphasis on end-of-life care as part of provision for older people are as follows. First, most people know that, as they age, they move closer to the time at which they will die. Most people in older age groups are aware of this, have thought about it and often planned for at least some aspects of it. Therefore, it is denial on our part of the reality of this stage of their life's journey to concern ourselves *only* with a positive emphasis on maintaining their lifestyle or keeping them going. It is the equivalent of doctors and nurses only talking about cure, without being open about the fact that some of the conditions they are treating are progressive and will lead to death. Including the end of life and communicating with them openly and with the courage to address the realities of their position is crucial to treating them as adult citizens. I have said already that this openness and preparedness to address the hard stuff is one of the valuable things about social care's contribution to services for older people. Second, end-of-life care allows us to help whole families and communities and their social institutions to be supportive of people in the dying phase of their lives and in bereavement. Many people who are dying and bereaved feel isolated because their friends and neighbours melt away, avoid them or talk only about everything other than their illness and death. Keeping up hope is all very well; but enabling people to express an important reality in their lives is also important. It requires communication and coping skills which are new to many people. Third, many people are not particularly planful: they do not prepare for important aspects of their lives. We may put off or be unable to decide on thinking about and planning for things that are difficult or uncomfortable; and for many people ageing, becoming ill and frail and dying are things they prefer not to think too explicitly about. But if we can help them to do it, their planning will make the services and support they get much more satisfying and appropriate for them.

## The importance of multiprofessional services in the community

The importance of multiprofessional services for older people and focusing on the lives of older people and their families in the community follows from many of the points that I have been making about older people at the end of life being citizens in their journey through life. This means that services must be constructed to be holistic in several ways:

- They must see older people as whole people on their whole journey. They are not a bundle of symptoms or medical conditions or assessable social care needs in an unfortunate and unpleasant phase of their life. This older person is someone with a personality, life history and social context who is entitled to more high points in life.
- They must see older people as part of a family and community. This older person embodies the life and experience of a family and community, and this family and community must be helped to engage with their members who are older and may be approaching the end of life.

- They must see services for older people as part of a range of life provision for adults in their later lives. This older person receives health and social care services, and is a consumer of for-profit and not-for profit services sustaining life, safety and well-being, including food, energy, financial resources, housing, education and leisure.

No one profession and no one service can provide all this. A profession or service that is called upon must weave their personnel and their provision into this older person's life journey and will be doing so alongside family members and other informal carers and other services. They must take the other professions and services into account, and in doing so, they will have to work with a range of other provisions. The milkman, the corner shop, the supermarket, the landlord, the computer engineer may all need to be engaged alongside official and not-for-profit housing, social security, education and leisure services.

### Advance care planning is integral to ageing and end-of-life care

Advance care planning is a healthcare technique in which people are facilitated to consider their preferences for services at the end of life. A related term, anticipatory care planning, often used in Scotland, refers to engaging people in planning their social and healthcare from the outset of their engagement with care services. In describing the journey through ageing towards the end of life, I emphasized the importance of planning to citizenship, thinking through options and opportunities. Unless services help people to plan, they cannot help older people to fulfil their citizenship to the highest degree, because services will be struggling with the unexpected, and older people and their families and communities will react to negatives instead of achieving positives. Unless advance care planning is part of services for older people at the end of life, we will be working mainly with current incidents rather than incorporating our service into the journey that older people at the end of life are making.

### ADDITIONAL RESOURCES

#### Books

The following books provide the theoretical basis for the present book:

Marshall, M. and Tibbs, M.-A. (2006) *Social Work and People with Dementia: Partnerships, practice and persistence.* Bristol: Policy Press.
This book brings out ideas of citizenship social work as a basis for working with older people.

Payne, M. (2011) *Humanistic Social Work: Core principles in practice.* Basingstoke: Palgrave Macmillan (with an Introduction to the UK edition).
Originally published in the US, this book is an introduction to the humanistic principles that underlie citizenship social work.

van Ewijk, H. (2009) *European Social Policy and Social Work: Citizenship-based social work.* London: Routledge.
This book, by a leading Dutch social work thinker, and including contributions from other social workers in mainland Europe, provides an important theoretical and policy basis for a broad citizenship social work, with a wider focus than older people.

## Websites

The following websites are useful sources of up-to-date information about ageing.

For general information, Helpage International provides wide-ranging global data, with an emphasis on the developing world. There are many publications and policy documents: http://www.helpage.org/ (accessed 3 July 2015).

Another useful website is the International Longevity Centre (ILC), with many well-informed publications and downloadable information: http://www.ilcuk.org.uk/ (accessed 3 July 2015).

There is an international alliance of ILCs, and from their website, you can surf through to the ILC for other countries: http://www.ilc-alliance.org/ (accessed 3 July 2015).

For researchers, the Gateway to Global Aging Data gives access to information from a variety of research organizations across the world. It covers all longitudinal health and retirement studies: https://g2aging.org/ (accessed 3 July 2015).

# 2

# CITIZENSHIP PROCESSES

## Citizening, de-citizening and re-citizening

The main aim of this chapter is to build on the points that I made briefly in Chapter 1 to show how thinking about older people as citizens helps us to practise social work with them, their families and their carers. It is divided into three sections:

1. Understanding citizenship and its importance for practice with older people.
2. Understanding citizenship as a process that forms the basis of citizening, de-citizening and re-citizening.
3. Unpacking citizenship thinking as we practise.

Citizenship thinking means holding in our minds throughout our social work that this older person shares a common human heritage with us.

## Citizenship and social citizenship

Citizenship is a status and identity, enjoyed by most people, which denotes their affiliation with a country. The legal status of citizenship is confirmed by official documents and by rights to participate in politics and government. While an individual's citizenship recognizes their legal connection with a country (Faulks, 2000), it implies much more. Identity is connected with citizenship: citizens belong both to a nation as a legal entity and also to its cultural, economic, political and social associations. Citizens are enabled by their belonging to participate in that country's life by interacting with other citizens who share citizenship: 'co-citizens'. Their identity as citizens is expressed through the social relationships that they have with co-citizens. Social citizenship is citizens' rights and duties to take up and pursue these social aspects of citizenship. If there are rights and duties that go with belonging in a society, those same rights and duties also imply inclusion for the citizen and exclusion for people who do not possess the same citizenship. Older people's social citizenship implies that they are alongside social workers, belonging and sharing important aspects of identity. We can work more respectfully and get better outcomes if everything we think, speak and do says 'This person shares my citizenship.'

Citizenship provides a structure of social order: it connects a population with the right to control of a territory and with the economic, political and social life that creates patterns of power relations within that territory. Marshall and Bottomore's (1992) analysis, developed from an earlier theory of Marshall's (1949), linked citizenship with three sets of rights:

1. civil rights to legal protection of their freedoms and equality;
2. political rights to vote, stand for election and participate in political processes;
3. social rights to welfare and participation in social relations with others.

The extent and nature of social rights associated with citizenship have become controversial in social policy (Evers and Guillemard, 2012). There is no set of rights naturally associated with citizenship: these rights have been fought over in political debate. Citizenship rights have also been seen as conditional on people participating in society, by being 'active citizens' and by contributing to a society economically. For example, social security benefits for unemployed people may be conditional on past employment and contribution to insurance. Older people might not be eligible for a pension unless they have made contributions to insurance or a state pension scheme during their working lifetime. Changes in demands on welfare systems, like the increase in the proportion of older people in the population that I discussed in Chapter 1, will affect the political and social perceptions of rights associated with citizenship. Citizenship rights may be seen as flexible in policy-making, according to economic and social conditions. The balance of rights and obligations changes over time, and this may affect older people who set out on life with one balance, to find that expectations of them have changed as they approach greater dependency on social benefits in later life (Gilbert, 2012).

Janoski and Gran (2002) identify four political positions about citizenship:

1. Liberal theory views citizenship as individuals pursuing their own interests according to accepted social and legal conventions, while being tolerant and respectful of others' rights.
2. Consensual order theories view citizenship as a social good, in which citizens learn that societies are most successful if people work together to develop good social relationships.
3. Participatory republicanism sees citizenship as complex, and requires active participation by citizens, respecting individual rights, so that a more respectful social order can be built up.
4. Postmodern pluralism sees citizenship identities as complex and multiple, depending on social groups representing particular interests, such as women, or disabled people, and focuses on social movements to promote rights of particular interests.

Most people's views of citizenship contain elements of all these positions. Older people may pursue their individual rights taking a liberal view, building up their pensions and insuring themselves for their health and care needs. Studies of care needs have found that even the richest people will not be able to provide for the most severe care needs, and rights to public or charitable services are also engaged. An example is my experience working in a hospice providing end-of-life care. Occasionally, we worked with patients who took a liberal view of citizenship and whose health insurance had paid for treatment for serious illness. Private hospitals' focus on treatment procedures often meant that such patients were transferred to the hospice for end-of-life care. They were distressed by this when they found that payment could not provide for the kind of care they needed, and they found it hard to imagine that high-quality care would be available in a service that was provided free by a charity. In another example, I know an older woman who is prepared to pay for care in a costly private care home, but struggling with the risk that her money will not last for the whole of her lifetime, meaning that she would be dependent on public services. This goes against her philosophy of life, and even though she can see that the care would be adequate, it is not her ideal. People with less money similarly struggle with compromises between remaining in their own homes and moving to a care home.

## Citizenship as process: Citizening, de-citizening and re-citizening

Janoski and Gran's (2002) typology of views of citizenship, therefore, helps us to see that citizenship often involves the creation of collectives, social groups in which civil and political rights are invested. Taking the more complex views of citizenship also leads us to a process view of it: people are always in the process of becoming citizens, or losing and regaining elements of their citizenship. This becomes obvious when we look at two important areas of scholarship in citizenship studies: how young people move from becoming children depending upon their parents, through education and increasing life experience, and how citizenship for migrants changes as they lose their previous citizenship and build up a new citizenship in a new location. Thus, I identify three processes that might affect older people:

1. Citizening, the process of gaining aspects of citizenship that facilitate rights in later life and at the end of life.
2. De-citizening, the process by which they lose elements of citizenship through ageing.
3. Re-citizening, the process of building lost elements of citizenship that enable successful later life and end of life.

All kinds of processes are relevant, but an important aspect of these processes is the capacity to engage with other people in communicative relationships (Habermas, 1996), so that they can relate to others that are important to them and in ways that help them to build relationships. This is why I emphasize the value of group work and arts work in end-of-life care and active social lives in later life. To facilitate citizenship, however, social relations need to be rooted in communities. This may be in a locality where there are strong continuing links. This is why in care during later life I emphasize ageing in place and the environment of care. Alternatively, citizenship processes can be rooted in strong patterns of shared interests, such as movements representing special needs and interests (Delanty, 2002). This is why I highlight participation in policy and provision in later life.

An important collective affecting older people is the state: the political system that maintains the nation in the interests of its citizens, who of course vary. The state, therefore, is not monolithic, not one collective, but many. Participation in social citizenship is not only a matter of social collaboration but also of social conflict. There is a national state, but there are many and perhaps conflicting departments of it, with many different roles; and there are local and regional states, too. The appropriate roles of the state and elements of it in relation to citizens are controversial: what services should it provide to its citizens and on what basis does it make demands of them? Are these services and demands absolute, or are they a form of exchange, in which services are only provided to the extent that citizens make a contribution? If so, the notion of deserts arises: are only deserving citizens entitled to some rights, and how is their entitlement to be defined?

Communitarians argue that citizenship is two-sided: rights go with membership, but so also do responsibilities. Radical communitarians see this as a criticism of individualism and a demand for mutual cooperation, while conservative communitarians see it as a demand for appropriate exchange, so that people only receive the benefits of citizenship if they also make a contribution (Dwyer, 2004: 28–9). In most countries, citizens are expected to make contributions to the social order by being law-abiding, and they may be valued if they make contributions by becoming parents, caring for people who are sick or frail, in their families or in their neighbourhoods as volunteers.

A question of concern to social workers, then, arises: what provision is made for people who through no fault of their own are unable to make a contribution to a society, or whose contribution is not recognized? Do they become non-citizens completely, or is their citizenship conditional? An older person's non-employed contribution to social relations (e.g. by grand-parenting) and the economy (e.g. through voluntary work or investing their pension in wealth-producing stocks and shares) may be devalued. Consequently, concern for entitlements and exchanges also raises questions about the power relations in a society, because they are provided for only to the extent that their provision can be enforced: powerful people can exclude the less powerful from receiving their entitlement, or can devalue the contribution of less powerful people. Feminist writers note that women are often excluded by the social assumptions of patriarchal societies from receiving equal citizenship with men (Lister, 2003). For example, their contribution to parenting as an important social role may not be as valued as men's employment as a contribution to the economy. Inequalities of this kind arise for ethnic minorities, people with physical and mental disabilities and illness, and people in other devalued or stigmatized identities: they may be excluded from 'social citizenship' (Dwyer, 2004), excluded or disadvantaged by their social categorization.

## Exclusion from citizenship: Older people at the end of life

Being older and being at the end of life are both social characteristics that lead to devalued social citizenship: older people approaching the end of life may legally be citizens, but their role in society is devalued to the point that they become almost non-citizens (Tonkiss and Bloom, 2016). For example, their citizenship may be devalued because they are unable to participate actively in civic life (Martinson and Minckler, 2006). Alternatively, they may be criticized because their participation is out of tune with young people; for example, older people were criticized for their disproportionately high support of leaving the European Union in the UK referendum on this topic (Abrahams, 2016). Common groups seen as noncitizens include stateless persons, refugees and asylum seekers, non-citizen workers such as seasonal agricultural labourers and domestic slaves, victims of trafficking, and children. Common experiences of such groups of people include:

- discrimination in housing and employment;
- abuse;
- arbitrary detention and expulsion;
- irregular movement and high-risk travel;
- women being deprived of relationships and social connections (Weissbrodt and Divine, 2016).

Many of these factors also apply to older people. They may not be allowed or may be discouraged from remaining in their family home when it gets too big for them; their social benefits may not allow them to pay for housing that most appropriately meets their needs; and younger people may be favoured as employees. They may experience physical, emotional and financial abuse. They may be kept in a hospital or care home inappropriately because they are at risk of injury if allowed to go home. Services to allow them to return to or remain at home securely are not provided either at all, because of expenditure limits or cuts, or not quickly enough or to a good enough standard through pressure on services. On the other hand, they may be expelled too soon from a hospital without services as 'bed blockers'. In many areas, public transport may be too irregular to provide for their needs, or un-adapted to physical frailties. Loneliness, particularly of widowed women, is a big issue for many older people (Victor et al., 2009).

Older people at the end of life may, therefore, easily face many of the same issues as other non-citizens. An important part of citizenship social work practice (see Chapters 7 and 8) is avoiding de-citizening and promoting re-citizening when we are working with older people. More than this, citizening work is required throughout the life course (see Chapter 6), in childhood and adulthood, so that we do not build up the social attitudes that lead to the expectation of non-citizenship for older people.

Many cultures value older people who are no longer economically active individually as grandparents, ancestors of currently active generations, and collectively as the past history of that society who have made contributions to achieving its present position. Citizenship in developed industrialized societies, however, has not always valued older people, because in a capitalist society, economic participation is an important source of social value. Many de-citizening processes are at work. When older people retire and no longer work, they are not part of important networks of communication, support and relationships, and their time is not structured by the need to attend a workplace. Moreover, there is extensive international evidence of abuse and ill-treatment of older people (Cooper et al., 2008). Since dementia is associated with increasing age, older people who experience the multiple medical conditions typical of advancing age may lose rights to treatment because they lack 'cognitive citizenship' (Graham, 2014); their failing minds exclude them from full participation in society. Younger people may regard them as irritatingly slow and obstructive in everyday life, out of touch with modern thinking and technology. Efforts may not be made to promote their ability to use new technology (Piaggesi, 2003). They may be perceived as unable to benefit fully from some medical treatments, or their lack of capacity to express pain and distress may mean that their need for treatments typical of older age groups such as hip or other joint replacements is not recognized by care staff. All of these attitudes de-citizen, removing aspects of citizenship from previously fully-citizened people.

> **CASE EXAMPLE: MELINA'S ARTHRITIS CAUSES PAIN**
>
> A social worker, Karen, visited an elderly client, Melina, who had severe dementia, to the point that she was unable to communicate in words. It was quite cold in the care home lounge, and Karen asked a care worker to fetch a cardigan from Melina's own room; respecting Melina's privacy, she usually did not visit clients' own rooms in a care home. As the care worker helped Melina on with the cardigan, Karen noticed that she flinched, so

she asked the care worker whether Melina experienced any pain. The care worker said that she sometimes seemed to find dressing difficult. Karen asked the care home manager to seek medical investigation, and it emerged that Melina was experiencing problems with undiagnosed arthritis, for which he provided treatment.

This case example shows how, particularly with older people who have communication problems or have lost mental capacity through dementia or other illness, respecting cognitive citizenship means that practitioners must be alert and observant to compensate for the loss of opportunities that come about because an older person cannot fully communicate their wishes and needs. If you cannot communicate, you cannot participate with others and it is more difficult to have your needs met. To meet the needs of older people with communication difficulties, practitioners need to be alert to signs that needs are not being met.

As we saw in Chapter 1, the social settlement for older people – that is, the accepted expectations about ageing and social provision for older people – is changing across the world. Thus, a larger population of older people will be practically and economically dependent on a smaller population of working age. In private life, dependence creates ties within people's relationships; many cultural traditions value interdependence (Sennett, 2003); this is citizening for people. An ethics of care view of human life proposes that care is an integral part of all human existence. It is not a rational, calculating approach to our relationships, but based on shared humanity, shared experiences and mutual interdependence in relationships (Barnes, 2012); those relationships are also citizening. Liberal and neo-liberal political philosophies see dependence as infantilization and connect independence with the work ethic: if people work to look after themselves, they contribute to society rather than drawing from it. The concern about dependence among older people is particularly informed by healthcare services, whose main task is to prevent physical deterioration. If it is possible to prevent people from becoming increasingly frail, it may be possible to prevent patients from becoming practically reliant on informal carers or formal services to carry out everyday tasks of life. The healthcare approach to later life is to manage illnesses and disabilities, treat medical conditions that develop so that people recover from them, moving on to provide respite and rehabilitation so that they can be returned to independent management of their healthy lives. Following this approach often unthinkingly de-citizens older people by seeing care and dependence as a loss of aspects of valued lives, instead of a citizening engagement with others. Long-term help with activities of daily living and eventually care substituting for independent management of everyday life is provided (Audit Commission, 2004); this may be de-citizening because it confirms officially the loss of aspects of citizenship. Recent research suggests that policy should move from this medically oriented preventive stance because it is de-citizening. It should be replaced by a re-citizening stance of positive maintenance and promotion both of personal independence and also of interdependence between people in a local community (Audit Commission, 2004).

These changes in the present economic system for the dependence of a rising population of older people lead to de-citizening personal uncertainty for individuals and wider social insecurity. Informal arrangements are used in most societies to sustain older people who are unable to provide fully for their needs. They are based on a system of family and community exchange and reciprocity: family and community citizenship. There is a fear that in many developed countries there is no practical way of continuing this as older people may be cut off from family and other contacts by labour mobility and lack of contact with the means of living. What does this mean for the citizenship of older people who are dependent and no longer able to reciprocate in the implied exchange in developed industrialized societies?

The cultural ideals that value older people highly as citizens in spite of their dependence require a preventive approach to economic and social processes that exclude older people from full participation in society. Adopting a concern for maintaining the citizenship of older people suggests that policy should focus on preventing dependence by emphasizing older people's full participation as citizens in all the different aspects of their society. Social and healthcare services should only need to offer help when older people are not able to carry out the everyday tasks of living, referred to in the professional literature as the 'activities of daily living (adls)' which guide many assessments of social care need, and cannot maintain social contacts so that they become socially isolated; I look again at these in Chapter 7.

Similar issues arise for people at the end of life. Although we all die, many people do not dwell on this reality while they are living. Avoiding active discussion of death may be healthy because it allows people to continue with their life tasks. Writers such as Ariès (1974), however, see death as a taboo in 20th-century Western society. The death rate has been reduced by medical advances, so that people do not experience death very often or very early in their lives. It is hidden from ordinary social experience, because the dying process is often managed by healthcare staff in medical settings such as care homes, hospices and hospitals rather than occurring in people's homes. Dead bodies are dealt with in a depersonalized way by specialist professionals such as funeral directors in rarely visited places such as cemeteries, crematoria and mortuaries. People generally are less inclined than at one time to participate in formal rituals of bereavement and remembrance. Instead of formal mourning rituals, less formal and populist rituals have developed, seen in the funerals and memorials for celebrities. It is important not to exaggerate the extent to which death and dying have become hidden; it does not mean that people do not experience grief. Avoiding public grief and mourning is not unique to modern society, but commonplace in many societies (Walter, 1992). The period when death was a taboo subject in Western society was a specific period occurring in the mid-20th century after two major world wars and the death of many Jewish people in the Holocaust at a time when medical progress seemed set to banish premature death. This has changed with better psychological understanding of death and bereavement and the development of the hospice movement.

Instead of a single ritualized approach to death and dying, people have a range of frames for viewing death and bereavement: the practical, the spiritual, the biomedical, the lay and the semi-psychiatric. In the practical frame, a funeral has to be arranged and money and property sorted out. In the spiritual frame, people reflect and meditate on the meaning of life. In the biomedical frame, reasonable standards of treatment and care are expected; people must visit the sick and support the family and caregivers. In the lay frame, people express their regrets, buy flowers, organize for people leaving work. In the semi-psychiatric frame, people recognize that there will be distress, stress, anxiety and depression and allow for it. A public health frame covers many of the procedures for certifying death and disposing of bodies, a theological frame provides for some of the ritual, and a psychological frame provides for explanations and actions around grief and bereavement.

## Citizenship social work and rights

This discussion about citizenship in principle now leads us to develop a citizenship social work practice. An important aspect of creating a citizenship social work for older people is a concern about rights for older people, especially as they approach the end of life. Among the reasons for being particularly concerned about older people's rights are:

- The rapidly growing number of older people in the worldwide population, which means that failure to accord them their human rights affects a significant and growing number of people.
- Age discrimination and ageism are widely tolerated and deeply ingrained in many societies and rarely challenged.
- There is no protection for older people's rights in the same way as for children and disabled people, and for people affected by racism and gender discrimination.
- Because of their physical frailty, older people are more vulnerable to violence, and because of mental frailty, they are more vulnerable to emotional abuse than some other groups whose special needs are respected
- Older people are often treated as the object of charity and special services rather than having rights respected, and the needs associated with their stage of life responded to.
- Older people are an increasingly significant group because a higher proportion vote than some younger groups, and their needs and interests are shared by adults as they age, so their rights and interests might have a strong impact if they are appropriately organized. On the other hand, their political significance is sometimes attacked because their interests are said to engender selfishness in maintaining political and economic support for their pensions and care services. In turn, older generations make unreasonable economic demands on younger generations, who do not get the same level of support and will not get the same financial and social benefits when they reach later life.
- There are large gaps in legislation against age discrimination, so obvious courses of action to enforce their rights are not easily available.
- Respect for older people's rights benefits society as a whole, because older people who are participants in a society are able to make a strong contribution and generate support for meeting their needs as well as broader social solidarity (Graham, 2014).

Many of these factors also link to rights to end-of-life care:

- A growing number of older people means that there will be a growing number of people close to death.
- Age discrimination and ageism means that many people avoid thinking about the end of life – both their own and the death of other people.
- If older people are vulnerable to abuse and neglect, this vulnerability extends to the dying phase.
- Palliative care has been strongly associated with charitable provision in hospices, and this tends to confirm the tendency to see end-of-life care as a matter of charity, rather than a matter of meeting people's rights and needs.
- Intergenerational conflict about the priority accorded to the rights and needs of older people may lead to lack of support for end-of-life care. For example, when resources for

healthcare are tight, priority might be given to curative medicine rather than caring for older people's needs. At the extreme, there might be stronger support for arguments in favour of hastening the death of dependent people at the end of life in debates – for example, about assisted dying.
- Limited recognition of the rights of older people in discrimination legislation also extends to rights at the end of life.
- The experience of people whom we know and love dying well creates well-being among the relatives and the community who surrounded them in life, strengthens coping skills in families, reduces adverse effects of loss and bereavement, and fosters stronger resilience in dealing with other adversities in life.

## Citizenship social work ideas

'Citizenship social work' is an approach to social work practice that emphasizes the citizenship of social work clients as a value base and a source of direction for deciding appropriate interventions. By thinking 'citizenship', we are enabled to create strategies for how we should approach social work. It may be applied with many different client groups, but emerged from practice with older people (Marshall and Tibbs, 2006; Payne, 2011). Therefore, to understand how it contributes a distinctive approach to social work, it is helpful to explore its origins with that client group. Marshall and Tibbs (2006) describe three main approaches to social work practice with older people:

1. Medical or organic approaches are the mainstream model, reflecting the dominance of healthcare practice and research with this client group. These approaches focus on resolving and managing problems that older people experience as ageing processes lead to increasing physical and mental difficulties in their lives. They aim to reduce or remove physical and mental damage and manage the effects of it on the older person's life. Social work in this approach contributes to healthcare by strengthening the older person's emotional and psychological resources and community, family and practical supports. Interpersonal practice with the older person and informal caregivers is combined with mobilizing and coordinating services from the practitioner's agency and elsewhere in the network of formal and informal services.
2. Social approaches focus on the impact upon the older person's social relationships and surroundings of any physical and mental impairments that they experience. Social work aims to help older people and people 'age in place' – that is, manage the effect of any physical, mental and social impairments that affect them within their social surroundings (Brittain *et al.*, 2010). Community services meet the needs of older people alongside others as part of their everyday provision. Social care services provide substitute help with the activities of daily living if older people cannot remain independent.
3. Citizenship approaches emphasize the right of older people to participate in society and make a contribution to it, in particular using their creativity and other personal emotional strengths. The aim of services is to help people identify and maximize their strengths and contributions to their family, community and society. This incorporates citizenship aims in our practice when ageing reduces older people's participation in and contribution to society.

The alternative and contending perspectives are as follows. The medical or organic model focuses on older people's health and social care needs, when this is necessary. The social model proposes that health and social care services should incorporate a broader focus on promoting the roles and opportunities of older people to achieve independence within wider society, incorporating health and social care provision within that. Citizenship practice accepts responsibility for enabling older people to strengthen their contribution to that society.

Thus, citizenship social work practice gives social provision and social work a positive focus: facilitating and empowering effective social responses to the issues that societies face. It is de-citizening to assume that older people are waiting for death: working with them in co-production of services offers an opportunity to empower solidarity in our society. It enables co-production in which older people and their carers participate with services and practitioners to identify the ways in which ageing requires extra help. Co-produced help enables older people's equality in respect and dignity as citizens to be expressed in the quality of their lives and the opportunities they have to fulfil their human potential.

## Citizenship social work practice

A cross-national study (van Oorschot *et al.*, 2009: 6) about disability offers a useful analysis of areas of participation which gives us clues about appropriate strategies to build citizenship practice:

- education;
- work and employment;
- income and social protection;
- mobility;
- information and communication;
- political participation;
- cultural participation;
- discrimination.

My first strategy is that social work practice should not hinder but promote participation in worthwhile activities through interaction with co-citizens. To practise social work in ways that see and treat our clients as citizens, therefore, we must help them to feel included with co-citizens. A social work that fails to help with participation is inadequate. Social work agencies need to provide for practice that engages older people with their co-citizens.

My second strategy is that social work must maintain and enhance people's lifelong personal identity and developing social identities, as they are expressed in their participation in social relationships.

My third strategy is that social work must protect and facilitate people in accepting and exercising the civil and political rights that go with their citizenship.

My fourth strategy focuses on the social rights of citizenship. This is not just about being able to participate in social interaction; it also means that people have rights to receive services from the state, their co-citizens operating in the collective interest. Social networks may be where older people are de-citizened, and social workers can usefully pay attention to them:

- Family and neighbours and influences from the community in which they are situated may value and provide for ageing and older people in their midst or may not do so.
- Intimate relationships, friendships, marriage and divorce may facilitate ageing or limit opportunities for successful ageing.

- Employment, retirement and income from both may finance and support successful and creative ageing or make for difficulties.
- Civil and social life, including leisure and recreation, travel and transport, money, political engagement, local government services, personal safety and human rights may all make provision for ageing, retirement and older people, or may hinder older people from taking up opportunities.
- Media portrayals of old age and death in newspapers, television and film may stigmatize and devalue ageing and older people or present them positively.
- Health and social care services may present barriers to older people through restricting access and by labelling and stigmatizing them as devalued (Thornicroft, 2006; adapted).

---

**CASE EXAMPLE: VALUING AND DEVALUING OLDER PEOPLE'S SEXUALITY**

Felicia lived in a care home for older people provided by a religious foundation. She formed a friendship with another resident, Honoria, and this developed into a lesbian relationship. Eventually, they asked to share a bedroom with a double bed. The managers of the foundation took the view that this was unacceptable to their religious values. Felicia's social worker was unable to persuade the managers that the residents' citizenship should give them the right to pursue the intimate relationship that they desired, even though the women's families (while one was unenthusiastic) were prepared to acquiesce in this arrangement. In addition to their principled opposition, the managers feared that press publicity about scandalous relationships in the home would damage their foundation's reputation. Living in this care home thus restricted the women's freedoms in ways that would not have occurred in their own homes. The social worker therefore applied for them to live together in a sheltered flatlet scheme, where there would be support from a warden and care could be delivered by community services but the women had greater privacy. The women combined their incomes to be able to afford this move.

This case example shows some of the limitations in intimate relationships that may arise through loss of citizenship rights and barriers to freedom in a social care service, combined with fear about media portrayal of older people's relationships. Fortunately, the women's combined financial resources enabled them to have the flexibility to take up the option of a more independent life in a flatlet, and their family relationships were not a barrier in this case.

---

Can we do anything about these risks of de-citizening? Balloch and Hill (2007) collected studies that show how community and care services for a variety of service users might avoid risks to citizenship and promote social participation, often in unlikely circumstances. Among the possibilities were the following ideas, which I have generalized from a specific service context:

- Where there was pressure to enforce conventional social assumptions, practitioners should avoid rough justice but seek flexibility in supporting a range of options for the people they are working with. This came from working with unemployed young people.

- Practitioners should aim at community involvement for people who experienced traumatic incidents in their lives. The aim was to reintegrate them into valued sets of local relationships. This came from working with domestic violence.
- Practitioners should aim to give people increased choice in and control over what was happening in their lives. This came from working with ethnic minority communities.
- Practitioners should try to get people with support and care needs to work together to find ways of dealing with these. This came from work with people needing community care services.
- Practitioners should try to challenge stigma and combat social exclusion by using befriending schemes to encourage the development of social relationships between excluded people and the wider community.
- Where paid workers are employed to help and care for people with social needs, maintaining the social elements of their role in relating to service users benefits both paid worker and service user because the job does not just revolve around programmed physical care tasks, but has a wider importance to both participants. This came from an Australian project.
- Service users were encouraged to find alternative ways of engaging in formal community organizations and service planning. This came from German policy.

The main principle behind these examples is to develop a social element to enhance all health and social care interaction. Therefore, important principles of citizenship social work in action include:

- Integration of services so that they support one another and interweave formal services with informal family and neighbourhood support through involvement of older people and their families in careful advance care planning (Payne, 2010).

### CASE EXAMPLE: ADVANCE CARE PLANNING FOR AN OLDER WOMAN

Penelope, aged 72, who lived with her son and daughter-in-law and their two sons, was diagnosed with an inoperable brain tumour. She returned home to die, and the family members agreed to care for her for the few weeks that this would involve. They were concerned that they would not be able to manage as Penelope's condition worsened, and the social worker sat down with Penelope's son and daughter-in-law, discussed the range of services that would be available and planned in detail how they could apply for each as Penelope got worse. A few weeks later, the son approached the social worker to say that his sons were being noisy and disruptive in the house, and asking them to respect the need for quiet had not worked; neither had remonstration. The social worker found that the sons were being kept away from Penelope, in order to protect them from seeing how ill she was becoming, and she suggested that they visit her in her room regularly for an agreed period and watch television or play games with her. His involvement allowed them to talk to their parents about their fears about an unpleasant death for Penelope, and allowed them to feel involved in her care, rather than just trying to get them to be restrained in their behaviour.

- Identifying generalized, low-cost services, where older people can be involved alongside younger age-groups, as opposed to specialized care services, where they are separated into specialist provision, can be improved to maintain independence and dignity for older people.

> **CASE EXAMPLE: IMPROVING LEISURE SERVICES**
>
> An association for older people responded to a consultation about leisure services in the area. They complained that although theoretically older people could use the local swimming pool to maintain and improve their health, a lot of younger users wanted to plough up and down the pool and this made it more difficult for frailer and less confident swimmers to use the pool. They asked for special sessions for older people to be introduced. A social worker reported that a hidden factor was that some older people were embarrassed because their bodies were not as conventionally attractive as some of the 'ladies in lycra' using fitness equipment in the same building, and this also put them off. The centre also introduced a special fitness session for older people as a result.

- Ensuring that healthcare, housing and social security services are appropriate and work well together since these are the priority domains for quality of life among older people and therefore for social work intervention and participation. Increasingly, the effectiveness of services can be enhanced by using assistive technology and telecare as part of care for older people. Telecare uses telecommunications technology to monitor vital signs or safety and security in the home, or to provide information and support. It includes video or audio surveillance devices, or radio call buttons on a necklace, so that older people can feel safe even though they are alone for part of the day (Payne, 2012). Effective telecare interventions include automated vital signs monitoring (for reducing health service use) and telephone follow-up by nurses (for improving clinical indicators and reducing health service use) (Barlow et al., 2007).
- Enabling older people to take part in creative and group activities so that they can continue with personal self-development and education, and to feel involved with other people.

> **CASE EXAMPLE: THE ART GROUP AND HENRY'S RELATIONSHIPS AT HOME**
>
> Henry, aged 85, was quite disabled and isolated at home, and so was referred to attend an older person's day centre. He was doubtful about this at first, but became involved in mosaic work, which he thought was more 'masculine' than basket work or painting activities. Eventually, he created mirrors with mosaic surrounds for family presents and a mosaic coffee table for his grandson's bedroom in the colours of his grandson's favourite football team, which he proudly displayed (Butchers, 2008). He said that this craftwork enabled him to give something tangible back to family members for the time and trouble they took in looking after him. He also found that he was able to talk about his craftwork and people he met at the centre, whereas previously he never met anyone or did anything new, so he had no sources of conversation when family members or neighbours visited him.

Many medical and healthcare practitioners do not understand social provision well. Because of a focus on their specific responsibilities, they may not be aware of the possibilities of stimulating ageing in place and ways in which older people's independence can be supported. Reporting back on social work actions is a crucial aspect of practice, so that they can see what is happening with their patients, feel more confident in and see results from social work involvement. Seeing successful work on emotional and psychological issues affecting older people and people at the end of life helps to strengthen healthcare provision, recognize citizenship and makes healthcare professionals more aware and accepting of potential social work contributions. Among the difficulties is that staff unfamiliar with social care services may not be aware of possible options.

> ### CASE EXAMPLE: PLANNING SUPPORT TO REDUCE RISKS OF ABUSE
>
> Henrietta was a frail woman in her 80s, living in her daughter's home, who was admitted to hospital for treatment of some symptoms of cancer. Nurses noted that she had severe bruising, and one of Henrietta's sons said to the doctor that he feared that his sister was misusing Henrietta's money. The doctor consulted a social worker, who suggested he had a private interview with Henrietta to find out her views. She said her daughter was rough with her, but she did not understand the money issue, and wanted to return from the hospital to her daughter's home. Therefore, the social worker had a discussion with the daughter, who was finding it expensive to care for her mother, and had used money from her mother's purse to pay bills. No discussion about finances had occurred when Henrietta had moved into her daughter's home: the daughter had not wanted to worry her about this, but now it was proving problematic. The social worker reported back to the doctor, and hearing what he had found out, suggested that he arrange for a physiotherapist to train the daughter in lifting and moving Henrietta. These procedures were not intuitive for the daughter, and the social worker arranged for a community physiotherapist to visit the home to reinforce the daughter's learning by providing additional training on the spot. The social worker explained to the doctor that she would sit down with the daughter and son to plan finances for the family, to ease the additional burden of Henrietta on the family finances. In discussion with the daughter, the social worker arranged for a community nurse to visit regularly, and planned with the nurse that the social worker, nurse, physiotherapist and a community doctor would organize their visits so that a professional saw Henrietta every alternate day, and could check to see if there were any problems. The doctor afterwards said to the social worker that he had not realized how coordinating changes in Henrietta's arrangements at home could help to reduce the risk of physical and financial abuse taking place.
>
> This case example shows how concern for both emotional and practical issues, and coordinating health and social care services can free even quite frail older people to 'age in place'; it also demonstrates the importance of reporting back on social care issues to healthcare staff who may be unaware of what can be achieved.

### The broader social context of participation

The broader context of participation connects with citizenship social work practice strategies:

- the importance of social class and other social and health inequalities;
- the role of social power relations;
- the role of the state (de Vos *et al.*, 2009).

Achieving participation for older people through citizenship social work takes place in societies with social divisions. These lead to social inequalities and, in turn, to health inequalities, which affect how people age and how they are affected by illness throughout their lives. Social divisions are bound up with power relations in society between different social groups.

Many of these economic and social issues are worked out in the role of the state. State health and social care services are a medium to redistribute resources between the generations, since older people are a more significant user of these services than younger adults. If the state reduces its role in social and health provision, and prefers a market economy, the capacity of these services and of social work within them to provide for older people is reduced. Citizenship social work sees the state as a mediator between the interests of older people at the end of life and other groups within any society.

By reducing the role of the state in social concern and expanding the role of the market, current politics negates the value of citizenship social work practice. But not entirely. By addressing practice strategies, social workers can adjust the impact of pressures upon the role of the state as mediator on behalf of the interests of older people. A citizenship strategy enhances older people's participation, respecting and valuing the contribution of informal care and community. Every time social care works with older people and their carers, it generates more social and community resilience and solidarity, not just for older people themselves, but for all social citizens.

## Conclusion: Citizenship and citizenship social work

Citizenship is a legal and social status that is part of the formation of a social order in any nation, by associating civil, political and social rights with emotional and cultural belonging. It is a controversial status, since in some political views, citizenship is part of an exchange in which citizens receive rights and services provided by the state in return for an economic and social contribution. Since older people may become progressively economically and then socially less active as part of a community, and eventually reach dependence and death, this conservative position may lead to questions about their entitlement to the benefits of citizenship and their contributions to society. A radical communitarian position, however, proposes that community cooperation and engagement with older people and end-of-life care builds community solidarity for everyone, not only older people themselves. End-of-life and palliative care, with its emphasis on transparency about dying and participation of families and communities in caring for dying people, further illustrates the radical communitarian view that engagement is a more appropriate response to dependence than exclusion.

A citizenship approach to social work contests dominant medical and social models of provision by ensuring that social work practice focuses on identifying and strengthening the contributions that older people and people at the end of life can make to their families and communities and promotes their participation in community and family life. It focuses particularly on responding in areas where older people and people at the end of life may experience de-citizening barriers or limitations. These include family and neighbourhood relationships, intimate relationships, restrictions and opportunities offered by employment and income, engagement in civil and social life, the influence of media and barriers in health and social care services to older people, and people at the end of life taking up full participation in society.

Citizenship practice strategies include re-citizening by focusing on integrating formal and informal services to provide effective support for freedom and advance care planning. By enabling older people and people at the end of life to take part in generalized rather than specialized services, this avoids de-citizening by forcing them into a care ghetto, in which we only think about care needs instead of human needs. Citizening seeks policy and practice acceptance that using healthcare, housing and social security as well as new technology is needed to enhance citizenship rights. Enabling older people and people at the end of life to take part in creative activities and personal development opportunities is a re-citizening enhancement to their social engagement with society.

## ADDITIONAL RESOURCES

Bartlett, R. and O'Connor, D. (2010) *Broadening the Dementia Debate: Towards social citizenship*. Bristol: Policy Press.

A good practical and conceptual introduction to working with people with dementia from a social citizenship perspective, particularly important because of the way in which we may exclude people with cognitive impairments from social citizenship.

Dwyer, P. (2010) *Understanding Social Citizenship: Themes and perspectives for policy and practice*, 2nd edn. Bristol: Policy Press.

An excellent general introduction to ideas about citizenship in general and exploring the meaning of social citizenship.

Scharf, T. and Keating, N. C. (eds) (2012) *From Exclusion to Inclusion in Old Age: A global challenge*. Bristol: Policy Press.

A more broad-ranging study including perspectives from many different countries covering issues of international concern, such as migration, globalization and social inclusion among different ethnic groups.

van Ewijk, H. (2009) *European Social Policy and Social Work: Citizenship-based social work*. London: Routledge.

An analysis of citizenship as an organizing concept for thinking about social work, and useful also because it emphasizes the European social model of the state as having an important role in social policy.

# 3

# SOCIAL WORK AND PALLIATIVE CARE

## Contributions to end-of-life care

### Aims

The main aim of this chapter is to introduce how citizenship social work with older people at the end of life is enriched by knowledge and understanding of palliative care. I also look at how end-of-life care may gain from a citizenship social work perspective. This helps us to clarify:

- the distinctive role of social work in healthcare settings; and in
- services for older people;
- in particular, by distinguishing the learning social workers can gain from an understanding of the positive features of the healthcare specialty, palliative care.

The main points are set out in Figure 3.1.

### Starting points: Social work's social role

Any specific role in social work is built up from, first, the general tasks of social work and, second, the specific tasks that come from the needs of the particular client group and the services that meet those needs. The general social work role with older people and the specific client group 'at the end of life' are my starting point. We can use knowledge and skills from related specialist areas, in this case palliative care.

Three main starting points are:

- social work's focus on the social;
- its application to social work and social care services for older people at the end of life;
- the contribution of palliative care.

### Differences between social work and palliative care contributions

#### *Qualities of social work and healthcare with older people at the end of life*

The first point is that social work is part of social care while palliative care is a healthcare service. This means that each is part of different service structures with different administrative, financial

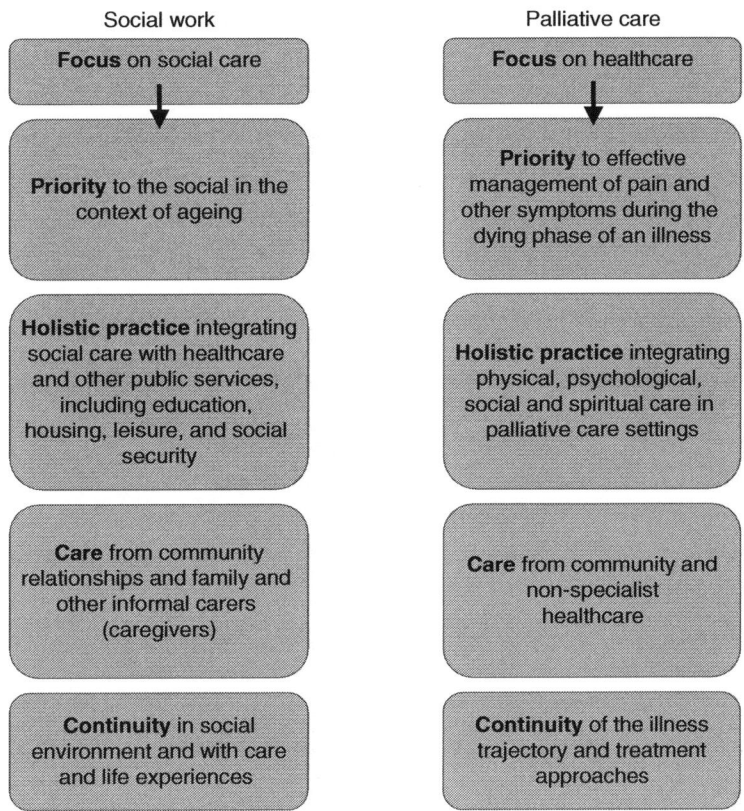

**FIGURE 3.1** Social work and palliative care contributions to end-of-life care

and legal systems. In England, for example, law and professional practice are generally developed and regulated through the Department of Health, and so is finance for healthcare, while financing for social care is routed through local government. In some countries social work is connected with social security; in others, social welfare services have their own ministry, separate from health. The service structures and their systems affect daily practice, and it is useful for practitioners to understand the consequences for their work.

Social work and palliative care are also not direct equivalents. Palliative care is a specialized multiprofessional practice, which often includes social work, within a wider healthcare service. Social work, on the other hand, is a profession within the social care sector of the economy and the public services. The qualities of each emerge from engagement in their particular sector of the economy and professional roles. For example, both healthcare and social work in the UK are in the public sector. There are considerable private-sector involvements in social care for older people; this is less important in palliative care. A significant aspect of social care for older people is informal care in the community by neighbours, friends and, most importantly, relatives of the older person. Palliative healthcare is largely professional; it does not have this informal care focus in its professional roles, although it comes into contact with family care for its patients.

The connections between health and social care and between palliative care and social work are not standardized in any particular country or across the world. We need to think through generalized understandings about the contributions and linkages of social work and palliative care to end-of-life care with older people in our particular locality and service.

Social work's focus on the 'social' and its role in social care services are confusing for many older people, their families and the public. Public and political recognition of medicine and nursing is secure, compared with public doubts about the value of social work. Such differences in recognition and value stem from many factors. These include the following points (developed from an analysis by Barnes *et al.*, 2007):

- Press and official criticism of social work interventions in exceptional but well-publicized cases of child death has devalued the potential help that social workers might offer in general and in other spheres.
- Social workers may be socially devalued by their association with issues such as addiction, mental health, offending, child abuse and homelessness, affecting socially stigmatized individuals and people often in lower socio-economic groups. Such groups are socially disapproved and subject to surveillance and policing by the state; social work is involved in that and healthcare professions less so.
- Social workers in many countries are state employees, and this often puts them in an ambiguous position at the intersection between public concerns and private issues. For example, social work offers personal support and counselling, helps people to make arrangements for care, but also has responsibilities that may involve curtailing liberty in child protection and mental health, assessing parental competence in child protection and adoption cases, or persuading older or disabled people to accept care arrangements that they don't want. Healthcare professionals, although often also state employees with surveillance and social management roles, have, in public perception, mainly been involved in helping and supportive roles.
- Social work draws on a wide range of human and social sciences which often raise ambiguous and contested understandings of social life and may have a critical perspective on current policies and practices. Healthcare professionals draw primarily on medical science knowledge which appears much more certain, is generally less contested and does not contest accepted social perspectives.
- Social work's knowledge base is, compared with healthcare, relatively complex and layered, accepting alternative perspectives on the situations in which people are involved, while healthcare knowledge appears to provide more certain prescriptions for action.
- Social work research and social care services are generally much less well financed than healthcare research and services, and are consequently less advanced and concrete in the understandings they offer to service development, policy and practice, and have fewer resources to offer.
- Social care services are financed and managed from local government provision and appear more constrained by political and organizational demands than healthcare, where services are more explicitly provided in response only to professional decisions.

Social work's focus on the social gives it a broad concern with people's well-being in daily life as part of interpersonal relationships in a social community. This distinguishes it from healthcare's focus on the impact of particular illnesses or combinations of illnesses on people's ability to carry on their preferred way of life. These focuses overlap: a serious illness or multiple conditions which increase a patient's frailty affect people's ability to pursue their relationships and daily life. Problems with relationships and maintaining a desired quality of life impact upon people's ability to deal well with an illness. The following case example illustrates this distinction.

> **CASE EXAMPLE: WELL-BEING AFFECTING RESPONSE TO HEALTHCARE AND ILLNESS AFFECTING DAILY LIFE**
>
> Mrs Jones was an older woman who regularly provided care for a teenage grand-daughter who had difficulties at school and a poor relationship with her father, who was separated from Mrs Jones's daughter. An education social worker was involved and encouraged this, even though neighbours and friends worried that the burden would make her condition worse. Although she suffered from Parkinson's disease, this was well managed by medication, and involvement with her grandchildren was an important aspect of her life. For one thing, it meant that she still kept in touch with the younger community of mothers caring for young children, so she felt involved with the world of work and child care, and said she felt younger as a result. Her doctors were surprised about how well she coped with the level of her disability, using the treatments that were available; social workers might interpret this as her being buoyed up by the valued social role and social connections that came from her grand-parenting. When serious symptoms began to emerge and she needed social care services, this prevented her from being involved with her grandchildren to the same degree. By this time, however, they had moved on to school, and her daughter did not need her active caring role in the same way. They found, however, that the grandchildren were prepared to keep in touch with her, now she was housebound. This made social relationships during her shortened period of severe disability before death much more satisfying.

Social work and social care services, because of their focus on the social, can therefore make a useful contribution to end-of-life care by pursuing prevention at an earlier stage of life. Citizening aims to help build family and community relationships and facilitate connections between people at times of difficulty. This aspect of practice is often neglected in social care practice in favour of person-centred care planning at a late stage of older people's ageing. In this case, Mrs Jones benefited in later life by the health and social care efforts earlier on to support her in caring for her grandchildren. We can't know at the time how this will work out. But generally, building and maintaining connections is a contribution to citizening that will always bring benefits in the long term, as well as satisfaction now. As a result, social care seems only to make a minimal 'service-providing' contribution to care for older people and to end-of-life care, and the priority appears to be heavy-duty healthcare and medical intervention. This is not to neglect the importance of those healthcare interventions. Mrs Jones coped with her disability with healthcare treatments, including physiotherapy and medication, serious symptoms which were diagnosed and managed by medical and nursing help. But a strategy of prevention that builds and maintains connections for the long term makes an important contribution (and primarily a social work and social care contribution) too.

I have therefore given priority to a whole-life focus on ageing in Chapter 6. Another emphasis throughout the book is the 'ethics of care' approach to caring practices and services, which identifies building social and community connections as important elements of care.

This is an important ethical basis for social work because it emphasizes building connections as part of services for older people at the end of life, and as we saw in Chapter 2, this helps with re-citizening.

This is not a counsel of perfection, unrealistic in the face of the pressures of the day job. It is a strategy for making some space around the edges of your professional tasks, and you and your team planning your career and your practice individually and together to enhance this social role (see Chapter 4). This helps to make the social contribution a natural part of everything you do to build better connections for people's long-term support. If you do, it will help to create more of a community supporting the people you work with, making your job easier.

## *Better well-being prevention strategies*

Chapter 1 pointed out that an important change in the political and social settlement around ageing was increasing separation between the phase of life concerned with bringing up children and being in the workforce, and old age. There is an increasingly elongated phase of life where people's children have moved into adulthood. At some point, as they age, people may leave the workforce, perhaps first partially and then fully. During this phase, they are very clearly citizens, often making big contributions to the community with caring responsibilities for grandchildren, neighbours and community and perhaps their own elderly relatives. As a result, many people do not think of 'old age' until they are frail and living on the threshold of the end of life. Social policy for social and healthcare has increasingly responded to this change with a stronger awareness of how important it is to identify when the end of life is near, as part of responding to older people with health and social care problems.

Clarkson (2012) notes research that suggests three scenarios of later life relevant to this greater emphasis on the end of life:

- 'Compression of morbidity', in which people age successfully, have longer lives and are generally healthy, with medical advance reducing the length of time that they are ill and frail as they approach the end of life.
- 'Expansion of morbidity', in which people live longer but more disabled lives. Such increasing disability in later life is potentially de-citizening, losing life opportunities, but it does not have to be if we take a re-citizening approach of finding ways of managing and transcending disability.
- 'Dynamic equilibrium', in which people have some serious disabilities, but decreases in other forms of disability, compensates for or reduces the impact of the serious conditions on older people's quality of life.

There is a class distinction here, in which poor people are more likely to lead longer lives than the previous generation, but their lives will contain disability and illness because they do not have the resources throughout life to maintain a healthy quality of life (Commission on Social Determinants of Health, 2008; Marmot Review Team, 2010). This suggests a practice strategy for health and social care services: to try to shift people towards compression and equilibrium scenarios, by encouraging people to achieve better well-being throughout their lives. This helps them prepare for ageing and reduce their demand on health and social care services. In particular, for social care, if older people manage daily life successfully for a longer proportion of later life and if good parts of their lives compensate for any difficulties, social care resources can give priority to people who need help most when they have high support needs.

## *Palliative care and its social work role transferred to end-of-life care*

Compared with the broad remit of social care's role with all older people needing services, palliative care has a more specific focus on pain and symptom management where people are in the dying phase of their lives because of a diagnosed medical condition. As older people move into end-of-life care, we can transfer ideas from palliative care into mainstream social work practice. Luptak (2004), writing with a palliative care perspective, identifies three important social roles in social work at the end of life. Contributing these to end-of-life care services for older people, she enables us to form useful practice strategies:

- Facilitating self-determination through person-centred care planning. This clearly transfers directly to the personalization in self-directed social care services. This can avoid the de-citizening that arises when people are blown off course because they are not prepared for things that might happen to them.
- Working for social justice in providing end-of-life services for older people. This is important for every client group; but Luptak's point makes it clear that unless social work includes end-of-life care in older people's lives, we shall be de-citizening them in their rights to the best possible care.
- Preparing healthcare and social service priorities for a more complex, holistic form of care for older people at the end of life. Simply focusing healthcare for older people on treating an escalating series of medical conditions or increasing frailty de-citizens older people by ignoring how all their needs fit together in complex ways.

Her view envisions a rights-based, quality-of-life focus in end-of-life care for older people, a concern for citizenship so that services are equally available to the whole population. Re-citizening people's experiences means acknowledging and incorporating a complex view of older people's needs in this phase of their lives. The aim should be not just healthcare and care provision, but equal right to a high quality of life until death, at least a step up towards the best quality we can help people to achieve.

Medical practice in palliative care has built on the experience of working with the end-stages initially of cancer, and later of other major illnesses. In particular, there has been a focus on the effective diagnosis and management of pain and other distressing symptoms. You can see this if you look at medical palliative care texts. Dealing with each condition requires a careful analysis of the symptoms that a patient experiences, where they experience them in the body, the seriousness of the problem they have with them and reactions to carious medications and other treatments. With pain, for example, doctors and nurses will be checking where in the body the patient experiences it, whether it moves, whether it is worsening or variable and the severity of it. Because pain and many other symptoms vary all the time, very detailed discussions are needed with the patient and other people who are seeing how pain affects them. When it comes to treatment, complex prescriptions of multiple drugs often used in combinations will be administered and evaluated, and how they affect each patient will be carefully charted over time and variations made frequently.

The consequence of this focus on the detailed analysis and management of symptoms is that wider issues that concern social workers cannot be a priority when palliative care patients meet with the doctor. But while it is de-citizening to miss the social in people's lives, it is also de-citizening to neglect the importance to older people of effective healthcare.

> **CASE EXAMPLE: THE DOCTOR'S FOCUS ON PAIN AND THE SOCIAL WORKER'S BROADER FOCUS**
>
> The consultant palliative care physician, at the hospital bedside with a specialist nurse practitioner and with Jane, the team social worker, started off her consultation with Mrs Calthrop, a woman patient dying of cancer, by introducing the members of the team. An immensely empathetic discussion followed about how pain was affecting the patient and involved careful rating of her different experiences of pain in different areas of the body. There was also discussion of how the patient had experienced the several medications being used. Finally, the consultant asked about support from the patient's family, and was assured that they were very supportive. After more than half an hour's discussion, changes in prescription and non-drug treatment were discussed with the nurse, who would be making the arrangements. The physician suggested the patient should pick up, with the social worker, the arrangements for returning home after the treatment was established and her condition was stable.
>
> After the medical consultation, Mrs Calthrop was clearly exhausted, and the nurse went off to make her a cup of tea, while Jane continued informal conversation about how the patient had come into hospital and how she had experienced surgery some months before. Cups of tea in hand, Jane introduced herself and gave Mrs Calthrop a visiting card explaining that this would help the patient remember her name in future and she could pass contact details onto family members. She then asked an open question, which any social worker knows is often a useful opening gambit: 'I wonder what the main thing on your mind at the moment is.' This question encourages focus on the patient's main priorities, and is characteristic of social work's priority to start from 'where the client is'. The medical priority in the consultation did not ignore or disparage the patient's experience; rather, it focused on pain and symptom management, to enable the doctor to use her powerful and important professional expertise in using medication and other techniques to manage the patient's pain. So both professionals worked in partnership with the patient, but with different priorities.
>
> Answering the social worker's question, the patient talked about how her husband was very distressed by the further recurrence of her illness, and feared all the consequences of her death, and was having practical difficulties in managing the home in her absence. Her daughter, a single parent of a child with attention deficit hyperactivity disorder (ADHD), was also living in their home and relied on the patient for support and care: her husband would be unlikely to be able to provide this to the same degree. A son was at college and relied on the family's income to enable him to complete his course. The social worker had much to do, it seemed.
>
> Afterwards, Jane reported this and her plan for getting to grips with the family problems to the consultant, who was puzzled. 'But why did she say the family were supportive?' she asked. Jane's discussion had revealed this. The patient felt that they were supportive and concerned about her, for one thing, and also she had been concentrating on working with

> the doctor on her pain, which was important to her, so she had reserved discussion about family matters to the social worker: 'I didn't want to bother the doctor with it.'
>
> The nurse had also seen the social worker get from the patient the names, ages and contact details of the various members of the family, and expressed surprise that the social worker in a hospital had left a visiting card. Although they had worked together for some time, this was the first time she had sat in on a social work interview. The medical records contained information about the family in the following form, a de-humanizing and therefore also de-citizening form: 'Next of kin: husband, above address'. After several years of treatment at the hospital, there was no record of his name or any details about the rest of the family: the file referred throughout to 'pt' (an abbreviation of 'patient') and 'husband'. The consultant's name appeared on a notice above the bed, and on the medical record front cover, but the patient did not know the name of any other member of staff. If she needed to contact someone, she asked a ward nurse to call the consultant or the specialist nurse. The focus on the detail of their professional responsibilities meant that the human and family details which were a natural starting point for the social worker were unknown to the hospital, and once the doctor's consultation had been channelled into the detail of pain management, the patient had thought it inappropriate to move onto family matters. Also, her lifelong experience of doctors was of brief consultations, with purely medical responses. She immensely valued the amount of time and trouble that this particular consultant had taken with her: this was the longest medical consultation she had experienced in her life and with a senior doctor, too. She felt privileged and cared for. To go on to deal with family concerns just seemed irrelevant.

I take several things from this case example, and many experiences like it. First, healthcare is an important issue for service users. So, it is de-citizening, neglectful of their rights to good healthcare provision, to be hostile to a 'medical model' of disability and illness. A focus on disability and illness, as a common critique of the medical model points out, is de-citizening in one way by dealing with bits of the body, rather than the whole person, and by focusing on illness rather than well-being. But clear focus on symptoms and treatment, diagnosis and prognosis, is a socially important priority to patients and their families because it symbolizes care. It is a citizening social recognition of their illness, acknowledges the importance of health to many people, and a prerequisite of successful and comfortable social relationships. For many older people and practitioners working with them in healthcare, pain and symptom relief and physical comfort achieved by successful nursing is a foundation for enabling patients and their families to concentrate on re-citizening them by enhancing social relations that are also important to them. Untreated physical discomfort is a distraction from addressing the social.

The second point is connected to the importance of the medical model in healthcare service priorities. It means that it is easy for healthcare staff to miss important aspects of the social patient. Feeding back to healthcare staff about social issues that have arisen and how the social worker is going to tackle them is re-citizening. It helps healthcare staff maintain balance between their work and the social, and also to value what social workers are doing as essential, not peripheral, to healthcare. Healthcare colleagues are rewarded by seeing through the social worker's reporting back what becomes possible because their treatment has helped the patient to return to at least some of their normal social life.

The third point is that an important social work contribution to the healthcare system is the recognition and prioritizing of the social. In particular, this means helping to make the connections to the social life history and family relationships. To some degree all healthcare intervention is temporary, because its aim is to put the patient in the position to recover or, in palliative care, manage symptoms to the point where medical intervention has come to an end. This is why the medical record often concentrates on medical issues to the exclusion of social relationships. Social work plays an important role in recognizing and documenting the continuity of patients' social connections within healthcare records and systems.

## Holistic practice in social work and palliative care

### *The social work contribution to holistic care*

An important principle of palliative care is that it is holistic care, often described as the incorporation of emotional, psychological, social and spiritual care with the physical care provided by nursing and medicine. Among palliative care professionals, however, these different aspects of care are not well differentiated, because the priority is to the physical. The terms emotional and psychological are sometimes used interchangeably to refer to non-physical responses to dying. This explicit commitment to holistic care fits well with the broad objectives of social work, and indeed most surveys of palliative care knowledge incorporate social work and refer to the valid contribution of social work to palliative care. The terms psychological and social are often combined as 'psychosocial care' as in, for example, Sheldon's (1997) well-known textbook. A close look at the palliative care literature, though, reveals that psychosocial care is often equated with the psychological, and the social aspect of this concept is not distinguished. In the NICE manual of guidance (National Institute for Clinical Excellence, 2004), for example, the content of social work intervention is ill defined, and limited to financial assistance and assessment for social care services. More recent guidance from NICE since it assumed responsibility for social care provision similarly recognizes the importance of social care as an aspect of end-of-life care (National Institute for Health and Care Excellence, 2011).

Social workers often find, therefore, a greater valuing and recognition of their role in end-of-life care than they experience in other healthcare specialties, although understanding of what they are doing may be diffuse and confused. To respond to this, a useful social work practice strategy is to be clear with colleagues and service users and carers about the precise aspects of the social, as well as the psychological, that they are concerned with. For example, making family, friendship, community and carer links and contributions explicit raises the social directly, while the psychological is more concerned with patients' and family members' personal reactions to the illness or disability we are working with. Another example is making clear the different service links contributing to the patient's care, which other professionals may also be hazy about. This is particularly important where difficult problems are involved – for example, safeguarding issues. Healthcare staff can have better confidence in their patient's security if they understand how community services have developed strategies for dealing with the risk of abuse or neglect.

As a social profession, social work is integrated with a wide range of public and community professions, as well as healthcare. Where re-citizening is our aim, therefore, social work offers a connection with the civic sphere beyond healthcare. Social care services are part of broader public provision, usually in local government, so the working base of most social workers and their career experience centres them on local government experience and on services in the community. Social work education and training involves practitioners in building up a picture of a wide range of social provision, including criminal justice, education, housing, information services and social security. Therefore, an important professional area of knowledge and skill for social workers is keeping a wide range of such services informed and involved and helping healthcare colleagues with procedures to use these services.

Healthcare practitioners, on the other hand, have all their early experience, education and training in healthcare organizations and often in large-scale institutions, the hospitals where most practical medical and nursing education takes place. Community experience is more peripheral than in education for social care professions and later on in the career path. A strong focus on the importance of biomedical knowledge and healthcare professional skills means that healthcare professions are typically not aware of or interested in social policy. Their focus on healthcare means that social policy is often seen through the lens of healthcare needs. For example, poor housing would be criticized in healthcare if it makes people's health worse and poverty because it prevents people from having a healthy lifestyle.

An important strategy for social workers, therefore, is to identify social issues that make it difficult for healthcare interventions to be effective and, on the other hand, social opportunities that might enhance healthcare. You can then raise these issues specifically, propose and take action on them, and feed back to healthcare professionals what has been achieved.

## *Spirituality: Some interactions with social work*

Chaplaincy is an important area of palliative care that interacts with social work, with these professions often being seen as overlapping areas of practice (Lloyd, 1997). A recent authoritative systematic review of spirituality in end-of-life care (Holloway et al., 2011) notes that palliative care literature, particularly in the US, conflates psychosocial and spiritual care, seeing it as dealing with a connected range of concerns. Social work practice has generally been a secular practice, and Furman et al.'s (2004) study of UK social workers identified that many practitioners demonstrate 'caution' in taking up concerns about spiritual care, with end-of-life care being an exception. This is mirrored by similar surveys in other countries. In countries where there is a strong cultural commitment to a religion, social workers' professional approach of open-mindedness about people's attitudes may mean that they struggle with family or community assumptions about religious and spiritual issues. For example, a high proportion of communities in the US expect strong overt Christianity, and permitting more flexible attitudes may be difficult. Working with communities committed to Islam or Judaism may also lead to conflicts in expectations that social workers have to deal with. Whereas chaplains have a clear commitment to their religion, expectations of a social worker may be less clear when they are trying to tackle social issues which have a religious or spiritual aspect. Even among people committed to a particular family or denomination, however, there is a considerable variety of practice and commitment, so a practitioner can never make assumptions about what people should do.

> **CASE EXAMPLE: ON NOT FACING MECCA**
>
> In a care home, a prayer room allowed Muslims to pray facing Mecca, and staff had been advised that it was helpful, if a resident was at the end of life, that their bed might be turned to face Mecca. Hussain, however, although committed to his faith, did not see this as important and preferred to keep his window view of the garden. When asked if he wanted his bed moved to face Mecca, he refused.

Social workers might benefit from becoming more conscious of spiritual care issues both because end-of-life care often raises such issues, but also because spiritual issues are part of responding to ethnic and cultural difference. Studies of older adults show that religiosity and spirituality are important to successful ageing and dealing with mental health problems in old age, too (Holloway et al., 2011), so transferring the importance of working on spiritual issues from palliative care into social work with older people could help to bring the two specialist areas together. It is de-citizening for older people if we avoid spiritual issues when these are important to them; it is re-citizening if we can include the spiritual back into their lives. A number of hospices have linked the management of social work and chaplaincy staff. The approach of the two professions, however, is different, with social work seeing spirituality as a potential area of concern to be tackled as a problem, whereas chaplaincy staff are more prepared to acknowledge 'mystery and paradox' (Reese and Sontag, 2001; Holloway, 2007; Holloway et al., 2011).

Spiritual distress is often associated with concern about 'meaning' (Payne, 2014), which Speck (2004) clarifies as being 'existential meaning', whether the fact of an individual's existence has meaning and purpose for them, what that meaning is and how the individual may discover it. A substantial part of working with spiritual issues is understanding what spirituality is and its interaction with religion. American studies give more emphasis to religiosity, while from elsewhere in the world spirituality is concerned with more secular concerns, bordering on social and psychological difficulties. Kernohan et al.'s (2007) Northern Ireland palliative care study identifies six worries: to have time to think; to have hope; to deal with unresolved issues; to prepare for death; to express true feelings without being judged; and to assess important relationships and the dying person's impact within those relationships. These are all issues which a social worker might look out for in discussions with older people and their carers, taking them up as they arise. This is because being able to tackle concerns about such issues may help people to deal more effectively with end-of-life care decisions. Another important spiritual issue is sometimes described as transcendence: the sense of a wider power to 'rise above' current difficulties and achieve a sense of hope that a dying person will achieve a successful route through the process of dying. Applying this idea to work with older people, practitioners might find it useful to work with older people on the positives they can get out of their present life experience. For example, some people moving towards the end of life talk about having enhanced appreciation of nature, music and other things that interest them.

Spiritual need is not something that is dealt with once and for all, and may emerge in different ways as practitioners work with older people and their carers. The Department of Health systematic literature review (Holloway et al., 2011) noted a number of models of practice seeking to integrate professional responses to spiritual issues in end-of-life care, and social workers might usefully take up some of these approaches:

- Develop awareness and understanding of spirituality and spiritual care.
- Develop, critique and refine theory and ideas about spirituality.
- Map spiritual care provision; this is something that can be done in the team by identifying both formal religious organizations and less formal courses and activities that may be helpful.
- Organize frameworks for the delivery of religious and spiritual support.
- Engage with spiritual needs in their practice.
- Develop knowledge, skills and competency in doing so.
- Respond to diversity of belief.
- Develop culturally sensitive practice, which includes sensitivity to spiritual care.
- Enhance the experience that older people and their carers have when they raise spiritual care issues.

In particular, this review noted that most approaches to spiritual care were multidisciplinary, which meant that all professions including social work needed to engage with spiritual care, alongside each other. Practitioners can usefully explore issues that may raise spiritual concerns under five main headings. By doing so, they can incorporate a social work perspective into the support offered by spiritual care professionals and other healthcare colleagues.

1. *Fulfilment*. People often talk about things they have not achieved and things they want to achieve. If they seem discouraged, practitioners can ask them to think through and spell out what they have achieved in their lives. This might be in their relationships, in contributions they have made to organizations or in practical things they have done or objects they have made or built. It is important to help clients think about and plan for how they can achieve what they want, and who they know who could help them. Canda (1998) points out that you can increase a sense of fulfilment in two directions. One way is inwards through introspection and revealing more about the true nature of our selves. The alternative is concentrating on outwards fulfilment, through mending damaged relationships or building new ones.
2. *Diversity*. People may talk about feeling uncomfortable with increasing ethnic, cultural and spiritual diversity. This might occur because the neighbourhood they live in is changing, or they are presented with alternative cultures and spiritualities that they disagree with on television or in organizations they are involved with. Practitioners might help people to become better informed and more tolerant of something they have experienced or that they need to get involved with. For example, they do not have to get to know all the different cultures in a multicultural neighbourhood, but they could concentrate on learning about their nearest neighbours or the relatives who are most important to them. Clients may also be helped to see links and similarities, as well as differences. It is (re-)citizening to help people understand and value spiritual links with others around them.
3. *Self-determination*. People often see respect for their right to make their own decisions about how they are cared for and how they live their lives as a crucial part of their humanity. This means having the right to alternatives from which people can choose. Presenting people with only one practical care option and being unable to work through their own priorities makes people feel non-human. Therefore, practitioners are building spiritual resources for people as well as (re-)citizening when they help clients and carers

think through decisions that are important to them, and plan for how they will retain in their lives important priorities as this becomes more difficult
4. *Environment.* Many older people are stuck at home; many dying people are limited by their frailty or illness. People interact with their environment, including their home and their neighbourhood, so limiting or controlling their environment diminishes and de-citizens them as human beings. Practitioners might do this unintentionally when for safety reasons they restrict people from moving about their home or from going out, or clutter up their home with lots of care equipment. Sometimes practitioners and agencies feel they have to press people to accept living in a care home; or in community care plans practical pressures of organization and staffing fail to maintain consistency in the carers who visit a client's home or room. The lack of a stimulating environment, and lack of change in client's surroundings, including the inability to take a holiday or a break from routine can also limit people's spirit. All of these pressures are potentially de-citizening, and we can aim to prevent or reverse such processes. Practitioners can look out for small opportunities or flexibilities that at least retain some elements of an environment that a client likes, and can look for ways of introducing variety.
5. *Helping relationships.* Responding to people's spirituality involves accepting and working with their quirks in practitioners' own quirky ways. People are unable to develop and fulfil their spirituality unless they can be active in thinking and talking in their own words and ideas about the problems that they are facing that they want help with. Their spirituality is not respected if practitioners mainly focus on tick lists of identifiable problems or diagnostic labels, another de-citizening process that we can avoid or reverse. Dialogue which enables discovery of each other is a crucial part of any helping relationship – this is true for professional practitioners, paid and unpaid carers and family members. Empathy involves not only the formal skills of listening carefully, reflecting on what clients say and feeding back practitioners' own responses to it. It also involves sensing unspoken elements of clients' communications, including feelings that they are holding back, and anticipating the spiritual implications of what they are saying (extended from an analysis by Canda, 1998).

In addition to having opportunities to talk about such issues with professionals and others, Dane and Moore's (2006) American study found activities that people find useful in dealing with spiritual issues include yoga, prayer and meditation. Practitioners might usefully suggest to older people and carers that they set aside some time for reflection each day if they have no experience of such techniques and no involvement in formal religion. This may form an indirect re-citizening, compensating for social losses by coming at them from a different direction.

There are a range of assessment tools and scales for assessing spiritual care needs in end-of-life care, hospital care more generally and in social work that practitioners may find helpful. These include, for UK practitioners, King et al.'s (1995) Royal Free interview for religious and spiritual beliefs, and various techniques proposed in social work by Hodge (2001).

## Social work and palliative care sources of caring

In this section, I want to distinguish social work and palliative care approaches to caring and the care tasks that social and healthcare services and professionals undertake. What is needed to care is in one way ambiguous and complex, founded in basic human emotions. In another way, the detail of the tasks that we must perform to care is specialized and we need to work out and train for the best ways of achieving it. We can see these different aspects of caring as we look at the contributions to caring ideas and expertise in palliative and social care.

One important distinction is that because palliative care is a specialized healthcare service, it is mainly concerned with delivering care by paid and often highly qualified healthcare practitioners attuned to helping people through the dying process in a small range of highly specific illnesses. It started in cancer, and is still strongly connected to cancer services, in the medical speciality of oncology (Reith and Payne, 2009). It has begun to open out. At first this was by supporting people at home, rather than in hospital and hospice settings. Now, end-of-life care has begun to transfer its specialized expertise to non-specialist services in general hospitals, general practice, community healthcare and recently to community social care. Nevertheless, its assumption about care is focused on good-quality care where there is a diagnosed illness, or at least a fairly clear indication that an older person is within a year or so of their death.

> ### CASE EXAMPLES: FEEDING MUM AND MANAGING PAIN CONTROL
>
> An example of this may make the point clearer. When I was working in a hospice, I was approached by a community nurse specialist with concerns about safeguarding for a frail older woman with end-stage cancer who was being cared for by her three daughters in one daughter's home. The daughters were concerned that their mother was not eating properly, and alleged that the daughter who had the main role in caring was neglecting to feed her. In a family meeting, the nurse and I shared a discussion with the daughter who was the main carer about what was happening. All the daughters agreed that eating was a problem, and they had all been assertive in producing meals and feeding them three times a day to their mother, to the extent that she was choking and then had refused to eat. One of the things we had noticed was that all the daughters were large women, and one of the concerns was that the mother had lost weight rapidly. We wondered whether this family had a culture of enthusiastic eating. We explained that as people approached the end of life they lost interest in food and because of their illness, they did not need the amount of food that they did in normal circumstances. We tried to persuade them that 'force-feeding' was not necessary, indeed it might be dangerous. After the meeting, in discussion with me, the nurse saw what the daughters were doing as cruel and oppressive behaviour. She said: 'Everyone knows that this is not the sort of thing you should do.' I explained that I did not think the average person would know this, particularly if eating was an important social aspect of life in a family. I certainly hadn't until I got involved in palliative care. Everyone the nurse worked with was aware of the same things that she knew, and we came to the conclusion that the team, although they had explained the changes that the family might expect, had not done enough to change their lifelong experience that food was part of caring.
>
> Another example often arose when we were arranging for people to return home from the hospice. Well-established and successful pain control on a hospice ward often goes awry when a patient returns home. One problem is that people often leave taking medication until they feel pain, rather than using it regularly, which is the best medical practice. You can probably imagine that the family caring for a sick older person at home, with a

> household to run, and lots of other things to do, does not check on medication on the same rigid timetable as the carefully recorded medication provision on a hospice ward. To the palliative care specialists, this was an unfortunate reduction in the quality of care offered in a home environment, compared with the high-quality care they offered in the hospice. Thus, we accepted the reduced effectiveness of pain control because of the social and citizening benefits of people being cared for by their family in their own home in the community, even if it did not provide the optimum quality of care. Re-citizening meant that we tried repeatedly to emphasize to their patients and their carers the best ways of organizing pain control medication.

I take from these experiences an inevitable difference in approach between palliative care and social work. While palliative care staff concentrate on the best quality of care they can provide professionally, the social work approach to care sees such institutional care in hospitals and similar places as the exception in people's lives, and concentrates on the caring that mostly takes place within the existing relationships that people have. It is part of the life journey and the relationships we make within it, and we feel a lack of care or a failing in care provision if we cannot maintain care within those relationships. The citizening social work caring task in working with older people, then, is to identify, maintain and build our care on the patterns of caring they have experienced during their life.

Daly and Lewis (2000) identify three dimensions of care that we should think about as we get involved in caring and in organizing care from colleagues in paid-for care services and in interweaving this with informal care from neighbours, friends and relatives:

1. It is labour, so we have to consider the ways in which it is similar to other forms of work and the conditions in which it is undertaken. I would add to this point that it usually involves *emotional* labour, because caring for older people, particularly at the end of life, usually engages both the carer's and the older person's emotions about their situation as a more or less dependent older person and carer. Caring labour may raise feelings about dependency for the older person and the carer, and it may also raise feelings for carers about the loss of other kinds of labour – with children and grandchildren, and employment and career opportunities – that because of the caring role may be put on hold or lost forever.
2. It takes place in a normative framework of moral duty and responsibility. It is this that leads to the association of care with respect and dignity.
3. It incurs costs, both emotional and financial, to everyone involved.

Caring may also have spiritual dimensions. For example, it demonstrates to people that they are significant to others in their lives, worth someone taking trouble over. It also includes being non-judgemental and sensitive about cultural values, physical preferences and social needs (Narayanaswamy, 2006). The 'ethics of care' view deriving from Gilligan (1993) and subsequently developed by Noddings (1984), Tronto (1993), Sevenhuijsen (1998) and others proposes that responding to need by caring reflects an alternative perspective that exists within society focused on connectedness within social relationships. Practice in caring services may have to respond to uncertain and conflicting views of what informal and paid social carers are trying to do. Uncertainties and conflicts are mirrored in the perceptions of social care and palliative care, and carry over into end-of-life care for older people.

Older people at the end of life, therefore, sometimes perceive a culture clash in their dealings with healthcare. They enter the healthcare system expecting cure, as they did when they were younger. Where there is a clear condition to be treated, this is often what they get. At some point, though, the focus shifts towards continuing care for conditions that will not get better. Some aspects of their healthcare will continue in 'cure' mode, while others will be more concerned with managing conditions that cannot be cured. Towards the end of life, there would ideally be an explicit recognition that only palliative care will be offered, and that death can be expected soon. This seems to require a different mode of care. Some people are comfortable with, indeed in old age and at the end of life welcome, this shift of modes from the decision-making rational model of care to the connectedness model; others are less pleased with the change, and want to maintain attempts at cure.

Such ambiguities also assail social care for older people at the end of life. We saw earlier that healthcare may be more valued than social work in general. It is also less clear that social work is about caring in the same way as healthcare and end-of-life care. Social care services may therefore have an uphill struggle because people may not assume that it is caring, in the same way that they would of a healthcare service. This is partly, as we saw, because it is associated with involuntary and perhaps oppressive helping, surveillance and public-sector assessment of need. Second, its caring is not bodily or intimate caring, as medicine and nursing are. Nevertheless, social workers spend much of their time concerned with caring in various ways. For example, social workers ensure that parents' care of their children is as good as possible where there are questions about abuse or the quality of parental care, to maximize the child's personal development. They are also involved with organizing care for adults who are unable to be completely self-caring.

In some ways, palliative and end-of-life care in its connectedness mode is more like social care than healthcare. For example, the shift to concern with quality of life in longer-term conditions rather than cure should, you would think, lead to a stronger focus on social relations and family support. The context of healthcare, however, means that palliative care has a primary focus on managing symptoms, and its history of emerging from cancer care leads to a strong focus on managing pain. This makes it seem less about connected caring and more about treatment.

## Palliative care and social work contributions to continuity

We can bring together the issues I have been discussing in this chapter by looking at the palliative care and social work contributions to the idea of continuity. We have seen that continuity with the life course experience of people and their families is an important part of maintaining their citizenship. Continuity across services and professions is also relevant in multiprofessional and multiagency practice, considered in the next chapter.

Figure 3.1 distinguishes the social work and palliative care contributions to continuity. Social work is concerned to maintain lifelong continuity: the community and social environment and the life and care experiences of the older person. Healthcare is concerned primarily with the consistency and continuity of the healthcare services and improvement in the response to illness. To make the most of the social work contribution, a useful practice strategy for social work practitioners is to spend time exploring and understanding the cultural, social and emotional background and history of an older person and the community and family context that informs their response to their ageing and the end of their life. They can then bring this perspective into the wider services that they are part of.

An important aspect of palliative care practice in end-of-life care is skill in dealing with the transition between curative and palliative care and discussing prognosis as well as diagnosis – that is, the likely medical outcome, as well as defining the condition that is causing the illness. This is an important stage because it marks the shift to palliative care. Crucially, it involves making clear to patients that no more progress with cure can be made, and that the illness will lead to their death. According to the widely accepted World Health Organization (1998) definition of palliative care, it affirms the value of the life that remains, while regarding dying as a natural process which should not be hastened or postponed. The WHO statement says dying is a normal process, but death is not commonplace in everyday life, so experiencing it is not 'normal' to most people. Discussing death with people, therefore, I prefer to say that it is natural. Palliative care does not mean doing nothing: in the course of the illness, therapies that prolong life and investigations and tests that help to understand and manage symptoms are important parts of care. These principles indicate how palliative care is not a separate or different form of healthcare, but continues on from curative treatment.

The crucial area of skill in this field for social workers to incorporate into end-of-life care practice with older people is techniques for raising and discussing the prognosis of terminal illness or the reality that people are dying. Without doing this, it is not possible to help people with the end of their lives, since this means accepting impending death and, in the case of family members, bereavement. Evidence about how healthcare professionals do this (Pino *et al.*, 2016) suggests that they start by asking open-ended questions about patients' perceptions of their situation. This gave patients opportunities to talk about end-of-life worries. If, in the reply, there was a cue that gave a further opportunity, healthcare professionals would then pick up that cue and ask more explicit questions about end-of-life issues.

### CASE EXAMPLE: TELLING JUNE THAT HER HUSBAND IS DYING

Carl, June's husband, had a longstanding progressive disease and was admitted to a hospital for treatment for some of the symptoms, including a difficult-to-cure lung infection. After a period of treatment, the lead doctor among the several medical teams treating him decided that no treatment was practicable; this was explained to Carl, and, aware that he was weakening, he asked June to bring his children to see him after school (normally in his frequent periods of in-patient treatment, they visited at weekends), without explaining why. June sought a meeting with the ward manager, who involved the social worker and a junior doctor. The doctor took the lead in the meeting, introducing the people present, all of whom June had met before. June asked how the latest treatments had gone. She was puzzled that Carl had asked to see the children, as this was not the usual way they managed things. The doctor explained that Carl had completed his course of treatment, but it had not had any effect on his lung infection, and the lead doctor had decided that there was now no treatment that would help Carl, and he would be remaining in the hospital, but would not be expected to recover and would not return home. The ward manager, a nurse, explained how they would make sure that Carl remained comfortable over the next few days, until his condition worsened. June asked what they were going to do now. The doctor asked June how she felt her husband was, after the course of treatment. June explained that she had seen some improvement, but that Carl had now gone backwards and seemed not to have improved after the initial

> treatment. The doctor repeated that there was no further treatment, and that the ward would provide the best possible care for Carl until he came to the end of his life. As he spoke, June collapsed in her seat with a wail, and said: 'I've just realized; you're telling me he's going to die, aren't you?' The doctor confirmed that this was so, and June went on that she understood now that he must know this, because he had asked to see the children. The social worker asked what the children knew about their father's condition. June explained that he had been ill for many years, and they took his periods of treatment for granted, and knew that his condition was serious, but they were not aware that death was so close. She pulled herself together and said that she would talk to them about this, and then bring them in to see Carl. The social worker arranged an appointment to talk with her after this had taken place.

Although each situation is unique, this case example is in many ways typical because it takes some time for people with their own thoughts and feelings to pick up even quite clear explanations about impending death. It is often important to people to maintain a balance between hope and reality to be able to continue with their lives in the face of serious illness (Reith and Payne, 2009). They maintain hope that there will be a positive future, such as successful treatment, while also keeping in their minds the reality that the end of life is probably nearing. Maintaining hope sometimes inhibits reality. Bringing them into contact with reality by inviting them to make their own judgements about the situation – for example, how the symptoms are worsening – helps them to make contact with the reality. Once they accept that they are dying, they often move into taking actions that they have planned or that they think are important in the time they have left. This may include completing tasks, organizing their affairs or, as in this case, seeing people who are important to them to say 'goodbye'.

This was a relatively clear situation. Incorporating end-of-life care within social work practice with older people, however, means dealing with the realities of dying at an earlier stage. Practitioners therefore need to build skills in responding to clues that someone wants to talk about the end of life. These are not 'worries' but addressing reality, because it is a reality that people are nearer the end of life in old age than in earlier phases of their ageing. One of the important things to do is to talk at the same time hopefully about the things that the older person is still able and wants to do, while addressing the reality of an approaching end of life.

## Conclusion: Social work practice strategies and learning from healthcare and palliative care

In conclusion, I summarize here two aspects of the practice identified in this chapter for social workers concerned with end-of-life care with older people. These are, first, the learning gained from the particular contribution of palliative care as part of healthcare services and, second, the practice strategies identified that stem from the social focus of social work. The aim of these is to help social work practitioners bring palliative care understandings together with social work with older people in social care services. If we are able to do this, social workers will provide a more effective citizening practice of social work with older people.

The learning gained from palliative care that can help social work practitioners make a useful contribution to end-of-life care of older people is:

- The importance of effective diagnosis, and medical, nursing and physiotherapy management of frailty and disability, which maintains the best health status for older people. 'Management' of health problems and their consequences, not just medical treatment, is crucial to enabling social care to make its contribution to the best quality of life as people age towards the end of life.
- Careful attention to the healthcare difficulties experienced by older people, so that we understand the importance of healthcare to them and how they are affected by their health problems. It is only by doing this that we can help them gain support in their social networks for the specific healthcare needs that they have.
- The importance of effective hands-on care as older people approach the end of life.
- The palliative care social work role with its focus on using social work personalized care planning to facilitate self-determination, ensuring that older people are enabled to achieve their rights to appropriate end-of-life care and ensuring that the complexity of their social needs are adequately represented in end-of-life care services.
- The importance of incorporating emotional, psychological, social and spiritual care in end-of-life care for older people, and making the social work contribution of defining and clarifying the 'social' within different elements of people's needs.
- The role of spiritual care professionals and awareness of spiritual care as a potential need for older people facing the end of life.
- The skill and priority given to open discussion of the end of life and planning for death and bereavement.

The practice strategies deriving from the social focus of social work are as follows:

- Build and maintain connections in families and communities as part of your practice for the benefit of long-term caring relationships.
- Aim to generate community support as a natural part of professional social work tasks.
- Shift people towards maintaining healthy lifestyles, balancing adverse health impacts with positives in their lives.
- Be precise about the aspects of the social that you are concerned with, feed back to colleagues on these aspects and clarify friendship, community and carer links and family relationships of benefit to older people receiving healthcare services, especially at the end of life.
- Maintain colleagues' confidence in the security of their patients by clarifying safeguarding strategies and their achievements.
- Develop awareness of spirituality in older people's lives; be prepared to explore spiritual issues with them, using specific assessment resources and identify these issues to colleagues.
- Identify and explore ambiguities in expectations of caring among different people involved with an older person, including professional colleagues.
- Explicitly identify social issues making it difficult for healthcare objectives to be achieved and the impact of health problems upon older people's family and community lives.
- Build skills in discussing the reality of an approaching end-of-life or dying phase, while maintaining hope for useful aspects of life continuing.

## ADDITIONAL RESOURCES

### Broad introductions to palliative care

Three comprehensive texts may be found in specialist libraries:

Hanks, G., Cherny, N. I., Christakis, N. A., Fallon, M., Kaasa, S. and Portenoy, R. K. (eds) (2010) *Oxford Textbook of Palliative Medicine*, 4th edn. Oxford: Oxford University Press.
This is a comprehensive and authoritative collection of articles on palliative care in general.

Watson, M., Lucas, C., Hoy, A. and Wells, J. (2009) *Oxford Handbook of Palliative Care*, 2nd edn. Oxford: Oxford University Press.
This is a smaller-scale reference book used by many palliative care services and provides serviceable information.

Altilio, T. and Otis-Green, S. (2011) *Oxford Textbook of Palliative Social Work*. Oxford: Oxford University Press.
Another authoritative collection of articles, mostly American-based but with some world coverage.

### End-of-life care and economic and social development

The World Health Organization sees palliative care as an important aspect of social development in healthcare, leading towards greater equality in healthcare outcomes across the world. Its website contains important information and resources, including a global map of palliative care developments and the WHO cancer pain ladder for adults, which helps us to understand the progression of increasing pain relief required for effectiveness. See http://www.who.int/cancer/palliative/en/.

### Spirituality

The following texts are useful in exploring spirituality in social work further:

Holloway, M. and Moss, B. H. (2010) *Spirituality and Social Work*. Basingstoke: Palgrave Macmillan.
A thoughtful practice text.

Holloway, M., Adamson, S., McSherry, W. and Swinton, J. (2011) *Spiritual Care at the End of Life: A systematic review of the literature*. London: Department of Health.
An authoritative review of the literature on spirituality in end-of-life care, from a range of professional positions, with strong social work content.

Mowat, H. and O'Neill, M. (2013) *Spirituality and Ageing: Implications for the care and support of older people*. Glasgow: Institute for Research and Innovation in Social Services. Retrieved 30 October 2015 from http://www.iriss.org.uk/resources/spirituality-and-ageing-implications-care-and-support-older-people.
A brief account of spirituality issues, with commentary on the evidence base, which is limited.

> **Websites**
>
> Social Care Institute for Excellence (SCIE) website on 'dying well at home' with access to two downloads offering good evidence summaries on working in an integrated way, and 'dying well at home' in general.
> http://www.scie.org.uk/publications/guides/guide48/practiceexamples/practiceexample03.asp

# 4

# PARTNERSHIP PRACTICE STRATEGIES

Like any other citizen, an older person needs to be treated as a whole person, a human being in the round, rather than as a cluster of needs and demands. This chapter is about making links between social care and healthcare services, so that they work together effectively, meeting the needs of older people and their carers in their community holistically. Citizening means a focus on the citizen and carer and community needs, not on the services.

Nobody would argue against doing this and mostly people have goodwill about it. We have to ask the question, therefore: why is there a long history of attempts to do this, symbolized by many concepts that try to express what we are trying to achieve? These include ideas such as collaboration, cooperation, joint working, partnership and integration. All of these ideas have picked up positive and negative connotations. The first section of the chapter examines the healthcare and social care contributions to successful practice in this area of work, drawing on a similar diagram to that in Chapter 3. Then, I seek to understand the difficulties and possibilities wrapped up in a complex parcel of ideas. Finally, I examine both structural and practice approaches to working together successfully for older people, their families and carers. I argue that a citizenship approach to services implies that services need to work in partnership if older people at the end of life are to be treated holistically within their families and communities.

The chapter's aims, therefore, are to:

- Examine the healthcare and social care contributions to multiprofessional practice.
- Understand the importance, the difficulties and the possibilities in working together for older people.
- Identify structural approaches to working together.
- Establish good professional practice in working together.

## Palliative care and social work contributions to multiprofessional care

In Chapter 3, I discussed different approaches to 'continuity', with healthcare professionals focusing on healthcare integration, and social care focusing on life course and broad public service integration. In this section, I extend these points to looking at multiprofessional care.

**64** The role of social work in end-of-life care

```
Social work                              Palliative care
┌─────────────────────────┐      ┌─────────────────────────┐
│ Focus on linkage across │      │ Focus on teamwork within│
│ organizational boundaries│     │ healthcare professions  │
└─────────────────────────┘      └─────────────────────────┘

┌─────────────────────────┐      ┌─────────────────────────┐
│ Priority to horizontal  │      │ Priority to vertical    │
│ integration in community│      │ integration of healthcare│
│                         │      │ services                │
└─────────────────────────┘      └─────────────────────────┘

┌─────────────────────────┐      ┌─────────────────────────┐
│ Concern to incorporate  │      │ Concern to respect      │
│ families and carers     │      │ confidentiality and patient│
│                         │      │ autonomy                │
└─────────────────────────┘      └─────────────────────────┘
```

**FIGURE 4.1** Social work and palliative care contributions to multiprofessional care

Figure 4.1 summarizes important points of distinction in the two approaches, around different focuses, priorities and concerns.

## Different focuses

The first point is that social workers' professional roles, in many settings, are about making links between services to benefit the people they work with. Healthcare professionals often see themselves as part of a healthcare system, ideally holistic, but with glitches. They therefore expect to be able to achieve good results for the health and care of their patients by contacting others with the same concerns and professional backgrounds. They do not see themselves as having wider responsibilities for the social fabric as social workers do, even though they sometimes get frustrated by non-healthcare issues that get in the way. A practice strategy for social workers, making use of their distinctive expertise and training, is to take responsibility for linkages with non-healthcare services and in the wider community. In this way, they can balance the healthcare priorities of healthcare staff. We saw in Chapter 3 that to make this work well, reporting back to healthcare colleagues about the links made and achievements in doing so is crucial. This helps in three ways. First, healthcare relationships operate on personal trust in individual professionals, so feeding back helps healthcare colleagues to see you taking action and helps them to trust you to do this in the future. Second, they have little experience of liaison work with other official organizations, such as housing trusts, social security or with pension companies. As a result, they often underestimate the complexity of negotiating arrangements and express astonishment at what social workers have to do and, on the other hand, what they can achieve. They value and understand social work more by getting feedback on what you do. The third benefit is that all good multiprofessional work involves people understanding the wider picture of what is happening to the patient, and they can adjust their own work to take account of the things that social workers are dealing with. They may also be enabled to take it on, or at least parts of it, in the future, rather than needing to call on the social worker. A further option for social workers is to act as a consultant to other professionals experiencing an issue, rather than taking over a linking role from them.

The second point connects with this. Healthcare staff are strong on facilitating their patient's use of healthcare services, so they are comfortable with referring patients for services from other healthcare professions, such as physiotherapists or for tests such as x-rays or blood tests, and often pursue such connections with creativity and tenacity. They are also accustomed to passing patients on to other parts of the healthcare system, including community health and intermediate care services, and sharing appropriate information. Linking with external services often raises questions in their minds about confidentiality of patient information, and they are unaccustomed to advocacy of patients' needs. They prefer a shared professional ethos when presenting their patients to other agencies, which is what they expect in healthcare. Consequently, they are less accustomed than social workers to pressing the case, appealing against decisions, and arguing strongly for exceptions and special circumstances.

A useful practice strategy to deal with these points is that social workers should pick up situations where they can contribute their experience and skills in working with external agencies, in presenting applications for discretion and for services and in advocating for the needs of clients. On the other hand, where the liaison involves interaction with healthcare staff, it is often better for nurse to speak to nurse, doctor to doctor. In this case, it may be helpful if social workers arm their healthcare colleagues with the arguments that might be presented and information about the procedures and criteria by which decisions are made. This is another example of being explicit about what social workers can offer. In this way, citizening older people by getting their rights is extended from a social work role into the healthcare element of the service, and the whole service becomes more about citizening

## Different priorities

Connected to the different focuses, social work and healthcare priorities when making contributions to partnership also vary. Healthcare staff make a strong contribution in ensuring that the elements of the healthcare system work together well. This includes referrals, providing discharge reports and ensuring that appointment systems and support such as transport to clinics are working well. The social work priorities may usefully emphasize support that can come from a wider range of relatives, friends and neighbours than appear at the ward or clinic and from a wider range of community agencies. For example, with carers, healthcare staff often think about referral to counselling; but social workers usually have better links with community carers' organizations and understand the contribution that group work may make to carers' support.

## Patient rights and family concerns

One area that may lead to tensions between social workers and healthcare staff is the requirement in healthcare law and practice that patients have individual rights to make decisions about their care. Patients, as citizens with rights, are the only persons entitled to give permission for their healthcare treatments and operations. Relatives may therefore feel excluded from healthcare decisions, and action may be taken on the patient's say-so without involving their relations. It may be left to the patient, who may either not be fully informed about or has not fully understood, what is going on to inform the relative. Social workers will often have had the role of working with family members or liaising with external services, and citizening means involving the family and community in discussing these issues about treatment and thinking through what is happening so that they can be supportive. The legal right to make decisions is that patient's, but the need to gain family and community support should not rest wholly with the patient. Families and communities also consist of citizens with rights to be engaged properly.

Where the healthcare decision is unexpected or disputed, relatives may feel uninvolved. This may be particularly difficult where a decision is made not to attempt cardio-pulmonary resuscitation (CPR). This is a medical decision, about which patients should be, but sometimes are not, consulted or informed. It is a medical decision, because doctors cannot ethically give treatment that they consider is detrimental to their patient's interests. At the end of life, resuscitation may be uncomfortable or even damaging to the patient and is often ineffective. Relatives and patients sometimes feel, unless the decision and the reasons for it are carefully explained to them, that care and treatment have been abandoned. Patients and relatives may feel the same way when, at the very end of life, hydration and nutrition is often withdrawn because it is unnecessary and sometimes uncomfortable for many patients to receive food or water by the mouth. Such decisions are commonplace in care for dying people, and unless they are explained, some patients and relatives, particularly if they are of the Roman Catholic faith, may feel that the possibility of recovery and the means of sustenance have been withdrawn (Craig, 2004, 2008). This sometimes provokes strong feelings and protest. Many hospitals (especially older ones) do not have the private facilities for private interviews and discussions with relatives about such issues, and may not have senior staff on hand to give the information required authoritatively.

A useful practice strategy, faced with conflict about such issues, is to facilitate relatives in discussing the decisions made fully with nursing and medical staff. It may be necessary to press senior staff to take the time to meet with patients and relatives in a family meeting to do this. Family meetings between the patient, their family and social care and healthcare professionals are used for a variety of purposes. Information-sharing, raising concerns about care and treatment, clarifying the goals of care and developing a plan of care for the patient and family carers are common objectives (Hudson *et al.*, 2008). This is commonplace in palliative care; it is less common in hospitals or primary care, and good relationships with medical and other healthcare staff often make it possible to persuade them to take this possibility up. Hudson *et al.*'s (2008) study shows that careful preparation and ensuring appropriate attendance are crucial to using them to generate multiprofessional work that, to be citizening, also involves service users, their family and carers. Kissane and colleagues (Kissane and Bloch, 2002) developed a process of family consultation in end-of-life care and bereavement situations, although it is time-consuming and expensive.

### CASE EXAMPLE: EXPLAINING TO KARINA

Karina, who was in hospital undergoing the final dying phase of colon cancer and was receiving heavy doses of morphine, had a discussion with her doctor about withdrawing nutrition and hydration, although her mouth was frequently moistened with small sponges by nursing staff. Her son, Joe, who was having difficulty accepting that her death was close, complained about this to nurses, who explained why this was good practice, but afterwards told the family's social worker that he did not accept this. Karina was unable, and did not have much energy, to persuade him that she had agreed to it. The social worker asked the consultant (senior doctor) if he would meet Joe and Karina at the bedside one lunchtime when Joe was visiting to explain this, and he agreed to go with the social worker. Joe, mainly, and to some extent Karina, spent some time explaining to the doctor how difficult all of this was for them, and talked about some of the difficulties of visiting; and Joe talked about caring for his children, who were distressed by their grandmother's

> illness. The consultant listened sympathetically, but said little beyond explaining that the social worker would be able to help talk these issues through with Joe. He then explained the nutrition and hydration decisions carefully, and they both listened and accepted them. After the meeting, Joe and Karina both separately told the social worker that they had found this very helpful. The doctor privately said to the social worker: 'Did you listen to all that?' and confessed that his mind had been elsewhere most of the time. The social worker explained that it was important that the message had come from him, with his medical authority and responsibility, and made it acceptable to the family. This case example is another situation in which repetition of an important message, hearing it from the right people and at the right time, is an important communication skill.

## Resuscitation, the Liverpool Care Pathway and its successors

Issues about family involvement most recently arose in the UK during a public debate about resuscitation and the Liverpool Care Pathway, and in this section I look briefly at these issues using the example of the Pathway, and policies which have replaced it, developed for the UK by the Leadership Alliance for the Care of Dying People (2014), whose guidelines, created following wide consultations, are current NHS policy in England.

Responding to WHO policy and public demand, many countries have developed policy favouring palliative and end-of-life care provision. In the UK, the most important recent initiative is the National End of Life Care Strategy for England (Department of Health, 2008), implemented through a programme which produced guidance and training. An important part of the strategy was the development of three important 'tools' for development and training:

- the Liverpool Care Pathway (LCP);
- the Gold Standards Framework (GSF);
- Preferred Priorities for (originally 'Preferred Place of') Care (PPC).

The reasons for implementing these schemes are twofold. First, there was evidence and some campaigning about the inadequacy of hospitals in providing for end-of-life care. For example, in 2009, the National Confidential Enquiry into Patient Outcome and Death (2009), an organization that carries out expert professional reviews of practice within the NHS, enquired into care in hospitals during the last four days of life. Among the main findings were the following points:

- In 16.9 per cent of patients who were not expected to survive on admission there was no evidence of any discussion between the healthcare team and either the patient or relatives on treatment limitation.
- In 21.8 per cent of cases DNAR (Do Not Attempt Resuscitation) orders were signed by very junior trainee doctors.
- There were examples of where healthcare professionals were judged not to have the skills required to care for patients nearing the end of their lives. This was particularly so in relation to a lack of ability to identify patients approaching the end of life, inadequate implementation of end-of-life care and poor communication with patients, relatives and other healthcare professions (NCEPOD, 2009: 6).

LCP was an important vehicle for tackling this issue over the quality of care for dying people in hospitals.

The second reason was that, bearing in mind that hospitals are places for the treatment of care of acutely ill patients, they are not suitable environments for calming care of dying people. Care in hospitals was also more expensive and less desired by patients and family members than care in people's own homes or in care homes that are the usual place of residence of a high proportion of frail elderly people. GSF and PPC were particularly focused on this second reason.

The LCP was designed to raise awareness in ward staff when patients were approaching death, to discuss this with patients and their families sympathetically, and to check that everything necessary was being done to ensure their comfort. LCP itself became controversial. It was primarily a protocol, based on hospice practice (Ellershaw and Wilkinson, 2010), consisting mainly of a list of things to do, and a service for testing improvement in each of the items of the protocol against a baseline registered by a care organization at the outset of applying the Pathway. The National End of life Care Programme sought to extend this programme across hospital provision, and many hospitals appointed coordinators to develop the programme in wards, primarily for older people. A substantial press campaign developed against it, with claims that people were placed on it who were not imminently dying, and this was done without adequate discussion with members of the family and carers. An important aspect of the criticism was the withdrawal of hydration and nutrition and the implementation of 'Do Not Attempt Cardio-Pulmonary Resuscitation' (DNAR) orders. This is common practice in hospices since there is evidence that many terminal cancer patients do not need nutrition and hydration, and that it may be uncomfortable for them (Partridge and Campbell, 2007). There is also evidence that seriously ill patients do not benefit from CPR and may suffer injury or distress if it is used (Ebell et al., 1998; Tunstall-Pedoe et al., 1992).

The press campaign on this issue was so intense that the government set up an enquiry into the LCP, which has led to its replacement by another protocol. Among the problems that the enquiry found (Independent Review of the Liverpool Care Pathway, 2013) was uncertainty about defining when the end of life had been reached, poor decision-making, instances where there was a lack of consent, poor communication with patients and their families, and poor record completion. There was also a lack of robust research evidence supporting the clinical experience which underlay the creation of the protocol. So the attempt at improvement by mandating widespread procedures failed.

GSF is a training scheme, originally for general practitioner (GP) practices but recently extended to care homes, allowing practices and homes to register for training and consultancy that allows them to claim 'gold standard' expertise in providing end-of-life care. PPC is a more diffuse programme which aims to encourage 'advance care planning', in which people approaching the end of life are encouraged to specify in advance the kind of care they would want as they come closer to death. I look at these processes in Chapter 5.

The guidelines published by the Leadership Alliance for the Care of Dying people (2014), replacing the Liverpool Care Pathway, offer a more complex set of priorities:

- Staff involved should recognize the possibility that a person may die within the next few days or hours and communicate this clearly to the dying person and their family. Decisions should be made and actions taken in accordance with the person's needs and wishes, which should be regularly reviewed and decisions revised accordingly. In hospital

or where formally organized end-of-life care is being provided at home, this would normally be done by nursing staff, and sometimes doctors, because recognition is usually only possible where contact with the dying person is frequent enough to notice minor changes in breathing and behaviour. Social workers may not get to hear about this, but sometimes they may be contacted by worried relatives who cannot get a response from community or primary health services. They need to alert healthcare staff that there is concern about death being close.
- Sensitive communication takes place between staff and the dying person, and family, carers and others who are identified as important to them. This means that social workers who are aware of important relationships should make sure these are identified to healthcare staff, who, as we saw in Chapter 3, may not have information about family contacts, especially more distant ones.
- The dying person, and those identified as important to them, are involved in decisions about treatment and care to the extent that the dying person wants. Not everyone wants to know every detail, and many older people may be content to let full knowledge and decision-making lie with the professionals, or with family members or carers whom they have chosen. In a busy hospital ward, or where there is a long period of care at home, where the older person experiences increasing frailty, it is easy to make assumptions about what they want, or to fail to make clear decisions. Family members and carers may want to protect older people from difficult decisions, and it is an important part of a citizenship approach to help involve older people as well as their family carers in decisions. Social workers may also be called upon to facilitate contacts, particularly where there are family conflicts or where family members are estranged. This may be an opportunity to reconnect family members who have been cut off from the older person. Citizening requires us to overcome or evade conflicts that get in the way of interpersonal connections.
- The needs of family and others identified as important to the dying person should be actively explored, respected and met as far as possible. There is a balance here between the dying person and the family's views. Social workers involved in these issues often need to balance the healthcare professions' assumptions about the patient's legal right to make the decisions with the family's right to discuss their views and needs. This may be particularly important, for example, if children or family members who have relationship difficulties in the family are assumed to be irrelevant.
- An individual plan of care, which includes food and drink, symptom control and psychological, social and spiritual support, is agreed, coordinated and delivered with compassion. This suggestion is citizening because it involves family members and social workers in understanding medical decisions about food and drink.

## Understanding working together

### *Continuity as an objective in partnership*

In this section, my aim is to disentangle the meaning and implications of different approaches to working together.

Why is this important and why is it difficult? For the older person, their family and carers treating their present as a development of their lifelong journey is an important aspect of citizenship. Citizening requires an understanding of and respect for the continuities in their needs and wishes. At the same time, though, we need to understand what is new in their present situation, because that very often responds to new events, new aspects of their personality and lives and new opportunities. For agencies and professionals, continuity is important because it has the potential to reduce financial costs that arise from duplication and overlap, and to avoid confusion and mistakes that come from unplanned intersections between different colleagues. Systematic reviews of research show evidence that identifying end-of-life care situations, assessing them, maintaining coherent management of cases across different settings and following up as older people move between settings reduces future hospitalizations and enhances self-care (Lorenz et al., 2008). Being prepared and organized is a crucial element of quality of life for older people and in managing services effectively (see Chapter 3 on person-centred care planning, Chapter 5 on advance care planning and Chapter 6 on life-long preparation for ageing). The practice strategy here, then, is to look for and combine both continuity and innovation in seeking the best quality of life in the older person's arrangements.

People use a range of different terms to talk about these issues. Examples that have come into fashion over the years include multiagency, multidisciplinary and multiprofessional, interagency, interdisciplinary and inter-professional practice and collaboration, cooperation, coordination, integration, partnership and teamwork. All of these words have slightly different emphases. The words that people use may, therefore, reveal different concerns. While in the next subsection I try to disentangle these, there are two main points: all of these are concerned with, first, continuity for, second, the people whom we are serving.

Continuity, the first point, is about making sure that the people we are serving have what in community care policy is called a 'seamless experience'. This phrase builds on a policy objective in community care to provide 'tailored services'. Even though they came from different providers with their own aims and methods, they feel connected to the service user and each other. The burden of coordination is on the social worker rather than the service user. Doing this is a counsel of perfection: a suitable practice strategy is to enable the user and carer to understand how the service is coordinated, so that they can participate in the planning to achieve the quality of life that they and their carers want.

Thinking about the people we are serving, the second point, should remind us that we need to consider not only the service user, not only the carer, not only professional colleagues in other agencies and settings but also, and crucially, the paid carers who are actively doing the hands-on job both in hospice, hospital, residential and day-care settings but also in people's own homes. In most cases, paid carers doing most of the practical work are relatively poorly paid, perhaps poorly trained and, in many countries, often also foreign migrants. Mostly they will do their best but often with a minimal training only in health and safety and in manual handling (the skills involved in moving bed- or chair-bound patients from one position to another). An important practice strategy for social workers is to take opportunities of contacts with such staff to help them pursue the more interactive human care tasks, rather than seeing the work as a checklist of practical tasks, without interpersonal content.

## *Partnership terminology*

The terminology of coordination and teamwork reflects the reality that these are aspirational terms and expresses hopes, plans or wishes that people will work together to provide services, and to plan and promote systematic attempts to create partnership. Reed et al. (2005), in an extensive literature review, note a shift in thinking from integration concerned with ensuring that older people can gain access to services towards the more difficult task of how services could work together. That means a shift in focus away from older people and other service users and towards a focus on service providers: perhaps an unfortunate move. This review also demonstrates how different objectives can be incorporated into similar language. In particular, reference to inter- and multi*disciplinary* practice may reflect a concern with different or competing knowledge and skill bases, while referring to inter- or multi*professional* practice may reflect a concern with the hindrance of practitioners' socialization into different professional backgrounds and training. Referring to collaboration and coordination or interagency practice may refer to organizational inhibitions to working together. During the early part of the 21st century, UK health and social care policy often referred to 'partnership' as an objective, putting forward a positive end-point, rather than, as previously, emphasizing the process.

While we can draw some theoretical distinctions, in everyday practice these terms are used more or less interchangeably and with the same aspiration. But from this account we can take two main distinctions. One emphasizes partnership that focuses on the people working together in their disciplines and professions and from their different working bases. If political leaders or agencies and their managers are playing a blame game, this approach runs the risk of blaming individual practitioners or professional groups for their failure to cooperate to the benefit of their clients. The other emphasizes partnership that focuses on getting the organizations to align their aims, policies and practices. This runs the opposite risk of blaming policy or management for organizational inadequacies, when it is professionals and paid carers who, as human beings, interact with the humanity of older people and their carers.

Strategies for improving each form of partnership are different, and potentially in conflict with one another. To avoid conflict, we should see the two emphases as complementary to each other. The next two sections explore opportunities for working on both.

## Structural practice strategies for partnership

### *Policy and organizational coordination*

The main direction of thinking in developing end-of-life care in the UK has been a pathway approach (Hayes *et al.*, 2014; see the Introduction and Chapter 3). I commented in Chapter 1 that this put the focus on the end-of-life care phase as determined by professionals and service provision, rather than on the ageing life journey. So while I do not dissent from the pathway approach, I want to take a broader look at coordination perspectives. Charnley (2001) usefully analysed the potential barriers:

- structural issues, such as differing geographical boundaries and management systems (agencies may be difficult to integrate if they come from different sectors of the economy, the public, private for-profit organizations and voluntary or not-for-profit organizations);
- procedural issues, where practitioners have different lines of accountability or degrees of discretion;
- professional issues, where different professional groups have different values and cultures;
- financial issues, where budgets are constrained or managed using different processes;
- policy issues where services have different priorities or there are conflicts, gaps or overlaps in services.

All of these barriers create difficulties and one way of responding to differences between organizations is to create structural relationships either at the level of the whole organization, or between sections of it or in a particular locality. These may include:

- shared support functions, such as information and training, which brings economies of scale and access to scarce skills;
- shared contract processes, which supports cooperation by financial incentives; either two or more organizations can issue joint contracts to others to do particular pieces of work, or can contract to make payments to each other to carry out particular pieces of work;
- shared working, where boundaries and strategies are aligned; this might be done through joint committees creating plans or by appointing an employee to carry out work in both organizations, or by out-posting an employee from one organization into a role in another;
- merger, where the joint working achieves greater permanence and a single identity for users and workers (developed from Whittington, 2003).

The integrated pathway approach used in UK end-of-life care policy tries to marry the first three approaches, without extending to merger: end-of-life care is only a small part of both health and social care services, so merger to achieve permanence in this area is likely to cause disruptions in other useful relationships. End-of-life care is therefore likely always to involve boundary-crossing between services. In the integrated pathway model of interagency practice, a typical journey of a client through the care system is identified, and the role of agencies at each point specified. We can see clients as progressing through a series of gateways, with a particular professional or agency responsible for assessing and deciding on access to the next element of the service. Social workers may find two problems with this approach. First, all older people are in some sense approaching the end-of-life phase of their lives, so selecting some people out for a special pathway is likely to mean that others are de-citizened by being excluded from help with end-of-life care. This approach is only useful where services are concentrating on a specified period of care – for example, those on end-of-life registers. Second, the pathway in end-of-life care is specified from a concern for healthcare provision in the dying phase of care, rather than starting from citizening older citizens who are receiving social care, or not receiving service at all, so that professionals engage with their end-of-life care needs. The end-of-life care integrated pathway, therefore, is de-citizening because social work and social care are required only in a healthcare-led dying phase, rather than incorporating end-of-life care into social work with all older people.

The starting point of developing a practice strategy for working on structural relationships for social work needs to consider who might be involved. In working with older people and in end-of-life care, we can identify a number of possible groups to be engaged:

- between practitioners, clients, their carers and families;
- between different professional groups;
- between professionals, paid carers and volunteers;
- between agencies with different roles in the care system;
- for social workers particularly, between healthcare, social work and social care agencies.

Structural practice strategies are often worked out in places where older people and their carers are de-citizened, absent. Emphasizing structural coordination can, therefore, exclude the citizenship of older people and carers, because they do not generally participate in planning or policy-making meetings. Kharicha *et al.*'s (2004) review of procedural and structural arrangements for collaboration between primary healthcare and social care settings, for example, identifies:

- named contacts for primary care staff in social care services;
- aligning link staff in social care with particular GP practices;
- attachment schemes;
- shared premises (co-location);
- joint primary care and social care teams;
- multiprofessional community teams.

They note that co-location, which is sometimes promoted as a structural means of improving health and social care cooperation, does not always achieve collaboration. Partington (2006) argues that a care pathway approach, which has been the English government's favoured approach to coordinating end-of-life care, has not always been successful in introducing end-of-life care in care homes. Kharicha *et al.* (2004) suggest that some GPs and some primary healthcare teams (PHCTs) may be more interested in and supportive of social work attachments, and this may lead to inequalities in service. This is because patients of interested and supportive practices may unfairly get a higher level of service than patients of less supportive PHCTs. Also, patients in PHCTs where there is an attachment are more likely to accept referral to a social worker than to an area team; again, this advantages patients in such PHCTs. All of these provisos make the more general point that it is the way in which people work together that creates collaboration: you have to actively develop teamwork and overcome conflicts. Thus, interpersonal strategies will always continue to be the main approach for social workers seeking to integrate end-of-life care into their broader practice and service delivery.

## *Settings for end-of-life care*

A useful way of examining how to develop social work engagement is to look at the social work role in the range of settings where end-of-life care may emerge from broader practice. The need for end-of-life care develops in a range of settings:

- People's own homes or the homes of relatives, friends or landlords are the most important setting. Many people would prefer to die at home, although this attitude is sometimes based on an assumption that they will be comfortable and surrounded and supported by family and friends. People without these supports may prefer professional care, and people with family support may shift their preference if they feel they are being a burden on their families or if they suffer from uncomfortable symptoms. While social care services are assessed and commissioned by their own practitioners, and social work involvement may have generated this care, it is often displaced by specialist palliative care at the end of life, commissioned from primary healthcare or specialist palliative care community services. Social workers may feel, even where they have longstanding relationships with the older person or family, that they are forced into a secondary role. While this may be a relief, particularly if the situation has been very pressurized, social workers sometimes need to assert their involvement by staying in constant contact with the palliative care

team. It helps if they are able to be responsive in providing variations in social care services, because people at the end of life often experience rapid changes in condition which merit a flexible response.
- Hospitals, where active treatment for a medical condition is being provided, but a dying process starts. One of the issues for social workers here is that where there is a long-term condition and treatment over a period is being provided, in a busy ward staff may not notice at an early stage the deterioration in a patient's condition. In day or out-patient treatment – for example, renal dialysis – the service may continue a routine of regular treatments when patients or their families are beginning to think about accepting that the end of life is approaching, and the routine excludes engaging with the professionals about this issue. It may be useful to relay relatives' queries and raise social workers' own uncertainties about how things are progressing to alert ward staff to this issue.
- Emergency healthcare facilities such as accident and emergency departments of hospitals, where death may arise as a result of accident, traumatic injury, self-harm and suicide, or a sudden deterioration in a long-term condition where the patient is being cared for in a care home or in their own home. Busy emergency staff may not be geared up to providing appropriate end-of-life care – for example, it may be difficult to find more than the obvious family members and community participants in the older person's life; social workers can perform a useful function in identifying them with patients and seeking them out. An important aspect of this may be identifying less obvious relatives or friends – for example, where a more distant relative such as a niece or nephew has a close relationship with an older person. Emergency staff may routinely ask about next of kin or close relatives, but more distant relatives and friends may lose an opportunity to say goodbye. Social workers may not always or often be present and have the opportunity, but when you are, do the social work thing and think family, because other people there have other priorities.
- Hospices, where care is provided for people known to be moving towards the end of their lives. Here, there is likely to be a stronger awareness of family and community involvement and the right environment for end-of-life care, but less awareness of the involvement of social care and other community staff. For example, there may not be an awareness of a social care worker or personal assistant who should be involved in the final few days, or have the chance to say goodbye. In many hospices, social workers are the main professional group who organize family meetings to plan arrangements for older people who may need a variety of involvements in their care.
- Care homes and nursing homes are locations where a high proportion of older people are likely to reach the end of their lives. Two problems may arise. The first is a lack of confidence among staff, many of whom may be poorly trained and paid, in caring for dying people. The second issue may be a concern among managers to ensure that every possible medical treatment and specialized nursing care has been provided. This sometimes leads to unnecessary admissions to accident and emergency departments, when a more measured provision of care may be possible in what is, after all, the resident's home. Although care home services are often commissioned by social care services, liaison and involvement in care after the initial assessment by social workers may be minimal. They may therefore not call on social work involvement, even if there has been a relationship built up in the community or hospital.

The Gold Standards Framework, a training and development project which tried to improve functioning in primary care and in care homes, found that training and support provided to care homes staff over a period enabled many more residents to be cared for until death in a care home (Badger *et al.*, 2010). One of its important focuses is collaboration between services, and this may encourage involvement by social care staff; a useful practice strategy may be involvement by social workers or teams of older individuals in such staff development activity. However, international research has shown that end-of-life care in care homes is variable in quality, and probably responds to the number of staff and level of other resources, as well as training (Ingleton and Froggatt, 2009). Care staff in homes may also be seen as marginal by other more mainstream healthcare professionals (Ingleton and Froggatt, 2009: 1813).

- Other institutions, such as prisons, psychiatric or other specialist hospitals, where people reach the end of their lives while being housed for some social purpose. Again, social workers may not be strongly involved and community connections not sustained in these settings.

In many of these settings, then, social workers may play limited roles. Hodgson (2005) suggests that the following roles may be important:

- Admission decision-making: social workers' assessments may contribute the perspective of psychosocial needs in hospices and hospitals; they may also be able to raise family and carers' needs.
- Discharge planning: social workers often help patients and family members to contribute their differing perspectives and have an important role in bringing together internal and external staff as part of their role in working across the boundaries of agencies and healthcare and social care systems.
- In-patient, day-patient and home care multiprofessional team meetings: social workers contribute a focus on family and community needs and psychosocial perspectives.
- Family meetings/conferences: social workers often take a major role in planning and chairing these and deciding whom to involve, bringing together appropriate professionals and family members.

## Taking up a full social work role

In discussing potential social work roles in end-of-life care settings, I have suggested that social workers may feel sidelined or left out. We saw in Chapter 3 that different concerns and priorities may devalue or simply miss the potential for a social work or social care role. A strategy for any social care and social work practitioner is therefore to build up support for our services and profession. This is not a given, although you may be lucky and have colleagues who already have a high valuation of social work and social care. If this is your experience, you need to plan to build on it; if this is not your experience, you can turn it round, and multiprofessional practice will be enhanced.

One answer to colleagues devaluing social work because there is no evidence that it is effective is to say that US research in the 1980s and 1990s has, in general, demonstrated effectiveness of social work interventions (Reid and Hanrahan, 1982; Rubin, 1985; Thomlison, 1984; Videka-Sherman, 1988) and that eight out of ten clients and families of older people who engage with social work services do better in achieving their and their practitioner's aims than the typical non-participating client (Gremier and Gorey, 1998; Gorey, 1996; de Smidt and Gorey, 1997). But note the words 'engaging with' and 'typical'; there's less evidence about people who resist being helped and people who have severe or unusual difficulties and so therefore might be harder to help. Of course, this is true of any helping professional, as any frustrated doctor or nurse will tell you. This is one of the things that we share, and gaining engagement from clients and their families is an important skill to demonstrate, especially if you can get them to engage with your colleagues' work as well – this gets social workers extra credit.

Another important strategy to support social work involvement in end-of-life care is for broader social care teams working with older people to develop resources to help practitioners become engaged with end-of-life care services. Since social work and social care is likely to be marginalized in or outside of end-of-life care services, social workers will only rarely have active involvement in them, so when there is need, their teams must have information and arrangements ready to build their experience in this rather specialized field. A team needs to have a variety of information resources to enable them to do their work successfully:

- contact details of specialist and non-specialist social care and healthcare resources;
- in the private, public and not-for-profit sectors;
- including the names of staff;
- and their roles in referral, assessment and case review;
- eligibility and selection criteria for services;
- monitoring and reporting arrangements, including requests from named staff for reporting back;
- limitations on contacts due to professional and commercial confidentiality (developed from Warburton, 1999).

## Interpersonal strategies for teamwork

Interpersonal strategies for developing teamwork in health and social care seek to:

- improve interpersonal relationships and group development;
- devise systems for cooperation among team members; and
- identify shared aims and ways of improving the quality and innovation of work.

An extensive review of research found that for most medical conditions and settings, successful interventions used multidisciplinary teams involving nurses and social services, ensured continuity across settings, and facilitated communication (Lorenz et al., 2008). A literature in palliative care teamwork mainly focuses on developing a multiprofessional team in work that concentrates on the end-of-life phase (e.g. Speck, 2006; Payne and Oliviere, 2008). The problem for social workers with older people is that unless they are a regular part of a palliative care team, they are unlikely to be involved in the group development aspects of teamwork because they will be more of an outsider. A suitable practice strategy, therefore, is to concentrate on the interpersonal and cooperative aspects rather than expecting to be involved in group team-building activity.

Interpersonal practice needs to build on the structures discussed above that your team has developed to provide resources for maintaining links and communications with end-of-life care teams. 'Everyday teamwork' (Payne, 2006) offers a practical set of strategies for relationships when you are an occasional member of a team:

- Take every opportunity to develop and maintain informal and social relationships, such as taking breaks with core team members, taking part in shared outings, parties and other social events. Peripheral team members have to work harder at these social connections than core team members.
- Be particularly generous with informal interpersonal help with the stresses of work.
- Participate in 'patient teams': groups of people planning work with particular patients.
- Participate in dealing with particular difficulties presented in a care home or on a ward – for example, responding to help with difficult behaviour from visitors or relatives. Since core team members are, in a sense, trapped in the care home or on the ward with any difficulties, it is important that they are supported in dealing with challenging or difficult behaviour.

It is useful to think about the cycle of practice with a view to identifying people, particularly older people and their carers, who might have been excluded, thus compromising their citizenship, and agencies whose staff might also feel devalued or unable to fulfil their role because you have moved quickly or older people and carers have chosen not to use their services:

- At the referral or assessment phase, think about other agencies, professionals and family members who can be involved.
- At the person-centred care planning stage, make sure to identify agencies, carers and professionals who need to be involved in any planning and commissioning, and also identify agencies, carers and colleagues who might be excluded (such as agencies that have been involved but now have no contribution to make, or relatives living at a distance) and keep them in the loop.
- At the review and evaluation stage, look for complainants or others who have dissatisfactions about what took place.

## ADDITIONAL RESOURCES

### Books

Speck, P. (ed.) (2006) *Teamwork in Palliative Care: Fulfilling or frustrating?* Oxford: Oxford University Press.
An edited book with many practical chapters about developing teamwork in palliative care settings, from which you can get ideas about particular issues that might arise in end-of-life care teamwork.

Glasby, J. and Sanderson, H. (2014) *Partnership Working in Health and Social Care: What is integrated care and how can we deliver it?*, 2nd edn. Bristol: Policy Press.
An excellent and brief general text on policy and practice in partnership working in health and social care, part of a series of similar guides from the same publisher.

Littlechild, B. and Smith, R. (eds) (2012) *A Handbook for Interprofessional Practice in the Human Services: Learning to work together.* London: Routledge.
A much broader collection, including chapters on older people and end-of-life care.

### Websites

These National Health Service (NHS) quality improvement programme websites connect end-of-life care and then care in the last days of life with care for long-term conditions, and provide useful links to a wide range of relevant sites:

http://www.nhsiq.nhs.uk/improvement-programmes/long-term-conditions-and-integrated-care/end-of-life-care.aspx

http://www.nhsiq.nhs.uk/improvement-programmes/long-term-conditions-and-integrated-care/end-of-life-care/care-in-the-last-days-of-life.aspx

This NHS Scotland website offers a learning programme on building your personal contribution to teamwork, including a range of exercises to help you and lots of useful links to non-healthcare sites:

http://www.flyingstart.scot.nhs.uk/learning-programmes/teamwork/

The Gold Standards Framework provides resources on working in the community with primary healthcare teams and with care homes to improve standards of end-of-life care:

http://www.goldstandardsframework.org.uk/

# 5

# ADVANCE CARE PLANNING

This chapter focuses on three aspects of planning that both social work and palliative care contribute to end-of-life care:

- Advance care planning (ACP) – the process of finding out and recording a client's preferences for how they want to be cared for or treated by health and social care services at the time that they enter end-of-life care. Originating in palliative care services, starting from advance decisions or directives about treatment, it extended to a wider use as end-of-life care developed.
- Care planning – part of care management in providing care services which developed in social work.
- ACP throughout the care career – ACP incorporated into the care management process throughout an individual's care career. It aims particularly to support people living with a long-term condition to plan for expected changes in health or social status. It incorporates health improvement and staying well. This idea developed in the Scottish health and social care system as anticipatory care planning – the idea that right at the outset when older people first come into contact with care services, practitioners should be mindful that they are moving towards the end of life, and plan for all the stages of that progression.

Planning is crucial for citizenship social work because:

- It is a good way of creating involvement between services, practitioners, older people and carers.
- Planning creates clarity and certainty and helps older people and their carers gain influence over how services respond to their needs.
- Advance care planning at the end of life enables older people to have influence over decisions that may be personally important to them, but they risk losing influence because of fading mental and physical capacity.

Figure 5.1 shows the sources within social work and palliative care for ACP. As ideas developed, care planning for social care services developed in social work to older people's entire care

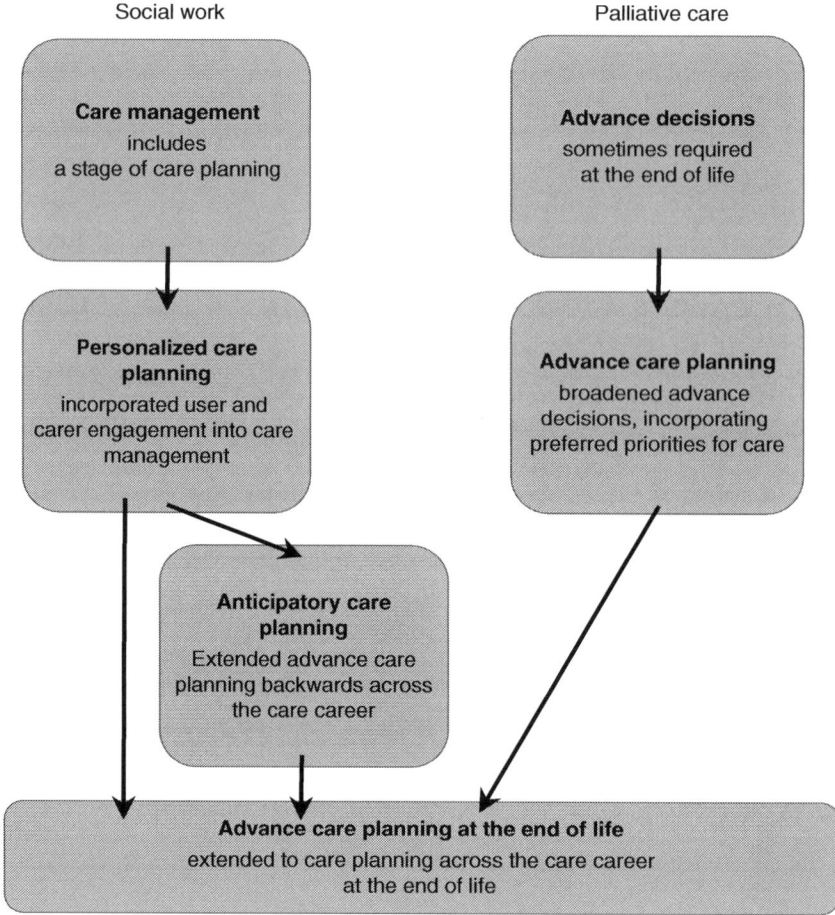

**FIGURE 5.1** Social work and palliative care contributions to advance care planning

careers, while advance decisions to refuse care at the end of life were extended into a longer and broader process of ACP, particularly developing ideas about dying people's preferred priorities for their care. These two sources came together to influence the development of ACP so that it became an increasing focus of practice throughout the care career, incorporating the idea of anticipatory care planning, used in Scotland to refer to planning undertaken as soon as someone entered care, and personalized care planning, designed to engage service users and their carers in tailoring care plans as older people became more dependent on formal services.

In the next section, I look at each of these in turn. The following section examines some of the implications of using ACP in practice, as an introduction to the discussion in Part II of its use at various life periods as people approach the end of life in older age.

The importance of advance care planning in end-of-life care means that its role in care for long-term conditions and for older people has developed, and social workers need to develop a practice strategy to originate ACP as soon as possible in an older person's care career. That plan can then be developed and communicated across to carers, both informal and paid, and forward to specialist teams as care passes from social care into end-of-life care.

## Advance care planning developments

ACP has three important direct sources:

1. the process of making advance decisions in end-of-life and palliative care; and, connected with this
2. managing decision-making where people have impaired mental capacity to make care decisions for themselves;
3. planning social and healthcare services for the long-term care population to ensure that they have good access to services.

ACP across the care career is an important development for achieving the citizenship objective of participatory engagement in social work practice because it enables clients' preferences to emerge at a stage in their care careers when there is a good chance that they can realistically have an impact upon resource allocation in later care decisions. Existing practice in both social care and end-of-life care tends to delay client engagement in decision-making until the point at which resource allocation decisions must be made, when the range of choices may have been reduced by preceding events. Also of significance, ACP is an example of the development of well-researched practice techniques in social work with people who have long-term care needs. Providing services for such people is increasingly a social work role because populations of older people are likely to have increased care needs.

### *ACP in palliative care*

An important source of ACP is how palliative care services approach decision-making where patients are known to have an illness that has reached an advanced stage that will lead to death. ACP involves 'thinking ahead' about a client's care arrangements to 'create opportunities to explore wishes and choices for the future for end of life, crisis, respite and rehabilitation needs' (LTCC-JIT, 2009: 9). As they approach death, patients may lose consciousness and then be unable to give or refuse permission for treatment or, more commonly, to make decisions not to accept treatment for their condition. The three basic choices are:

1. Life prolonging care: this involves cardio-pulmonary resuscitation (CPR) (see Chapter 4) – that is, stimulating the heartbeat using a defibrillator, and mechanical assistance with breathing.
2. Limited care: patients accept admission to hospital and antibiotics, but not CPR.
3. Comfort care: patients accept treatment only to relieve symptoms, such as pain relief (Volandes *et al.*, 2009).

Usually in this situation, staff must ethically authorize or provide treatment that they judge to be in the best interests of the patient. A document called an 'advance decision to refuse treatment' (the British term) or 'advance directive' (the US term) sets out the patient's wishes in a formal way in case they lose their mental capacity to make the decision themselves. These documents have legal force if they are clearly expressed. Patients need, therefore, to be aware of likely contingencies as their illness progresses. Many patients also experience periods when they are unable to make decisions – for example, because of advanced dementia.

Sometimes particular conditions, such as motor neurone disease, affect patients' ability to communicate their wishes, even though they have the capacity to make decisions.

It is easy to misunderstand the purpose behind making provision for advance decisions. For example, some patients are concerned that it offers a legal provision for physicians to assist people to commit suicide or denies care at the end of life. Thinking this through, it is important to remember that death is a natural process. At some point in everyone's life, death will take its course. Medical treatment, nursing care and possibly psychological and social support may postpone it; but in the end it must occur. Many treatments to postpone death are unnatural: they may be painful, use heavy medication that has side effects, reducing the patient's quality of life. Eventually, they will lose their effect and death will occur anyway. So the decision has to be made about the point at which treatment is more damaging than advantageous. Such a decision can only be made by a doctor with full knowledge of the circumstances and wishes of the particular patient: at what point is it too painful, unpleasant or counterproductive for them? When they are unable to express a view, an advance decision can inform the medical decisions about patients' best interests.

Csikai and Chaitin (2006) review the development of advance directives in the US leading to a focus on refusal of treatment in particular circumstances. Medical advances have offered a clearer picture of the typical states through which major illnesses will go at the 'end stage'. This has permitted a clearer specification of treatments that are available for an increasing range of illnesses at different stages and which the patient might wish to refuse. In turn, this has led to a process of detailed specification of the actions refused in advance. Csikai and Chaitin (2006: 77) draw attention to well-established medical protocols for drawing up advance directives in the US. Advance directives can only be given to refuse treatment; doctors cannot be required to provide treatment that they think will not be in their patients' best interests (Samanta and Samanta, 2006). These focus on clear instructions about limitations to medical treatment, particularly where it is invasive – that is, requires breaking the skin or penetrating the body. An example is the difficult decision for many people of withdrawing nutrition and hydration through tubes. Many people believe that offering nutrition and hydration leaves it open for patients to revive, whereas if it is withdrawn, patients will, in effect, starve to death. In many cases, however, patients cannot absorb nutrition and hydration through their stomach and feeding them or giving them water makes them uncomfortable (Craig, 2004). Gillick's (2006) discussion of ACP in the US stresses the importance of clarifying with patients and families the risks and benefits of nutrition support in a variety of common situations as a prerequisite to effective ACP, since without this understanding an advance decision cannot be made.

## Social work roles in advance decisions

Social workers involved in end-of-life care with older people need to understand these processes, because they may become involved in two different ways:

1. Raising with older people, at a suitable early stage, the value of making advance decisions and advance directives.

A difficult practice issue is the need to be able to identify when the time is right. Often, this will be when the social worker hears a mention about concern for where treatment is going, or what is going to happen in the future. To start on the discussion, it is helpful to say something like: 'Have you thought about how you want your doctor and the health services to treat you, if your illness gets worse?' or 'Would you like to make plans for your treatment in the future?'

2. Sometimes these issues are raised by healthcare staff as part of ACP processes, or decision-making about medical procedures, and social workers become involved.

When this happens, social workers, with their concern for family participation, may need to propose the involvement of family members in the decision-making, and make the arrangements for suitable consultations. Since, as we saw in previous chapters, in law treatment decisions may only be made by the patient themselves, it is easy for healthcare staff to concentrate on consulting their patient, particularly in emergency situations. If this has happened, a useful practice strategy for social workers is to review the decisions with family members, so that they understand what is going on, and if necessary call on healthcare staff to take the time to explain things to family members.

It is also valuable to think about members of the family whose involvement may be neglected by both healthcare staff and family members. Important examples are children and family members with learning disabilities, who may have a strong emotional commitment to the older person who is dying. They may, however, be excluded from decisions either because it is difficult to communicate with them appropriately in the rush of an urgent situation, or because everyone wants to protect them from upset. An American study (Ratner et al., 2001) found that a social work visit led to very high participation in ACP for end-of-life care arrangements in a community home care service, and greater compliance with patients' preferences. This makes it clear that social work skills can clarify and facilitate participation in decision-making.

A variety of factors may affect older people being prepared to engage with ACP and using advance directives. For people with long-term conditions, end-of-life considerations are only part, and sometimes a less important part, of a wider process of changing health behaviours and the management of daily living as people approach greater frailty and illness (Fried et al., 2009). Barnes et al. (2007) found that while some patients and caregivers would like to engage in ACP, others would not; they would often prefer to deal with wider care issues, not just medical decision-making. Also, informal caregivers providing everyday support may be different from the person nominated to make decisions in end-of-life situations and decisions change over time. Therefore, practitioners involved in ACP need to maintain a good understanding of the network of support used by patients (Dizon et al., 2009). Again this is usually an important focus of social work, as compared with nursing and medical, practice, and social workers can make an important contribution. For example, an American study (Bullock, 2006) of African Americans found low take-up of ACP because of their spirituality which in turn influenced their view of suffering, death and dying. Consequently, the social support networks available to them influenced them to feel that documentation was not required. Practical barriers to recording and transferring an advance decision document between care locations and, in particular, their mistrust of the healthcare system led to refusals to complete plans. While this study draws attention to particular issues for people in some minority ethnic groups, it also makes clear that good trusting relationships between staff and clients are likely to be particularly important in creating an atmosphere in which future planning can be achieved successfully. Long-term community engagement is likely to be an important aspect of building trust – another role for social work.

## Decision-making where mental capacity is impaired

The second area where ACP has developed is where a client's mental capacity is impaired, so that they become unable to make their own decisions. People's mental capacity may be impaired temporarily by, for example, a period of mental illness, or permanently – for example, if they are learning disabled. Some people's capacity may be progressively impaired by illness, increased frailty and particularly dementia in later life, so their incapacity varies but tends to worsen: they need to plan in advance. People whose mental capacity is impaired may need others to make decisions on their behalves.

The need for such a process is related to the palliative care services' need for ACP to respond to commonplace treatment decisions at the end of life. Most legal jurisdictions make some provision for (in the American terminology) 'substituted judgment' – that is, another person, usually a close relative, to become a 'healthcare proxy' (again the American term, which you can find in the literature), taking over decision-making for the patient. The alternative process is to develop ACP to the point of producing an advance directive, while the patient still has capacity. In the US, the Patient Self-Determination Act 1991 makes provision for this. These processes are hard to separate for many families because most would not take on the proxy role without discussion with the patient and consultation with other family members (Hirschman et al., 2006).

In the UK, the Mental Capacity Act 2005 established new procedures. People may register 'lasting powers of attorney' for people to act as proxies for them in financial and welfare (including health) matters. If this has not been done, medical decisions are made in patients' best interests, if necessary with an independent representative to represent the patient's interests. Often this is a social worker if no relatives are involved, government guidance on implementing the act focuses on enabling people to make decisions and maintaining that capacity by engaging them in decisions on everyday matters, for example in care homes (Department of Constitutional Affairs, 2007). This points to a developing role for social workers and care staff to build enabling practice in care homes and when people are cared for in their own homes.

## Social and healthcare services for long-term care populations

Building on the experience in end-of-life situations and in cases where there are mental capacity concerns, recent developments in ACP focus on providing ACP to wider groups, in particular people resident in care homes and receiving community social care services. Multiprofessional guidance issued by the UK Royal College of Physicians (2009) is an example of ACP developing for this wider population. Its extensive review of research shows that most people are happy to discuss ACP in the early stages of care in anticipation of future ill-health, and ACP discussions with patients with long-term conditions or as part of broad end-of-life care management increase patient satisfaction. While such discussions at entry into a care home may cause upset in a period of transition, they can be successfully implemented by trained care staff once residents are settled.

## Care planning in care management

Another important source of understanding is the experience in social care services of care planning as a stage in the care management process. This has formed the main social work practice in adult social care, and was developed during the 1980s from American case management (Payne, 1995). It was introduced by the NHS and Community Care Act 1990 as a way of managing a newly established quasi-market system of provision. This gave local authorities the role of planning services in their area from all the sectors of the economy, which enabled them to commission agencies to provide services. A plan setting out the services available having been established, the care manager assessed service users' needs and commissioned the services from the various providers. Local authorities themselves provided some services, including social work, usually provided directly by the care manager. The system established has been rationalized by the Care Act 2014, which reformed the legislation on adult care for the first time for many decades. Building on the previous practice, official guidance on the Act (Department of Health, 2016) emphasizes the local authority role of 'market-shaping'.

Some models of care management envisage social workers maintaining a continuing supportive relationship once they have assessed the need for and organized services. Financial, organizational and policy pressures have commonly led to the adoption in many areas of an administrative form of care management which militates against this with older adults. Administrative care management emphasizes a formal, and usually computer-based, assessment following which services are commissioned from a range of independent service providers, without continuing social work involvement from the care manager.

The care management process is a traditional social work circle, in which the assessments lead to a care plan, which defines the needs, the services to be provided, the charges and a date when the plan will be reviewed. The services are organized and the care manager monitors how the services fit together, making adjustments as required, and evaluates whether they are meeting the user's needs at a periodic review (Payne, 1995).

As we saw in Chapter 3, two recent developments have adapted this cycle of practice. Since the 1980s, a growing movement representing the needs of informal carers, and in particular family members, has grown up. In the UK, successive legislation has tried to incorporate within care management practice the growing public concern for the support of carers. As a result, carers are entitled to a separate assessment of their needs – for example, for respite, pursuing education or employment, and a plan for meeting their needs must be incorporated into care plans. This is maintained in the Care Act 2014. The guidance on assessment, for example, proposes that assessments should take into account 'the wider picture by considering … the impact on the whole family' (Department of Health, 2016: Chapter 6) and provide for a carer's assessment: '[w]here an individual provides or intends to provide care for another adult and it appears that the carer may have any level of needs for support, local authorities must carry out a carer's assessment' (Para 6.16).

Another development is personalized care management invoking direct payments or independent budgeting. These are part of an international trend, and of a 'public choice' policy agenda characteristic of many Western governments. The 'ordinary living' movement of physically disabled people sought to improve housing and public facilities so that service users could have lifestyles similar to those enjoyed by non-disabled people. After a negotiated assessment of needs, elements of a care plan are agreed, and the budgets to provide these are paid to the service user, helpers or families. Some people employ their own care assistants, called 'personal assistants', and this maintains continuity and user control of the arrangements in their own home. In some areas, user-controlled organizations offer an alternative way of managing services, without the practical difficulties for families of employing carers directly.

Although this is a more flexible system of care, which is supported by service users because of the freedom of choice it offers, there are concerns that not every person receiving social care wants to be entrepreneurial and manage their own provision or has family members willing to help them. They may also choose carers to meet their own preferences, without considering the training and general suitability of the employee for a career in social care in the future (Payne, 2010).

Professional care planning of this kind is part of care management practice, particularly in long-term social care provision in many European countries (Le Bihan and Martin, 2006). While clients and informal caregivers might be involved in the assessment, the plan that determines the care package is established by the professional usually following a system devised by the local authority, and often relying on commercially available computer programs (Payne, 2009). Guidance on the Care Act 2014 provides for 'person-centred care and support planning' (Department of Health, 2016: Chapters 10–13):

> The person must be genuinely involved and influential throughout the planning process, and should be given every opportunity to take joint ownership of the development of the plan with the local authority if they wish, and the local authority agrees. There should be a default assumption that the person, with support if necessary, will play a strong pro-active role in planning if they choose to. Indeed, it should be made clear that the plan 'belongs' to the person it is intended for, with the local authority role being to ensure the production and sign-off of the plan to ensure that it is appropriate to meet the identified needs.
>
> *(Department of Health, 2016: 10.2)*

The experience of personalized care planning and independent budgeting for care services has been taken up in the English NHS (Care and Support Planning Working Group/ Coalition for Collaborative Care, 2016). It is increasingly being used for care management across British social care and healthcare services, and potentially facilitates greater partnership, through shared understanding that arises from using the same administrative processes.

## ACP throughout the care career

This focus on developing personalized or person-centred care as a way of integrating health and social care has led to the idea that ACP could be adopted throughout an older person's care career. ACP discussions can be successfully led by a range of professionals. Used in this way, ACP is a fluid process, and if it is made continuous throughout people's care careers rather than a single event leading to a document at the end of life, it can offer opportunities to integrate different services more consciously, and enhance the involvement of older people in planning their care, an important citizenship objective.

While palliative care has, internationally, been an important driver of the development of ACP, as practitioners have sought to clarify and formalize patients' advance decision-making where they are likely to lose capacity to make treatment decisions at the end of life, this has led to the development of interpersonal work with both patients and families. The NICE Care Standard for end-of-life care for adults in all settings, but particularly focusing on care homes, sets planning as an important aspect of holistic care: 'People approaching the end of life are offered comprehensive holistic assessments in response to their changing needs and preferences, with the opportunity to discuss, develop and review a personalized care plan for current and future support and treatment' (National Institute for Health and Care Excellence, 2011: 22). An extensive American research review (Gillick, 2006) focused on end-of-life situations suggests that many people would value ACP discussions but do not have this opportunity, but that they have clear and stable views on how they would like to be treated. Many regard permanent coma, dementia, severe stroke and severe pain as worse than death and would not want life-sustaining treatments in such situations. They would reject treatments depending on how invasive and prolonged they were seen to be. Examples of groups who would benefit from such provision are people with dementia (Volandes et al., 2009), heart failure (Formiga et al., 2004) and serious mental health conditions (Foti et al., 2005).

This focus on family engagement and broader decision-making about care, taken up at an early stage in people's care careers, means that ACP is less focused on advance decisions, because it is hard to prepare for all the possible contingencies, but more on preparing people and their families for agreed 'in-the moment' decision-making at the end-of-life (Sudore and Fried, 2010). Involving informal caregivers and family members is significant in this implementation of ACP in long-term care (Fried and O'Leary, 2008). American studies found that social work involvement led to high participation in ACP for end-of-life care arrangements in hospital (Johnson and Stadel, 2007), community home care service (Ratner et al., 2001) and care home settings, and greater compliance with patients' preferences, especially if the intervention was 'culturally appropriate' (Morrison et al., 2005).

The shift to engaging families in decision-making reflects a greater emphasis in palliative care on the involvement of family carers (Hudson and Payne, 2009), and the European Association for Palliative Care has produced guidelines on developing support for family carers giving importance to their involvement in plans for patients (Payne and EAPC Task Force on Family Carers, 2010).

The Scottish government policies on 'anticipatory care planning' for people with long-term conditions was informed by a pilot project using a case-finding tool to identify patients with long-term conditions with a high risk of hospital admission. It evaluated help for them to plan their care proactively to anticipate and avoid admission. The study came to the conclusion that the location of anticipatory care planning should be standardized to care homes, to ensure its availability (Gallagher and Ireland, 2008). Patients, carers and practitioners have had positive experiences of the processes (JIT, 2015). Palliative care services often refer to care for people, including older people, with long-term conditions as 'supportive care'.

The implications of a shift towards personalized ACP throughout the care career and engaging family members as well as patients suggest that a significant change in practice affecting palliative care services has been taking place. Generating care planning discussions early enough to enable patients to express their wishes while they have capacity has been a constant ambition of practitioners in palliative care. Palliative care services have often been predicated on the diagnosis of a clear terminal illness, or the identification of a patient entering the end stage of a longer-term condition. ACP has focused on end-of-life decision-making because of patients' awareness in this situation of approaching death that arises from a transition into being provided with terminal care.

An important aspect of ACP is identifying the trajectory of the conditions that affect the older person. However, most people approaching the end of life in the general population are experiencing a trajectory of increasing frailty or a slowly deteriorating long-term condition. Black's (2007) review of US research showed that twothirds of adults die with four key conditions, congestive heart failure, emphysema, frailty and dementia, and these should be a marker of the need to plan care preferences. To offer a choice of home care options alongside nursing and care home options, she proposed that ACP should be an element of care at the early stages of a care career with anyone with these conditions. It can also be difficult to identify an appropriate point to undertake end-of-life care planning, and strategies such as the 'surprise' question (asking a practitioner if they would be surprised if the patient died within a year or some other specified period) seek to deal with this problem. Patients, family members and staff may all find it difficult to raise end-of-life care as an issue.

Such problems would be reduced if involvement in care planning was a feature of all care arrangements from an early stage. Personalized ACP early in the care career may helpfully enable everyone involved to progress naturally from more acceptable discussion of earlier care preferences towards end-of-life care preferences.

The consequence of this is that palliative care services increasingly make provision for identifying where earlier care planning has taken place, and updating it at the point of entry into palliative care. Specific medical and nursing guidance is required at this updating stage to document effective advance directives, once end-of-life care decisions enter the frame. Another impact upon palliative care is that earlier planning is likely to have involved family members. This is because it is a requirement of much decision-making in social care settings and because family members' informal caregiving is likely to be closely interwoven with the delivery of social care and community health care services. Therefore, patients with experience of earlier care planning are likely to expect a greater involvement in end-of-life care planning.

## Implementing ACP in practice

Extending ACP to the whole care career means that skills in facilitating ACP in palliative care settings will need to be transferred to a wide range of social and healthcare services. These will, in turn, require a stronger focus on the need to make preparation for end-of-life decisions when these arise at a later point in the planning process.

ACP early in the care career is, however, unlikely ever to be universal, mainly because not everyone takes a planful approach to their lives. Research in the US (Black, 2007) and UK (Samsi and Manthorpe, 2011) found that tendency to plan was a personal lifelong preference and that the general public requires support to perceive benefits in thinking about potential future health problems. In the UK study, while financial and funeral plans were common, health and social care plans were less so. People often relied on family members to act in their best interests, rather than recording their preferences, and an important practice strategy is, therefore, to help people understand how family members may be helped by thinking these issues through with them.

Consequently, professional practice in developing ACP in end-of-life and palliative care settings is likely increasingly to be placed within a context of family meetings, or other forms of wider involvement, and skills in facilitating such meetings will need to be developed.

As wider ACP processes have developed, practice has also been extended from the focus on clarifying potential decisions to refuse treatment where the end of life is very close to a much wider range of situations, including care arrangement, such as those envisaged by the Care Act 2014 in England, but relevant everywhere. This means that practice is drawing on the skills of many different community professionals, increasingly social workers, as families and informal caregivers are drawn into the process and care homes and community settings are building ACP practice.

## The ACP process

Shanley *et al.*'s (2009) study of Australian ACP practice in care homes for older people identifies four main issues in ACP practice:

1. Initiation – at what point in their care career and how does a practitioner begin a conversation about future care planning with a patient?
2. Scope – who is involved in the planning and what areas of care are covered?
3. Follow-up – is the initial planning process referred to and used in everyday care and is the plan reviewed regularly?
4. Documentation – how is the documentation kept and disseminated and does it transfer satisfactorily to new care settings with the patient?

The general answer to all of these questions is to establish the process as early as possible to cover as broad a range of topics and interests as possible and ensure that it is continuous throughout the client's care career. Authoritative guidance issued by the UK Department of Health proposed three stages:

1. an informal stage of *discussion involving information giving* about patients' conditions, their likely progression and eliciting patients' concerns and personal goals in receiving care; leading to
2. documentation in a *statement of wishes and preferences*; followed, if necessary, by
3. an *advance decision to refuse treatment* (Henry and Seymour, 2011).

An American format, physician orders for life-sustaining treatment (POLST), enables discussion to develop in a positive rather than negative way by specifying treatments that are approved, rather than disapproved. It leads to two possible orders for resuscitation: do not attempt cardio-pulmonary resuscitation, or to attempt it. Scope-of-treatment orders consist of limited additional interventions and full treatment, which include hospitalization, and comfort measures only. POLST forms identify patients using name, birth date, sex and address (Fromme *et al.*, 2012). There is some evidence that these increase patient satisfaction with the process.

Initiation is important because, as we have seen, many clients and their families are not accustomed to thinking about the kind of issues that arise in ACP. Careful explanation can be enhanced by using video to support decision-making (Volandes *et al.*, 2009). UK Mental Capacity Act guidance (Department of Constitutional Affairs, 2007: Chapter 3) suggests preliminary steps before developing a document:

- Ensure that people have all the relevant information and access to alternatives.
- Communicate appropriately.
- Help people to feel at ease.
- Support them while they go through the process of making decisions.

Good professional interpersonal skills are therefore crucial in introducing what may be a difficult topic for some clients. These can be enhanced by introducing an effective organizational system. It is helpful to ask routinely for people's preferences as they are assessed for the first time, or at an early stage of care. Starting at this stage promotes clients' engagement in planning as a natural process; this is reinforced by regular reference to their plans and regular review. At a later stage, asking the 'surprise' question to medical staff and others who know the patient and family well ('Would you be surprised if this person were to die in the next six to twelve months?') enables them to integrate a holistic view of the stage of an illness or disability that patients have reached and may help practitioners to decide to instigate ACP processes.

A Scottish analysis of practice with long-term conditions, covers issues such as:

- What happens if your carer becomes unwell?
- What will you do if your condition flares? How will you access help, advice and treatment?
- What would you like to happen if you became acutely unwell with …?
- What is your preferred place of care – home, community hospital, care home or acute hospital?
- Is there a resuscitation status (LTCC-JIT, 2009)?

As the process moves towards documentation, it is important to consider how preferences can be best recorded. Many people prefer documents that state positively what they want to achieve, rather than directives about specific treatments in specific circumstances, but professionals find these more difficult to interpret in making treatment decisions. Therefore, the Royal College of Physicians' (2009) guidance suggests maintaining a balance of expressing personal preferences in a narrative and specific advance refusals. A clear format and guidance in asking concrete questions is also important; even the most articulate people may have trouble thinking what is good about their life. An agency setting up ACP can find many document formats on the internet to select from by searching for 'advance care planning'.

A useful start may be to ask about people's actual experience. Practitioners can ask whether they have experienced or have seen other people having 'a positive or difficult experience' with care, and asking 'what could have been done better or differently?' Moving on to ask clients about current social and healthcare needs provides a concrete basis for asking about any values or preferences that affect their views about it, future health or care needs. Another useful element is to ask about who should contribute to decisions about care needs in the future, or who might take them on a client's behalf. A comprehensive article offering guidance to community healthcare staff also offers useful ideas about initiating queries, which I have adapted to add some broader concerns:

- How have you been coping with your illness (care arrangements, looking after yourself) recently?
- Do you like to think about or plan for the future?
- When you think of the future, what do you hope for?
- When you think about the future, what worries you the most?
- Have you given any thought to what kinds of (care) treatment you would want (and not want) if you became unable to speak for yourself?
- What do you consider your quality of life to be like now (Mullick *et al.*, 2013)?

An Australian prospective randomized controlled trial of plans made up to six months before death (Detering *et al.*, 2010) demonstrated that ACP led to more patients' preferences being known and acted upon, significantly less stress, anxiety and depression, and greater patient and family satisfaction. One format for community use asks concrete questions about current important aspects of life, positive preferences and dislikes if care is required in the future. Another format used in care homes asks for specific preferences in most areas of care for example, from hairdressing to religious preferences (Payne, 2011: Chapter 2). Flexible documentation that can be kept by or disseminated among agencies involved in the patient's care or transferred with the patient between agencies is also helpful to practitioners, clients, informal caregivers and families.

## Barriers to ACP

Barriers exist in implementing ACP, and each of these may be de-citizening because they prevent someone either from knowing that planning is possible or from being fully involved in it. An American study of palliative care professionals, who might be expected to know of its value, showed only 35 per cent had made an advance directive, mostly because of lack of time, although most had had conversations about their preferences with family members. Patients and informal caregivers with chronic obstructive pulmonary disease (COPD) identified five barriers. One was inadequate information provision about the likely course of COPD at diagnosis. Then there was a lack of consensus among professionals about who should initiate ACP, how they should do it and in which setting, so some joint discussion and training may help introduce the process. There were psychological connotations of comparing COPD with cancer. These arise because the prognosis that the illness may lead to the end of life is better understood with cancer while COPD is not understood to be life-threatening in the same way. Another problem was that ACP discussions conflict with the process of focusing on chronic disease management rather than the end-of-life outcome. There was also a lack of understanding of the meaning of 'end of life' within the context of COPD because it was not seen as a life-threatening condition (Gott *et al.*, 2009). It is likely that similar factors would inhibit ACP with other long-term conditions; this research suggests that it is important to shift ACP away from the assumption that it operates only in end-of-life care, and transfer it more actively into long-term care situations. Relatives of older people may wait too long to have a conversation, avoid the topic or the older person may deny their increasing mental incapacity (Hirschman *et al.*, 2006).

A well-conducted study of care homes in England (Froggatt *et al.*, 2009) draws some of these issues together. It found that while many tried to implement ACP processes, because residents were admitted when they were already very frail, a wider commitment to ACP at an earlier stage from social work assessors and care home staff would have been beneficial. Where ACP was attempted, there were three main principles of the process: the plan was individually tailored and led as far as possible by the resident's wishes, a wide variety of people could be involved in the process alongside the staff member documenting the plan and the resident, including relatives and external professionals involved, and the processes were incorporated into existing planning rather than forming an extra task. This meant that residents' preferences and plans informed professional planning for the future.

One of the important developments of ACP in healthcare is a focus on developing appropriate participation in thinking through future plans, rather than on simply recording decisions. Examples of this trend are Henry and Seymour's (2011) guidance with its three ACP processes. An extensive review of American palliative care practice (Lorenz *et al.*, 2008) concludes that 'moderate evidence' supports ACP led by skilled facilitators who engage key decision-makers and interventions to alleviate caregiver burden. Kielmann *et al.*'s (2010) study of patients' attitudes to 'self-care' in long-term conditions suggests that patients can feel abandoned by professionals and that active engagement with them in planning programmes of care are important. Similarly, Hamann *et al.*'s (2007) study of schizophrenic patients' medication found that patients' involvement in planning for the future and shared decision-making about medication led to better long-term outcomes.

## Conclusion: ACP as a citizenship social work strategy

In this chapter, we explored a movement away in recent years from a focus in ACP on documentation of patients' advance decisions to refuse treatment and legal protection for medical decision-making in end-of-life situations towards a broader engagement of people with long-term conditions, their families and informal caregivers in decisions throughout their care careers. This shift is still incomplete, and in some countries and healthcare settings there remains a focus on end-of-life care situations, rather than extending ACP throughout the care career. The research and official guidance suggests that ACP provides a good opportunity for engaging people at a difficult time of their lives and achieves increased satisfaction and better attainment of their goals in receiving care. It is thus a good example of how to implement in practice the citizenship strategies that we explored in Chapter 2. Avoiding planning is de-citizening; facilitating it is re-citizening, especially where people are beginning to lose physical or mental capacity.

These developments lead us to seeing ACP as a crucial element in all social work practice with older people. It benefits clients and services for a number of reasons. First, it highlights clients' own preferences and empowers their influence within professional and social agency decision-making processes. Second, it protects human rights to freedom of decision-making through openness in professional practice, particularly about difficult issues that some people try to avoid. Third, that protection through openness is prioritized against legalistic, bureaucratic or managerial protections of clients' rights, which may be more restrictive of flexibility in meeting clients' preferences. Fourth, ACP emphasizes the importance in social work of its role in making arrangements for and provision of long-term care, rather than counselling or interpersonal or therapeutic problem-solving. Analysing ACP therefore identifies some of the interpersonal and human aspects of a service provision model of social work. It helps practitioners to understand the relevance in social work practice of what sometimes seems to be 'just' an administrative or management requirement of their agency. Fifth, connected with this, examining ACP also explicates practice with an important but under-explored client group, people with long-term conditions who require care for a period, rather than short change-oriented interventions as a focus.

Expressing preferences does not necessarily lead to clients being in control of care decisions, however. Often people have no choice about receiving care when they would rather not, and there are often not enough resources to meet their needs; or practitioners judge that alternative interventions are required. Nevertheless, there is evidence that ACP in healthcare leads to patients' wishes being met more often than where there is no planning. There are barriers to effective implementation of ACP, in particular people's preferences, their existing expectations and their understanding of their condition. When it is offered, though, it is a valued intervention which also provides an opportunity for engaging family members and informal carers in care planning as well as clients. Expressing preferences helps members of the public to accept that they have been treated fairly, since practitioners have clearly listened to, recorded and given themselves the best chance of being influenced by clients' wishes. ACP permits practitioners to identify when clients' wishes cannot be met and to find ways of meeting their wishes in other ways or to some extent, rather than just accepting a status quo that they feel is unsatisfactory.

## ADDITIONAL RESOURCES

### Official guides

http://www.ncpc.org.uk/freedownloads

The National Council for Palliative Care offers access to a range of useful documents which have disappeared from the internet; this includes access to the final edition of the valuable guide written by Henry and Seymour for the NHS England National End of Life Care Programme, and the regularly updated guide to ACP for service users published by NHS Improving Quality, which uses the same approach.

Henry, C. and Seymour, J. (2011) *Advance Care Planning: A guide for health and social care staff*. London: Department of Health.

NHS Improving Quality (2014) *Planning for Your Future Care: A guide*. London: NHSIQ.

https://www.rcplondon.ac.uk/guidelines-policy/advance-care-planning

This website offers well-regarded guidelines published by the Royal College of Physicians on behalf of a widely representative working party. The guidelines are as follows:

Royal College of Physicians (2009) *Advance Care Planning: National guidelines*. London: Royal College of Physicians.

The former Labour UK government published a quite informative website on Advance Decisions to Refuse Treatment, which has not been adequately replaced, but you can view the archived website here:

http://webarchive.nationalarchives.gov.uk/20121015000000/http://www.direct.gov.uk/en/Governmentcitizensandrights/Death/Preparation/DG_10029429 (retrieved 30 October 2015).

http://www.scie.org.uk/dementia/supporting-people-with-dementia/decisions/advance-care-planning.asp

SCIE offers a fairly limited website on ACP in dementia, emphasizing, as appropriate for this service user group, the procedures of the Mental Capacity Act 2005.

### Websites

This website introduces POLST, a US ACP protocol: Physician Orders for Life-Sustaining Treatment. The orders record statements agreed with relatives and patients, and are

focused on people experiencing extreme frailty, as well as diagnosed terminal conditions. The website includes a list of research and professional publications about the approach:
http://www.polst.org/about-the-national-polst-paradigm/

Advance Care Planning Australia offers an excellent range of resources and links to sites provided by Australian states. The 'Research and Publications' link offers links to PDFs of many useful research articles on ACP:
http://advancecareplanning.org.au/

As with the Australian site, the Canadian website 'Speak up' offers useful resources and links to publications for professionals and service users:
http://www.advancecareplanning.ca/

The National Institute for Aging, a semi-official academic and professional resource, offers an extensive website on ACP covering US practice:
https://www.nia.nih.gov/health/publication/advance-care-planning

# PART II
# Practice strategies for end-of-life social work with older citizens

# 6

# PREPARING FOR LATER LIFE

## Adulthood and the third age

### Chapter aims

In Part I, I discussed citizenship social work and citizening social care services. I argued that we should avoid practice that de-citizens older people. Instead, we should aim to citizen and re-citizen them as whole people, whose humanity includes their continuing connections with carers, families and communities. Holistic practice means respecting the relationships and communities in which they have travelled their life journey.

This chapter focuses on the contribution that social work and social care managers and practitioners can make to helping our society recognize and value older people and the processes of ageing and dying well. Part of this is good-quality professional practice and providing appropriate services, and I look at that in the next two chapters. First, however, in this chapter, I look at how we can draw on the experience of our professional practice to contribute to preparation and social action in this field.

The aims of this chapter, therefore, are to:

- Identify social work practice strategies that facilitate preparation for ageing and the end of life, enabling people to have a better quality experience of these phases of life.
- Argue for the significance of social action for better quality ageing and end-of-life experiences for all citizens.
- Establish policies and services that contribute to better ageing and end-of-life experiences.
- As part of better policies and services for older people, focus strongly on preparing and supporting carers.
- Review social action strategies drawing on social work and social care that can contribute to policy, practice and services concerned with ageing and end-of-life care.

### Preparing for well-being in later life and at the end of life

The starting point is that social care and end-of-life care professions need to incorporate work towards good provision for well-being in ageing and dying into their everyday work.

An example of including well-being at every stage in life is the objectives set out in the English Care Act 2014. The official guidance on the act helps us to see what a broad focus on adult lives our practice should have:

- personal dignity (including treatment of the individual with respect);
- physical and mental health and emotional well-being;
- protection from abuse and neglect;
- control by the individual over day-to-day life (including over care and support provided and the way in which it is provided);
- participation in work, education, training or recreation;
- social and economic well-being;
- domestic, family and personal;
- suitability of living accommodation;
- the individual's contribution to society (Department of Health, 2016: Para 1.5).

Aiming for an older person's well-being requires not only good everyday social work practice, but a focus on social action around ageing and dying and on policy that contributes to life preparation for ageing and dying. Most texts on social work and services with older people concentrate on practice with individuals who have problems as they become elderly, and they sometimes fail to deal with end-of-life issues at all. Moreover, as a consequence, they deal with carers as an adjunct to working with older people, whereas I argue that thinking about the nature of care and the role of carers should be integral to planning services.

The adulthood period, the 'second age', merges into the 'third age' of active later life; Figure 1.1 will remind you of the life stages of the four 'ages'. For many people, active adulthood continues, but increasingly people become aware of physical ageing and limitations on their active lives. The third age may last for a considerable period into people's 80s, or it may be more truncated if they are affected by disabilities or illness, and this is more likely if they are from socio-economic classes affected by poverty and deprivation earlier in their lives (Marmot Review Team, 2010).

## Practice strategy: Preparing in adulthood for later life

### Three alternative practice strategies

How can social workers have a practice strategy preparing for ageing, when most practitioners work only with older people who are already in difficulties because of increasing frailty? In this context, three different kinds of practice strategy are needed:

1. A personal strategy. Social workers can make contributions as citizens alongside other people. They can do this both by setting an example in preparing for ageing and the end of life during their own adulthood, and also by taking opportunities in their own communities and social networks to promote positive ageing and end-of-life care.
2. A career strategy. Social workers can consider working in policy and service development roles and in providing services, often through periods of work in not-for-profit

agencies, that promote better provision for ageing and end-of-life care, and for older people and their carers.
3. A team strategy. Working in a team with older people, social workers can use the team's expertise and experience in a planned way to support external services and community provision.

> **CASE EXAMPLES: PERSONAL, CAREER AND TEAM STRATEGIES**
>
> Julie, a social worker in her 40s taking up her second social work job in an older person's team, decided to complete a will and a 'lasting power of attorney'. She got her husband to do the same, and discussed it with their teenage children. When she worked with a woman moving into a care home as she was coming towards the end of life, she was able to talk about her own experience with both the older person and with her main carer. The carer was able to tell his own children about their grandmother's illness and the prognosis that she had only a few months to live. This is a personal strategy and some of its consequences.
>
> Harriet worked in an older persons' team and thought that she might eventually like to work in the local hospital. She decided to take up a job as coordinator of a new advocacy scheme for older people being started by a voluntary organization in her area, which had received a three-year grant for the purpose. She decided that this gave her opportunities to cooperate with a range of care homes and other organizations working with older people, and gave her a good basis for later applications for jobs in the area. This would be so even though she faced the risk of her job not continuing when the grant ran out. This is a career strategy and some of its consequences.
>
> A team working with adults with intellectual (learning) disabilities realized that many of the service users they worked with were living much longer than had previously been the case, and had ageing parents. They set out on a project to work in cooperation with colleagues in their older persons' team to provide training for staff in care homes and other services for older people on learning disabilities. Eventually, this experience led them to plan with the palliative care team at their local hospice commissioning a support service for people with learning disabilities at the end of life. This is a team strategy and some of its consequences.

In the next sections, I discuss briefly the main areas of preparation that may be useful, and offer a number of case examples to illustrate them, and to prepare the way for discussing some broad issues about planning for ageing.

## Planning for ageing

In Chapter 5, I looked at how advance care planning and its extension into planning for the whole care career is crucial to citizening for older people at the end of life. In this section, I explore how people can plan for ageing throughout their lives and how social workers can help them to do this.

There are three important difficulties in making general strategic decisions about planning for later life:

1.  Not everyone plans, either because temperamentally they are not proactive in life, or because their personal and family circumstances create pressures that make planning difficult or impossible. Helping people plan supports their citizenship because it allows them to exercise their choices.
2.  National, regional and local administrative, legal and service systems and the varying impact of markets mean that general rules are hard to apply to local situations. Helping people understand how these systems affect them specifically enhances their citizenship because it helps them to use their rights and opportunities.
3.  Societies change so rapidly that planning over a lifetime is difficult. Avoiding planning as a result is de-citizening, because it takes choices out of people's own hands.

So people give up, and social workers often deal with people without flexibility in making life plans. But there are some answers to these problems. First, having some plans, or a general picture of where you want to go, alerts you when things happen that mean you should change your plan. Second, total change in any society is rare, particularly in the relatively developed societies in which social workers often work. When changes occur, therefore, you can make adjustments to keep plans on track. Third, there are distant plans and closer plans. Plans for long-distant events, such as retirement or incapacity at the end of life, can be fairly general and can be firmed up later, while plans for your funeral when you are diagnosed with a life-threatening illness can be more specific and are less likely to change. Fourth, you can have plan A and plan B, giving yourself alternatives in case things go wrong. This helps to keep control of your affairs. People can be encouraged to plan as much as they are able, and take opportunities to plan as they arise. Planning enhances your citizenship because it helps you keep (at least some) control.

## Finances

Preparation in adulthood for adequate financial support as people age is perhaps the most important area of life to provide a basis for security. In the UK, most people of pensionable age gain the largest proportion of their income from the state pension and benefits, although private pensions are at present an increasing, but smaller, proportion of income (Adam *et al.*, 2012: Figure 2.1).

Most people are aware of this, even if they are unclear about their options. Everyday pressures of life in adulthood, such as family living expenses and care for children, suck up resources. Consequently, it can be hard to focus on financial provision for ageing. Social workers can help by making the arguments for financial planning with people as they come across them. It is useful for people to set themselves some basic rules:

- Contribute to a pension from the earliest possible age, because investments build up value over long periods; the longer you have them the more value they will gain. In most countries contributing to pensions also has tax advantages.
- Obtain employer contributions, because this adds to your eventual retirement income at no expense to you. Employer contribution is a form of wages, so you are entitled to it.
- Put part (if not all) of windfalls into your retirement resources. Adding lump sums to pensions or tax-efficient savings schemes can help them build up, without missing out on current spending. Such windfalls might include inheritances, bonus payments and prizes.

- If your pension is invested, review the investments every few years and certainly more regularly as you approach retirement.

Social workers often mainly work with people whose income is irregular or who are in poverty for much of their childhood and adult life. Even so, financial preparation for ageing and retirement is an important skill to develop for people you work with. If you are helping people find work, or supporting a family in child care, for example, use any chance to get them to think about how they are building towards retirement or at least not closing off any options. Many countries, like the UK, now pressurize people to sign up to pension schemes; but these are not good enough unless they find ways of adding to the minimum. Also, try to get people to think about ways of reducing their poverty in their own old age and among older people they are caring for.

As people move into the third age, they will begin to shift from work to relying on their pensions and savings as the economic basis of their life in retirement. This requires careful planning and thinking about what people want to do in their retirement. Even if the pressures on their current life are legion, it's always worth encouraging people to have half an eye on this future – it's also an inspiration of hope.

## Home, housing, shelter

Everyone has a home or at least is housed, and this is a major element in people's stability and human relationships. Even people living on the street usually hope to move towards greater housing stability and quality. In the UK, not enough housing is being built and older people are disproportionately housed in owner-occupied housing. This means they have responsibility for maintenance, which becomes more difficult as they age, and there is a lack of suitable, attractive housing to move to that is accessible for ageing people (Ota, 2015). A range of supported housing includes facilities for older people alongside living accommodation, set out in Table 6.1. This is not, however, universally available.

Our housing interacts closely with our experience of ageing and with care we might need when we reach later life (Victor, 2010). We have different housing arrangements at different stages in our lives, usually in mainstream housing to meet general needs. For example, during the period when we are young adults we might live with parents or rent fairly small-scale accommodation, to the point where we marry and have a family, when we rent or buy larger accommodation. There is then the question of how we should continue as we age and children leave home or we need less space for our adult life. In the UK, particularly, housing has been a good investment in the last part of the 20th century and many people have money tied up in their houses, becoming rich in housing assets but, as they age, perhaps not having the income to maintain or live in a larger property. In all countries, there is an issue of the extent to which it will become necessary to use property assets to finance care. Another related issue is the extent to which care becomes bound up in housing arrangements.

'Lifetime housing' suitable to accommodate people without moving permits 'ageing in place', 'living in the community, with some level of independence, rather than in residential care' (Davey et al., 2004). Although this concept mainly refers to having appropriate housing, it is closely linked to feelings of attachment to social connection, a sense of the home as a familiar, secure place and refuge and the community as a resource, and identity and

**TABLE 6.1** Supported housing

| Housing type | Aim | Facilities |
|---|---|---|
| Supported housing | Specifically for older people with access to support and care | Twenty-four-hour alarm system, a warden, shared lounge and programmes of activities |
| Very sheltered or assisted living | Independent living with managed care and support services | Meals, domestic help, assisted bathing |
| Extra care housing | Accommodation with managed on-site care and support services | Hairdressing service, 24-hour staff |
| Close care housing | Independent living with on-site care and support. | Linked to care home |
| Retirement villages | Large developments (often 100+) with a range of housing types | Range of levels of care and support on one site |

*Source*: HAPPI (2009: Figure 3)

opportunities for independence and autonomy (Wiles *et al.*, 2011). Other aspects include having a range of appropriate services available offering choice and flexibility and an environment in which the generations are mixed (Ball, nd).

A longstanding issue for older people is the extent to which their housing is segregated from people at other stages of their lives and the extent to which care is provided only in segregated settings, such as care homes (Butler and Tinker, 1983). There are tensions between a wish to remain in one's home with the need to adapt it as needs change in later life (Ota, 2015). If older people live in adapted housing (HAPPI, 2009), questions are raised. First, how do people decide that they want to live in a special place? Second, part of the first question is what reasons are there for segregation rather than integration? Third, another part of the first question is what are the human, practical and social consequences of segregation and integration in people's housing? Fourth, and finally, what are the criteria for deciding at what point older people will transfer from integrated housing? In the UK, a Disabled Facilities Grant (DFG) may be provided by local authorities where older people need to adapt their homes, but it can be hard to organize the adaptations (Ota, 2015). As they reach middle age and the third age, people might think about how they will deal with this and practitioners might encourage them at any time of life to think about future housing issues for themselves.

The HAPPI project has sought to provide design criteria for housing suitable for older people; this includes:

- generous flexible space, with three habitable rooms;
- good natural light;
- avoiding internal corridors and single-aspect windows; offering balconies, patios and plants;
- making homes adaptable and 'care ready';
- promoting shared spaces and avoiding an 'institutional feel';
- multipurpose space, activities serving the wider neighbourhood, guest rooms for visitors;
- connecting with the street;
- providing for mature trees and wildlife;
- energy-efficient, well-insulated;
- good storage;
- priority of pedestrians, suitable for people with navigation difficulties.

An older person's quality of life does not depend on their personal independence in housing. Being independent and self-sufficient, and forms of housing that most promote independence are desirable for most people. Many aspects of care involve, however, connectedness between people. Promoting independence may disconnect people. A good quality of life, therefore, balances connectedness and care with housing that separates, and other factors that decrease connectedness.

To think about these issues, a useful practice strategy is to give priority to maintaining and enhancing existing links across the life course. Many people want to stay in the same housing because it stimulates important memories about earlier stages in their lives. They may also have a network of relationships deriving from earlier days. They have networks that come from social involvements, in a local church, local community centre or that derive from work. All of these will vary depending upon the individual and their life history and the nature of the community.

Improvements in housing stock that benefit older people include improving the availability of accessible bathrooms and kitchens, access for people who are increasingly frail, and safety features for people who have difficulty in moving around or who might be at risk of falling. As people age, they may be helped to think about gradually adapting their houses to include such features, in their own property and in rented accommodation. Making housing accessible and easier to manage benefits people at every stage of life.

## Activities, including leisure, work and community involvement

An important aspect of adult life is developing and maintaining a range of activities, often building from school and university education, work and family life. Included in these activities are sports and social activities. Important social networks are often built up around these activities. Of course, in adult life, these activities are developed for all sorts of reasons, but one of them, particularly as people move towards later life, should be the possibility of maintaining them to help them maintain an active social life and a healthy lifestyle. People can be encouraged to think about leisure activities that can be continued economically, but that will benefit their health. An example might be swimming using public leisure facilities, which usually offer reduced fees for retired people.

Decluttering is often seen as a lifestyle choice, but it can also benefit health and safety and thinking about how you declutter and what you retain with an eye to your needs when you are older can help to maintain social networks and activities.

> **CASE EXAMPLE: KEEPING THE TOOLS AND THE TOYS**
>
> After her husband died in his 60s, Karen sorted out the shed he used as a workshop in the garden. She offered many of his tools to younger people just starting out on married life in her local church, but made sure she retained screwdrivers and a hammer so that she could still do basic jobs around the house. She gave away many of his media, retaining only the ones that she might want to watch and listen to, having them converted to new formats a few years later. She decided to keep toys left behind by their children, and valued this decision in later years, because it meant that grandchildren and their friends visiting her had lots of activities to interest them using 'retro' toys. They were much keener to visit her than other older relatives who did not have such interesting toys to play with, and this meant that they had a better relationship with her. When she became very frail, this meant that they visited her more often than she had expected.

## Health and safety

I suggested when looking at housing that gradually adapting housing, whether owner-occupied or rented, to improve people's safety is not something that just benefits ageing or older people: it benefits all members of the family. Encourage people to look around the house and make improvements which make life easier for everyone. My approach to this, consistent with my 'humanistic social work' approach which looks at security rather than risk (Payne, 2011: Chapter 8), is to concentrate on people's feeling of security. Ask people what would make everyday activities feel more secure. If they are doing something that makes them a bit anxious in adulthood, they are likely to feel more insecure with it as they age, so it is worth looking for better equipment or improving the layout of the house to create greater safety.

> **CASE EXAMPLE: FALLING FROM THE ATTIC**
>
> In adult life, Jan often felt vertigo when she looked down from heights. Her husband always climbed a foldout ladder to get into the attic, and balanced on joists while walking across the attic. When he died of a heart attack in her early 50s, Jan was forced to take this on. So she spent money from his life assurance payment to have a pull-down ladder with handrails built in so that she could gain access to the attic more securely. She also boarded the floor, so that she could walk across it safely. Arthritis made movement more difficult and painful as she aged and 20 years later she was grateful for these improvements.

## Holidays

One of the traditional things that older people did when they retired was to go on a round-the-world cruise. It was seen as a luxury, which rewarded a lifetime of effort at work and in raising a family. For some periods in adult life, people prioritize the needs of their children when arranging holidays: it is an opportunity to spend concentrated time with their children. Many people are unable to take holidays in adult life, because their income is low and this is not a priority. Even so, in later life, they can pursue economical leisure activities around their home. As they age and become grandparents, they may spend part of the holiday period looking after grandchildren for working parents in their family, or will go with children and grandchildren on family holidays. People who are better off may build plans to visit places that interest them, or take part in activity holidays. Some people buy second homes in holiday areas or in other countries in adult life, at least partly so that they have somewhere secured for holidays when their finances are less good. All of this is about planning for leisure time in old age. As people become frail, the inability to have a holiday, or loss of expectations of holidays can also be an important factor.

---

### CASE EXAMPLES: HOLIDAY PLANNING

Joe and Miriam had a second marriage late in life, and after a period in which both had stressful jobs, he was made redundant, with a good lump sum payment, but after a period of great conflict in his workplace. They had planned to pursue personal interests on holidays on retirement, having led very busy lives, and provided a lot of care to the grandchildren of their earlier marriages. Shortly after his redundancy, he was found to have pancreatic cancer, which has a very high death rate when diagnosed, and he died very quickly. Both told their social worker that they regretted having left 'together-time' until their retirement, and were both very miserable about the loss of their plans.

Catherine had a progressive disease, and was cared for by her husband at home: she eventually became very disabled, requiring almost total care, which he provided. Their social worker organized a holiday for a few days at a care home in the country, not an ideal or stimulating setting for a holiday, although it meant a change of scene. On their return, they told their social worker that the thing that they most appreciated about the holiday was the chance to be 'a married couple again', rather than 'carer' and 'cared for'.

---

## Care arrangements, including end-of-life care

A range of social care and related facilities are available to support older people, and I list common types in Table 6.2. An asterisk shows types of provision where specialist providers of palliative care, in the UK mainly hospices, offer specialized arrangements for this service user group. This arises partly because symptom management at the end of life often requires specialized nursing and physiotherapy provision. The main reason is that in the UK independent charitable hospices have been the main location of specialist palliative care. Until the early 21st century, these services had been seen as an extra service for a few days or weeks of high-quality care, what has been called 'a little bit of heaven for a few' (Clark *et al.*, 2005). Provision is also made for many of these types of care in specialist facilities for people with dementia, and there are also widely available specialist healthcare community services for common long-term conditions, such as chronic obstructive pulmonary disease (COPD), heart failure and Parkinson's disease.

Most older people experience only the generally available services as they become increasingly frail, and rely on family and friends to support their own self-caring. While most people feel anxiety about what care needs might mean to them and their families, they have little opportunity to plan and foresee what might happen. This raises the risk of

**TABLE 6.2** Social and related care provision

| Adult services | Description |
| --- | --- |
| Care homes and care homes with nursing | Provide accommodation, meals and personal care; nursing homes provide integrated nursing; specialist homes provide care for particular needs, including dementia |
| Supported housing | Housing providing independent living, with variable levels and types of care delivered; see Table 6.1 for further details |
| * Day care | Hospitals, centres, clubs, drop-in centres, social and rest centres, communal rooms in supported housing schemes, lunch clubs, work or craft centres, clubs and societies |
| * Respite care | Help in the home to offer a chance of time off or holidays for carers |
| * Care in your own home | Older people 'stay put' in homes suitable for their whole lifetime; care workers provide help with washing, dressing and eating and other practical tasks in people's own homes |
| Assistive technology | Devices and systems enabling people to perform tasks that they would be unable to do or that would be more difficult or unsafe without assistance |
| Direct payments | Help with cash payments made direct by local councils to enable people to buy assistance with care |
| Nurse agencies | Organize nurses to visit people who need care, in their own homes, and in care homes or hospitals |
| Adult support schemes | Organize to provide people in need with a family life in the carer's homes, or with 'co-housing', where people live together to contribute to meeting each other's needs. |

*Sources*: Payne (2009: Table 5.1); HAPPI (2009: Figure 3)

* Asterisk shows where specialist provision of this type is available at the end of life.

de-citizening because they are not ready to make their own choices when it comes to greater use of services.

Care arrangements, as they become necessary, are closely bound up with their finances and their housing: what can people afford? What does that mean for their housing? The services in Table 6.2 represent a progression from social care that involves the most integration of care and housing, and often the highest cost, to less costly and more flexible options. The use of these options varies. For example, day care has been declining in recent years, as fewer older people and service commissioners are prepared to finance what may seem a purely social or leisure facility. This is so even though there is evidence that they reduce the need for progression to care homes and hospital care (Manthorpe and Moriarty, 2014). Most older people will experience combinations of less costly options provided in their own homes in earlier old age, and progress through a series of transitions towards more costly options, requiring them to move into specialized housing, care homes, nursing homes, hospitals and hospices. At some point in that series of transitions, end-of-life care might be provided in any of these options.

The cost of care options interacts with income, including pensions, and wealth, as well as capital, which may also contribute to costs. Progress in reducing poverty in old age for many people in recent years reflects increases in incomes and capital resources, and in some countries and particular areas of countries increases in the value of housing have contributed to this. A report from the International Longevity Centre – UK (2015) notes three important points:

1. Reductions in resources for social care services and the 'care gap' described in Chapter 1 means that older people could face considerable levels of unmet need.
2. There is considerable diversity even among the post-war generation of 'baby boomers'. While this population group benefited from economic growth and the expansion of state expenditure and pensions in the last half of the 20th century, one third, particularly women, have no pension wealth at all. Others are insecure because they rely on housing wealth for resources in their old age, particularly if they require high levels of care.
3. Younger generations have less generous pensions, dependent upon the money markets, and these are likely to produce reduced returns to support pensioners in the future, compared with recent experience.

Costs of social care and healthcare rise, particularly in the last year of life, and give rise to concern about covering them, both in the UK National Health Service and social care services, where there has been a succession of reports about the issue from various sources. These include the Sutherland Commission (1999) on long-term care; the Wanless social care review, (Wanless *et al.*, 2006); the independent review of free personal and nursing care in Scotland (Sutherland, 2008); the Commission on Funding of Care and Support Fairer Care Funding (2011). There are insurance-based schemes such as the arrangements in the US (Riley and Lubitz, 2010). As with social care, there is considerable movement between various forms of care.

In adulthood and the third age, most people will not require care for themselves; they will, however, often become involved in care arrangements for others, including parents and older relatives and people in the local community. Experience in caring for older relatives is a preparation for planning your own care, conditioning how people react when questions about their own ageing come up.

Similarly, an important element of your attitude to your own end-of-life care is having experience of other people 'dying well'. So when someone dies or is going through the process of dying at your school, workplace or within your family it is good to get involved and contribute to care and a creative period of living for that person who is dying, or helping people around them experience a successful bereavement. This has led palliative care services to develop projects in schools to introduce young people, and through them their parents, to thinking about, understanding and planning for dying. The St Christopher's Hospice Schools Project is a community arts programme. Within a structured framework of four-week exchanges of visits between schools and colleges, children are given the opportunity to interact and engage in music and art-making together with terminally ill patients, culminating in an exhibition or performance. The main aim is to promoting healthier attitudes towards death and dying among children, their teachers, school peers, parents and carers (Tsiris *et al.*, 2011). Connected with this, it is important to consider how children in a family and community may be involved with someone who is changing because of their ageing, and who in later life is going through the dying process. Adults often feel the need to protect children and young people from unpleasant aspects of life, or from events in the family that might disturb their education and development (Reith and Payne, 2009). Children may therefore be excluded from knowing about illness, disability and death among family members, blaming themselves because they do not know the truth of what is going on or cut off from relationships – for example, with grandparents whom they have previously had a lot of contact.

Where social workers are involved with a family, it is helpful to encourage them to find ways of encouraging children to maintain contacts and activities with older people. As with the St Christopher's Schools Project, arts and crafts activities, even by the bedside of someone who is bedbound or housebound, can be a helpful way of achieving this. Park's (2014) systematic literature review shows that intergenerational activities in which younger people engage with older people, as in the St Christopher's Schools Project, bring emotional and social benefits for older people living in the community and improve older people's cognitive functioning.

## Social action for quality of life and end of life

The ageing journey may be travelled in many different ways. The fact that ageing is inevitable does not mean that the way we age is out of our control, and cannot be influenced by ourselves, our friends and families and the professionals working with older people. Lloyd *et al.* (2014) emphasize, in a study on dignity in later life, that maintaining a social self and social relationships also enables older people to maintain their identity. By managing, helped by families and friends, illnesses and disabilities, health treatments and social care arrangements themselves they are able to persevere against their difficulties. Lloyd *et al.* (2014) propose that perseverance is a valued sense of self, lying between resistance and acquiescence, rising above our difficulties through developing our own sense of direction in our everyday life. Achieving our own sense of direction and control of our lives in later life is a crucial part of citizenship, and this is equally true at the end of life.

Having personal, career and team practice strategies for ageing in adult life implies that all social work should include social action benefiting older people's citizenship. We often think of social action as being concerned with policy about ageing and social service provision. For example, each of the practice strategy areas identified above offer scope for development and innovation through social action. There is active campaigning on older people's finance for social care and other services, pensions, issues concerned with poverty, including fuel poverty and food poverty, housing, activities, holidays, health and safety and care arrangements for older people and in end-of-life care. Groups involved in these issues locally, nationally and internationally would benefit from involvement by social workers and older people, carers and other people in the community.

Older people's services have been developed in different ways, however, and engaging in social care services or community provision for older people and end-of-life care are equally valid objects of advocacy and social action. Verleye and Gemmel (2009: 49–58) identified four innovation strategies pursued by different countries to change services for older people:

1. decentralization, spreading services across a community;
2. deinstitutionalization, improving care which keeps people out of care homes or hospital;
3. integration, improving connections between organizations or people involved in the care of older people;
4. rationalization, reducing inefficiencies in organization or communication.

To stimulate innovation, they ran a competition to generate proposals, which were then evaluated. Three types of innovation were created:

1. New technologies. One example was a gadget to detect when someone living alone had had a fall and to summon assistance.
2. New care services. One example was a collaboration between groups of local organizations for older people to provide a pool of labour to provide night care for older people.
3. New general services. One example was a cyber café in an older persons' organization to encourage social activity.

> **CASE EXAMPLE: INNOVATION STRATEGIES**
>
> In one local authority area, a church had created a weekly meeting for people in a local community, mixing people with physical and learning disabilities, mental health problems and older people. A coordinating organization was created within an existing group in the town which so far only provided a central resource and drop-in centre for older people and whose grant was being reduced. The funding provided some stability to promote and support the model to community groups in other areas, aiming to develop groups across the whole town. This stabilized and gave a new focus for the central group dealing with its funding cuts. This was a project idea from a local councillor from a majority party, and therefore gained political support; it also engaged local adult social care managers and staff, local disability organizations and local mental health organizations. This is a decentralization strategy.
>
> A hospice developed its internal care assistant training to provide support and training in care skills to paid care workers to provide a home care service for social care clients, who were on the palliative care registers of local GPs. This was a deinstitutionalization strategy because it kept people out of hospital, an integration strategy because it got a healthcare organization involved in social care provision, and a rationalization strategy because it used healthcare training resources better and used the local palliative care register to bring together the health and social care needs of the service users.

Advocacy, political action and service development are not the only practical strategies for social workers. Drawing on a range of studies, Clifton (2009) argues that building social ties and relationships is the most important area for maintaining older people's dignity and social roles. Loneliness is a significant risk factor in many of the problems that older people have. He suggests that social ties are important because they provide:

- practical support and information;
- emotional support and advice;
- positive affirmation and a sense of respect;
- a meaningful social role in social groups;
- stability, social norms and routines;
- support that enables older people to live independently;

- connections and support that enable people to participate in activities;
- relationships that older people can contribute to, which are of greater benefit than relationships where the older person is simply a passive consumer of services.

Social action by social workers for older people, therefore, can readily focus on improving opportunities for interpersonal and social interaction through community organizations, and does not have to be focused on care services themselves or through political action or advocacy. Verleye and Gemmel's (2009) Dutch study of how to promote innovation in provision for older people identified a range of innovations in equipment and social provision in state, voluntary sector, private sector and in families and informal care. They identified five ways of introducing innovations in older people's care:

1. projects deriving from present practice including cost-reduced versions of existing products or enhancements;
2. new products and services ('breakthrough projects');
3. changes to products and processes;
4. creation of 'know-how' and 'know-why' which might underlie new technologies and practices; this might include researching service user or carer views or feedback;
5. forming new alliances and partnerships to pursue innovations (Verleye and Gemmel, 2009: 24).

The citizenship approach to social work with older people closely connects with two internationally developed policies for older people:

1. active ageing (World Health Organization, 2002);
2. creating age-friendly environments and particularly cities (World Health Organization, 2007; Arup, 2015).

'Age-friendly environments' policy proposes that all societies should create environments that enable older people to live their lives successfully as citizens in eight domains of life:

1. community and healthcare, with accessible, affordable care at home and in the community, with residential care available if required;
2. transportation, including affordable, available, reliable and frequent public transport with comfortable seating;
3. housing, including affordable, adaptable housing with a range of options for tenure;
4. social participation, including affordable, accessible, well-publicized opportunities, integrating the generations;
5. outdoor spaces and buildings, including places to sit and rest, safe pedestrian areas and walkways;
6. respect and social inclusion, offering places within the community and the family with respectful and responsive social opportunities;
7. civic participation and employment, including flexible employment, entrepreneurship and volunteering opportunities;
8. communication and information, including the right opportunities at the right time, with personal attention and the availability of support to use new technologies (World Health Organization, 2007).

According to the World Health Organization, age-friendly cities and communities:

- Recognize the wide range of capacities and resources among older people.
- Anticipate and respond flexibly to ageing-related needs and preferences.
- Respect older people's decisions and lifestyle choices.
- Protect those who are most vulnerable.
- Promote older people's inclusion in and contribution to all areas of community life (World Health Organization, 2007).

The World Health Organization's Healthy Cities Project also identified a range of community activities that could build understanding and knowledge of the end of life as a public health strategy creating 'compassionate cities' (Kellehear, 2005).

---

**CASE EXAMPLE: LEARNING TO TEXT**

Mrs Harcourt was a woman in her 80s who was admitted by ambulance in an emergency to hospital after a fall in the street. Graham, her nephew, who lived at a distance, visited her regularly, although infrequently. He became, in a way, the family's representative in helping her. He found that she was isolated from other members of the family who lived even further away and many of her friends had died. Although she had a smart phone, and had used it for occasional calls, she did not telephone people without making an arrangement to do this, not wanting to interfere in their busy lives. She had been frustrated with texting, finding that the predictive text feature of her phone made constructing words and sentences impossible. She could not see the point of texting. When she returned home, Graham showed her how to turn off predictive text and suggested she try texting him messages about how she was getting on. He explained that while he was at work, he was not allowed to phone, but he could look at texts, which accumulated for him until he had some time available. She tried some texting, receiving replies from him, and she found that texting became her favoured, non-intrusive means of communication with more active friends and family. As a result, she became quite proficient and much more connected to people, even though she was mostly housebound. When she needed to go into hospital again for a longer stay, with complications from diabetes, some months later, she used texting to maintain contact with people, and her numbers of visitors increased as a result. This was maintained when she was discharged to a care home.

---

Social workers may be unable to do this kind of practical helping in their everyday professional round, but they can do three things, individually and collectively, to maintain older people's social links as part of a concerned age-friendly community. First, as a personal strategy for individual practitioners, they can keep up with helpful new technologies and demonstrate their usefulness to older people. Someone who retires at 60 and does not see the point in keeping up with the latest technology will 20 years later at 80, when they need to use something to assist with their ageing, be so out of touch that they cannot make a start. Getting out of touch with technology is de-citizening, so we should always try to combat it. Social workers should be models of keeping in touch with modernity. Second, as part of the community, they can encourage education and social activities that can benefit older people, including school, workplace and community education around dying matters. Third, as part of commissioning services, care planning and advance care planning, they can include educational, personal development and leisure activities that will benefit older people and enable them to think and plan for the end of life.

## Preparing and supporting carers (informal caregivers)

### Some points about terminology

One of the most important areas for social action and development that benefits older people and prepares in earlier life for ageing is concern to develop caring resources. In this section, I discuss the importance of a practice strategy for supporting the role of carers, both in general with older people and as they approach the end of life. 'Carer' is the UK term for family members, neighbours and friends who provide care, of various kinds, for older people. The term that is used to refer to carers in the international healthcare professional and academic literature is 'informal caregivers', because it is thought to be more precise. For one thing, it distinguishes them from 'formal' carers – that is, people who are employed to provide care as part of the care system. Some British carers find 'informal caregiving' too official or professional sounding and prefer 'carers' as a more personal and warm term. When we use it, we have to be careful to distinguish family and friend carers from paid staff, but using the terms 'formal' and 'informal' is also unclear, because many family and friend carers organize and plan their work very effectively, often with clear agreements with the people they care for. They often see their caring as formally organized.

I use the term 'care staff' when talking with older people and their families when I want to refer to carers employed by agencies. As we saw in Chapter 3, a cadre of 'personal assistants', paid for caring work by or on behalf of older people themselves, has emerged as person-centred care policies have developed in which home care is funded by direct payments to older people rather than by agencies organizing packages of care for them. Such policies are sometimes known internationally as 'cash for care' services or by other terms. It is a sign of changing policy and practice that terminology is not agreed. As you read international literature, you sometimes have to interpret precisely what is being referred to (see Chapter 7 for some more about this).

### Being a carer

Research on a more practical analysis of the activities that carers carry out points to different types of care:

- personal care, such as dressing, bathing, helping people use the toilet;
- physical help with walking or getting in and out of bed;
- paperwork and managing finances;
- other practical help, such as preparing meals, shopping, housework and doing household repairs;
- keeping an older person company;
- taking an older person out;
- giving medication, including injections and dressing wounds;
- keeping an eye on someone – for example, checking regularly that they are safe (Parker and Lawton, 1994).

Some of these might be done by a neighbour, or a volunteer project, while others are only acceptable from a close relative or professional. Moreover, some roles are gender specific: men are more likely to become engaged with physical, financial and practical help rather than personal care, except for their spouses or parents. This range of tasks, however, makes it clear that roles can be developed that feel acceptable to anyone, both carers and older people.

English legislation has sought over the years to ensure that carers' needs are separately assessed from the needs of the person they care for. Providing a social work assessment is still, however, a professionalization of a personal connection, by defining a person as having the identity of 'carer'. Not everyone finds this definition of their relationship acceptable. Fink (2004) suggests that identifying oneself as a carer may be:

- resisted, negotiated or accepted as a valid and valuable role;
- changing over the life course;
- shifting as the needs of the person cared for change.

Lethin *et al.*'s (2015) Nordic study of family carers of people with dementia identified three main areas where carers needed professional help, and these are relevant for all carers of older people:

- At the point of the dementia diagnosis (and indeed any diagnosis of a major illness), family carers needed help to enter the formal care system as a novice carer, including information and explanations of what was on offer and what they could expect.
- When the older person's condition deteriorated, carers needed to understand how to get access to and use greater involvement with formal care to continue care at home.
- When the older person entered a care home or nursing home, they needed help with maintaining their involvement in their relative's care.

A useful strategy for helping carers when there are constraints on the time you can allocate, therefore, is to focus on these important transition points. In each of them, carers are helped by knowing what to expect, but also in working through the emotional consequences of these major signs of the progression of the older person's condition.

As part of a series of studies about carers, Barnes (2006) looked at carers' accounts of their lives to identify how a present caring relationship interweaved past history and future hopes for the people involved. Caring tasks are important, but carers generally saw caring as part of relationships that already existed, in many cases in gendered roles. Giving and receiving caring was part of longstanding connections between people. People who gave and received care saw this process as part of both political and human relationships. Caring was seen as a right in a shared human relationship (the human aspect) and expression of citizenship that should be offered to and received by people as part of society (the political element). Other studies by Barnes include a conceptual analysis from an ethics of care perspective (Barnes, 2012), which emphasizes the importance of continuing connections between carers and people being cared for, which informs the approach taken in this book.

A difficulty for adults in middle-aged adulthood or in the third age is 'sandwich care', in which families provide care for dependent children at the same time as supporting older adults in the family (Pierret, 2006). This means that carers, usually women, have to balance demands of work with social care for both older people and children (Ben-Galim and Silim, 2013), and may leave work to provide care. This reduces the length of their working life, and often decreases their pensions, and also lessens their sense of self and satisfaction in their life achievements. Where they are caring for older relatives with long-term conditions, this may involve considerable financial and emotional pressure on the family. Where retired grandmothers are caring for grandchildren, on the other hand, their caring contribution may enable mothers to work and improve family finances; but this is often not valued by the care system. As patterns of 'breadwinning' have changed in families, giving up work to provide care for older people in the family influences decisions about retirement and their care arrangements in later life.

## Sourcing a wide range of 'care'

I argued early in the chapter that it is de-citizening not to know about the range of care available, because you cannot use what you are not confident about, and you cannot be confident unless you know what you want. Social workers who want to re-citizen the older people need to find ways of educating older people and their potential carers about the opportunities for care. Possibilities include making information available widely in the community, helping people to arrange visits and organizing social events in care facilities so that people can gain contact with them.

Chapter 3 noted that social and palliative care services have different approaches to care, because social care is more concerned with community and family sources of care, and palliative care is primarily paid care provided in professional healthcare services. Social care services providing care for older people are the point at which people begin to enter the formal care system, as opposed to being cared for as part of their family and community, and as part of the universal healthcare system. Both primary healthcare and social care jog along together, but usually rather separately, until the level of frailty or illness moves people along to end-of-life care. Duration, intensity, complexity and prognosis are crucial dimensions of social care. People with high care needs will need care for long periods of the day, over a long timescale and covering many aspects of their lives (Parker, 1981).

The length of time and the range of aspects of people's lives increase over time. Many different aspects of care are relevant to providing caring services:

- Care may be paid or unpaid ...
- ... public or private ...
- ... be provided through cash payments or in 'packages' of services ...
- ... formally contracted or informally provided ...
- ... be seen to create dependence on the carer or promote independence for the cared for person (Daly and Lewis, 2000).

To add to this analysis, which is about the organization of social care:

- Care may be aimed at treatment or improvement of someone's condition or maintaining their present physical, mental or social status ...
- ... be primarily medical or social in focus ...
- ... be primarily by informal carers, minimally qualified paid carers, professional carers such as doctors, nurses or social workers ...
- ... be concerned with physical tending to the body, emotional tending of the mind and responsiveness to social ideas and beliefs, as in saying we care about justice and equality.

The complexity of range of different types of caring involved in services for older people and in end-of-life care and ideas about them makes it useful to think through and tease out colleagues' different approaches and attitudes and not to devalue or ignore particular aspects of care. Organizing volunteers to keep older people company or take them out can help maintain them in their own home, which is as valuable in its contribution to their overall care as changing a dressing or avoiding bedsores (nursing care) or checking how the impact of pain medication has changed and adjusting it slightly (medical care). They are all on their own minor points, and missing one out on a particular occasion may not matter too much. Over time, however, attention to details in every area of life does matter, and missing out a regular opportunity to socialize can be as important as a regular medical assessment. Generally, social workers are better placed to identify the full range of non-healthcare issues that are relevant to an older person's care than healthcare staff, and to add this focus to the overall response to an older person's needs.

## Conclusion: Practice strategies before later life

Building on the importance of advance care planning (see Chapter 5), I have proposed practice strategies for social workers' engagements with ageing in the earlier stages of life. Older people can be more secure in later life if they are helped to consider financing, housing and likely care costs when they reach the fourth age and before the end-of-life care phases of their lives. While people's preparedness and ability to plan varies, developing an age-friendly society is an important basis for active ageing and both of these societal strategies contribute to greater resilience in dealing with any difficulties that older people experience as they reach later stages of ageing. Social workers through their personal, career and team strategies can make an important contribution to creating the sort of society that responds to older people's needs effectively, naturally and consistently. This does not just mean social action campaigning and developing services, useful though that is. Social work skills can, in particular, contribute to making each community and society a place that improves social networks and human ties that will be the basis of future caring. Social work practitioners can also make an important contribution to promoting the role and value of carers in society as part of that. Informal caring is an important citizenship role.

All of this is an important precursor to making the social work role in the fourth age and in end-of-life care as useful as can be, and that is the subject of the next two chapters.

### ADDITIONAL RESOURCES

#### Books

Barnes, M. (2006) *Caring and Social Justice*. Basingstoke: Palgrave Macmillan.
Barnes, M. (2012) *Care in Everyday Life: An ethic of care in practice*. Bristol: Policy Press.
Two excellent books covering carers' life experiences and conceptual analysis of caring.

Victor, C. R. (2010) *Ageing, Health and Care*. Bristol: Policy Press.
A useful research-based study of the interaction between ageing and health and care services.

### Websites

This useful website provides information and advice on all sorts of housing and care for older people in the UK:
http://www.housingcare.org/index.aspx

The Organisation for Economic Cooperation and Development (OECD) is an international think-tank of industrialized nations. Its website provides helpful information on pension policy and comparative pension information from around the world:
http://www.oecd.org/els/public-pensions/

The American national Aging in Place Council provides a wide range of practical information for older people on how to remain in their own homes as they age:
http://www.ageinplace.org/

Useful guide to issues that carers may face: American, but its general advice is applicable everywhere:
http://www.caregiverslibrary.org/home.aspx

The 'Dying Matters' consortium seeks to improve awareness and responsiveness to dying and provides a range of resources to encourage schools, workplaces and community organizations to start 'conversations about dying':
http://www.dyingmatters.org/overview/resources

# 7

# DIRECT SOCIAL WORK WITH OLDER CITIZENS IN THE FOURTH AGE

## Chapter aims

In this chapter, we come to the stage in which people are more aware of ageing, and increasingly accept that social care services may be required in the future. Interpersonal social work plays a role in provision for older people as a result, and it has opportunities for opposing de-citizening and promoting citizening with older people and their carers. I focus on those opportunities, rather than the full range of social work with older people. The main aims of this chapter focus on social work roles to:

- Establish elements of a citizenship practice strategy for the fourth age.
- Identify specialized skills relevant to citizenship practice with older people.
- Examine the assessment and person-centred care planning roles of social work in person-centred care.
- Identify the issue of the balance between citizenship with over-protection and surveillance in social work's safeguarding role with older people.
- Understand the importance of citizening social work practice with older people who need considerable services, and who have dementia.

## Practice strategy for citizenship: social care in the fourth age

Practice strategy in the fourth age is much more concerned with direct social work than in the adulthood and the third age. Determining our strategy at this time in ageing people's lives particularly focuses on citizenship policy. At the completion of Chapter 2, I identified some important features of citizenship social work practice:

- Develop citizening practice as you use medical and social models of provision.
- Help older people and carers re-citizen by assuming greater control of decisions and generating independent support and care.

- Focus on integrating formal and informal services, so that you do not unintentionally de-citizen by poor collaboration.
- Generate freedom of action in activities of daily living for the older person by careful planning.

Because planning is at the heart of citizening, social work actions should build on preparations that older people, their carers and families made in adulthood and the third age, aiming for security in people's living arrangements. Helping people repair lack of planning can give service users increased influence and freedom of action. This means including realistic preparation for the end-of-life phase of their ageing, and for bereavement.

These strategies involve looking at how people are maintaining the quality of their living environment and activities, which for many social workers is not the focus of their official role. Research, however, has identified eight areas of life that social care users identify as important in achieving a good quality of social care provision:

1. personal cleanliness and comfort;
2. accommodation cleanliness and comfort;
3. food and drink;
4. safety;
5. social participation and involvement;
6. occupation;
7. control over daily life;
8. dignity (Netten *et al.*, 2012).

In such details of people's lives, the freedom of action and quality of life that citizenship requires can be maintained and improved. The last four are particularly important, because engagement, keeping active and maintaining control in a dignified way, without having to fight for rights, are significant in citizening. As in Chapter 6, I explore important areas of life to identify appropriate practice strategies for this phase of working with older people.

## Finances

In their third age, older people will have taken up enough of their pension to live adequately. As they become more disabled, maintaining the activities of daily living may increase in priority. Helping people review explicitly such changes in priority can be a useful aspect of citizening by maintaining their control of their life choices. Practitioners may also find it useful to find help through grants and whatever services are available to provide free or concessionary help with activities of daily living.

## Home and housing

Older people may begin to consider changes in their home or their housing arrangements, as they become aware of loss in capacity to carry out the activities of daily living (see Tables 6.1 and 6.2 for possibilities). Citizening strategy might encourage people to consider and plan helpful alterations or changes in good time. Adapting bathrooms and sleeping arrangements, putting in lifts and stair lifts may help people to stay on independently, or with minimal support, for longer. Quality of life is maintained by quality of the environment provided by someone's home. This might include help with decoration, replacing worn-out furniture, tidying, decluttering and gardening. Such help provided a generation ago by home help services has been displaced by personal care, but continues to be important to many people. Older people may be helped to identify simple aids that maintain cleaning and tidying; they can also be helped to gain access to commercial and, for those with fewer financial resources, volunteer cleaning and repair services. One consideration may be adapting housing and living arrangements to facilitate a live-in carer, since providing accommodation may be a more economic and congenial way of paying for care than offering low wages to unskilled visiting paid carers.

## Activities, including leisure, work and community involvement

Maintaining citizenship means older people maintaining social contacts and interests, adapting activities within the limitations of changes in their capacity. Aim to encourage them to keep things going, rather than give things up. Practitioners could ask about ambitions for personal development, or personal skills, in the arts and music, for example, that may facilitate involvement in activities to promote personal development. A principle of citizenship social work, and of human rights, is the humanistic objective that people should be facilitated to continue personal development throughout life, extending to the moment they die. Citizening involvement and participation in decision-making in community, religious, political and spiritual organizations can also continue.

## Health and safety

As they age, older people become more aware of growing minor illnesses or disabilities. Awareness may have been raised by prophylactic medication, such as statins to reduce high cholesterol, or medication to lower blood pressure. Such measures reduce the likelihood of cardiovascular (heart and circulation) disorders. Older people often experience hearing loss and use hearing aids. Common preventive treatments, such as new hips and knees, or cataract operations to improve sight, may be within their or community experience. Progressive conditions such as age-related macular degeneration or glaucoma are often diagnosed at this stage, too. There is an increasing incidence of Type 2 diabetes mellitus, which, untreated, may have serious consequences, leading to organ failure.

Social workers will rarely be consulted about these fairly routine health interventions, managed in primary healthcare by GPs and their staff. Assessing for or providing social care facilities for older people provides an opportunity to enable people to have health check-ups and become aware of preventive medicine and other services. Adaptations to living accommodation or their lifestyle may help to manage minor disabilities. People with the financial resources will often make changes to do this, but older people in poverty may need help with finances and discussion of options and encouragement to take up opportunities. Similarly, help may be needed to maintain or build up healthy living or fitness activities, such as regular walking, improvement in eating healthy food and swimming. Local authority leisure facilities and other resources offer financial concessions to older people for such activities, and older persons teams need to be aware of and promote such opportunities. It also avoids social work being seen as concerned only with undesired care options.

## Holidays

If older people have the finances and physical capacity, they usually maintain holidays. If they are more financially limited, they might be encouraged to find companions to travel or have holiday periods in homes of members of the family for as long as this remains possible for them. Another option is visits and day trips with family, friends or social groups.

## Care arrangements, including end-of-life care

During this phase of life, older people will increasingly need to make arrangements for their care, and they should also formulate or update advance care planning for the end of life. This will include arrangements for:

- Inheritance, including a will, discussing funeral arrangements and dispositions for property, such as jewellery or work tools, after their death.
- Proxy decision-making in the event of mental incapacity, which in the UK might include making lasting powers of attorney for health and welfare and financial and property affairs. As important as making and registering these with the Office of the Public Guardian is the opportunity to discuss such matters with carers, friends, relatives and paid staff of care homes.
- Funerals, including the possibility of using income or capital to pay for a funeral plan, covering the costs of funerals in advance, avoiding a burden on relatives. Older people can also discuss how they would like their funeral to be conducted, including discussion with musicians and ministers of religion or officiants at secular ceremonies.

Putting off planning becomes de-citizening. Helping to plan combats the tendency to leave things until they become a crisis. Absence of planning makes crises worse.

## Skills in practice with older people

### *Important interpersonal skills*

Skills that social workers use in communication with clients and others are also relevant for citizening work with older people. It is de-citizening if clients and carers are not secure in their relationship and communication with you:

- When introducing yourself, leave a visiting card or written record of your identity and note of why you contacted them. This enables older people and their family or carers who come along later to contact you. People do not always pick up your name or your professional identity, particularly in a healthcare setting, where you may be another of the many people who turn up to ask questions.
- Make sure you are in a good light and your face and lips are visible to an older person. Good eye contact increases your ability to communicate interest and commitment to the other person. Many older people have hearing problems, and although they have not formally learned to lip-read, seeing your lips and face aids communication.
- Listening is an important starting point and continuing priority. The voice of older people is often ignored, because of impatience and communication difficulties. You can indicate your

preparedness to listen by putting aside documents and agency requirements in the first instance and in an initial open question focus on the client's priorities: 'What's the thing that's most on your mind at the moment?' (see the case example, Mrs Calthrop, in Chapter 3).
- Communicating with a very frail and disabled person may be improved with colleagues' and family members' advice.
- Focus at first and regularly throughout your involvement with the older person directly, even if carers or other professionals are also involved; Biggs (1993) suggests that we often get involved in triads with others, and this, often unintentionally, excludes the older person. This can especially be so in family meetings, which social workers often have the responsibility for setting up and chairing. Meet carers separately, so that you can focus on them directly, too.
- Provide information in ways that the older person can understand; at times when it is useful in making decisions, explain why it is important and make clear how an older person can use it to make decisions for themselves. Provide written or printed reminders.
- Connect the person to their past lives and achievements, making the link between aspirations now and past wishes and hopes. This may help to identify social and other activities that can be picked up again and help you to value and respect this person. It also gives you topics for informal conversation, now and in the future.
- Be strengths-based, looking for and building up capabilities in the older person, their families and carers. It's more respectful and more likely to identify resources that you otherwise wouldn't know about.
- Challenge assumptions about older people's capabilities and avoid focusing on what people can't do by explaining how the older person can make at least some choices for themselves (developed from Naleppa and Reid, 2003: 38–73; Ray et al., 2009: 31–2, 68–9; Ray and Phillips, 2012: 99–122).

## Active intervention at an early stage, when things change and at end of life

Often people only call on social care services when they already have serious problems. Older people and their families go on trying to cope until daily living becomes impossible. People value perseverance in the face of adversity because it enables them to retain greater control of their lives, avoiding potential restrictions that services and equipment will bring to their lives (Lloyd et al., 2014). Part of the reason for delay is that social care is very much a residual service, and the first call will be made on friends, family and neighbours and healthcare provision. Morales-Asencio et al. (2014) explored care management with people with multiple long-term conditions. They identify three stages where proactive practice really helps:

1. the onset of conditions and their initial adaptation to it: this phase may be repeated as users are affected by additional conditions, with the need to adjust to new interactions with their initial problem;
2. the beginning of quality-of-life changes; and
3. a final stage, in which the users' lives are governed by the complexity of their conditions (see Chapter 8).

Ideally, relationships between local services should be good enough for healthcare staff to inform social care colleagues of an important diagnosis, or a shift in growing frailty. On the other side of the relationship, local social care services need to have the flexibility and resources to make some early contact with an older person and their family to become a more natural point of call in future difficulties. More resources at an early preventive stage are useful. But it also helps for social care managers, practitioners and their services to be open to using an early, perhaps inappropriate, contact from a service user to build trust for later work when an older person is more frail or a carer more under pressure. Even occasional regular contact enables older people and families to raise concerns and fears about changes in their quality of life. Later on, we should look to pick up burgeoning complexity, particularly where it affects family and social relationships. Citizening means not looking at each event separately as long-term conditions progress to assess whether to start providing services, but rather being willing to find ways of building relationships over a period.

## Openness to negotiation

Citizenship social work means being prepared to negotiate. Services have to meet needs as assessed on behalf of service providers and commissioners, but can do that in ways that respond to older people's preferences. When older people are difficult, even cantankerous, in insisting on their preferences, this is often because they feel anxiety about limited options, and about loss of capacity and lifestyle. Citizening involves negotiating between different stakeholders to clarify exactly what is causing the concern, and seeking to counter it through understanding. Lymbery (2005: 144–51) identifies networking (e.g. by bringing in a range of options), negotiation, mediation (e.g. by adapting the normal way things are done in a care home to demonstrate what flexibilities are possible) and administrative skills (e.g. in building care commissioning that responds to older people's concerns) as important assets in social work's toolbox with older people. Negotiation in the classical research in psychology involves setting exaggerated demands and accepting reductions until a compromise is reached. This is not appropriate in social work, because it leads to excessive expectations among clients and to conflictual or cynical relationships with partner agencies. Instead, a strong focus on evidence from assessment of needs and family plans can lead us to identifying acceptable and unacceptable choices. Practitioners can then adopt an advocacy approach, trying to achieve the best results. A partnership approach with other agencies of joint exploration of options is more helpful. Another common view of negotiation is to see it as a process of persuasion in which one party gets the other to understand and accept their point of view. This is an extreme form of the zero-sum game where one side of the negotiation is the winner. It is particularly inappropriate in a citizenship approach to use persuasion with a user or carer, and joint exploration is more appropriate with colleagues in other services.

The main way in which social workers do this is through care management, in its present methodology, person-centred or self-directed care planning.

## Person-centred care planning

### What is person-centred care?

Person-centred care aims at care services supporting older people to age in place, in the least restrictive way possible. The reason for this is to avoid de-citizening by cutting older people off from the continuity of their lives. Organizing person-centred care is the main professional role of social workers in the care system for older people, so it also comes into play as an important contribution to end-of-life care. Person-centred care is connected with ideas such as direct payments, personalization, self-directed support and individual or personal budgets. All these terms mean slightly different things, but they all describe the system by which we plan variable combinations of services to meet older people's needs. Its variableness implies both:

- a wide variety of different combinations, tailored to the person who receives it and their family and carers;
- preparedness to vary the combination as circumstances change.

Person-centred care can go wrong when variableness is missing. Sometimes, we go back to, or because of lack of resources we are forced back on, the same old services that are available to us, rather than thinking creatively about new ways of doing things. Another failure of variability is providing or financing services and failing to reassess and adjust them. Both are a failures of good social work because they are failures in responding to change.

> **CASE EXAMPLE: GOING TO THE PUB**
>
> An elderly man, a former factory worker, tried out a group for older people at a local drop-in centre. He told his care worker that he liked the contact with people of a similar age and background, but found a preponderance of women members who did not share his interests. The care worker mentioned this to a visiting social worker, who in turn talked this over with the organizer of the charity that provided the drop-in centre. In a local meeting for community awards, the organizer met the regional director of a pub chain, who wanted to develop a greater lunchtime clientele at local pubs, including one in the street where the factory worker lived. Local discussion ensued between the publican and several local men, and a cheap menu, which was attractive to several men in the area, was developed for weekday use. When this brought in quite a number of local people, including some women, it was picked up and used in other local pubs, to everyone's benefit.

One feature of this case example is how feedback from one individual passed through a number of organizations, some in the social care sector, others in the private sector. The original care user's experience was generalized to benefit a wider area. It also illustrates the importance of practitioners being engaged in wider community networks.

Person-centred care moves away from offering a limited number of well-established provisions such as domiciliary, day and residential care, towards greater flexibility in the range of care offered. The aim is to maintain an older person's independence. We do this preferably by 'ageing in place'. Place here means their physical place – home and community – and social and emotional place in continuity with their life course and personal wishes. It means enhancing the older person's freedom to live how they want. A logical follow-on is their freedom to make decisions to die how they want when it comes to the end of life.

Personal budgeting has been strongly promoted by enthusiasts as a way of ensuring greater participation in deciding needs and the services that will best meet them. As with the rise of care management in the 1990s (Payne, 1995), the aim continues to be to include less formal provision, such as leisure and personal development activity. But there have been three main issues about this, particularly for older people:

1. Person-centred care planning puts responsibility on service users for things that go wrong. Service users, particularly older people and their carers, do not always wish to become budget managers, rather than receiving well-planned and thoughtful service provision.
2. Allocating a budget in advance often provides just as powerful a straitjacket on flexibility as practitioners preferring services that are available, rather than a new pattern of provision. As resources for social care provision are reduced in many countries, and resources are not allocated to meet fully the needs of a growing population of older people, starting from the budget leads to restriction rather than flexibility in care planning.

    As an example of such reduced flexibility, Ismail *et al.* (2014) identified important limitations to care for older people arising from austerity policy and budget cuts in England. Consequences included ramping up requirements so that fewer people were eligible for help, fewer people receiving services, longer waiting times until services were provided and having to wait in more for hard-pressed social care workers, reduced contact time with paid care staff, and inappropriate indicators to monitor services, meaning that deterioration in quality of service was not fully identified.
3. People have wants, as well as needs. This means that allocating budgets to meet needs may not achieve a desired pattern of care. A care deficit (see the Introduction) exists not only because there are insufficient resources to provide for all the care that a growing number of older people might need, but also because paid-for care delivered in routine ways cannot always meet the desire for a highly personal care from well-loved relatives. This is another way in which personalization may come to be perceived as anything but person-centred.

These general points about person-centred care do not detract from the value of helping people participate in care decisions. Social workers carrying out the initial assessments are often the first contact for social care services with older people and their carers. Openness in care planning sets the tone and facilitates participation later on. It is also important, though, not to allow universal participation to become a 'tyranny' (Cooke and Kothari, 2001) which means that practitioners do not make enough input to enable older people and their carers to achieve their wishes. It is de-citizening to push older people and carers to meet agency interests or administrative convenience. Citizens are entitled to professional help in making their decisions, because they are facing new situations, without experience of the opportunities and limitations. They may also fear limitations, such as lifestyle limitations in a care home, when giving them some experience will remove their concerns.

## Outcomes approaches

Outcomes approaches focus on the outcomes of interventions or services provided for older people, their carers and families. The weakness in a long history of 'management by objectives' in residential and social care is that it sets objectives according to the aims of the organization, not older people and their carers. A political impetus developed during the 1990s to avoid this and research identified three types of outcomes that were important for social care services:

1. maintaining quality of life or preventing problems – for example, acceptable personal comfort, safety, a pleasant, clean and tidy environment, maintaining social contacts, meaningful activity, participation in family and community roles and control over daily life and routines (Netten *et al.*, 2012);
2. change – for example, improving physical and psychological symptoms, developing and regaining confidence in mobility, reducing risk, improving communication, regaining the capacity for self-care and using skills;
3. impact of the service process – for example, being treated as an individual, feeling valued and respected, having a say in and control over services, finding that services are well-coordinated in themselves and with family and community support and compatibility and respect for cultural and religious preferences (SPRU, 2000; Glendinning *et al.*, 2006).

An important point was that service users and carers had aims concerned with *how things were done*, and personal consequences for them, rather than *what services were provided*. These ideas have developed in several locations, and the following case study offers a documented and researched example of what might be achieved.

> **CASE EXAMPLE: 'TALKING POINTS' LEADING TO PERSONAL OUTCOMES**
>
> This project was developed by the Joint Improvement Team in Scotland project using informal semi-structured conversations with users and carers to set 'personal outcomes' (Cook and Miller, 2012). Rather than seeing the practitioner as 'assessing' a service user, the practitioner facilitates an exchange of information between the older person, carers, any agencies involved and their own judgements. The aim is to identify what changes are being proposed and the impact these will have upon the service user's whole life. This is carefully recorded in a shared record, rather than a computerized document solely for the use of the practitioner and agency. A negotiation develops over how the aims put forward by the people involved may be met. Intended outcomes are agreed, and then recorded.

This kind of approach to what is usually called 'assessment' uses communication and other professional skills. Both a greater sense of empowerment and involvement for service users and carers, and increased efficiencies for the agency, are achieved. Although sometimes people express aspirations, they do not necessarily expect services to be provided to meet these: often these are in the realms of an almost spiritual wish for fulfilment, happiness or success in relationships (Harris, 2006). We saw in Chapter 5 on advance care planning that a similar approach to talking points also works for end-of-life care planning. Gaining experience with an approach in general helps to connect it with using similar approaches in specialized settings or particular situations.

## Activities of daily living

One of the most important concepts for social work with older people is 'activities of daily living' (ADLs). These are the activities that people have to carry out so that they can continue to function independently in the community. They are usually measured by scales, which are widely used to assess older people's physical capabilities, and those used by healthcare professionals focus on self-care and physical disability. They include:

- bathing;
- dressing;
- transferring from bed to chair;
- ability to feed themselves (Spector *et al.*, 1987).

Instrumental activities of daily living (IADLs) scales are sometimes used in social care to assess more complex everyday skills. The five main areas assessed are:

1. housework;
2. travel;
3. shopping;
4. managing finances;
5. meal preparation (Challis *et al.*, 1994: 67).

In addition to assessment, a useful intervention strategy might also start from ADLs and IADLs. Because they are carefully specified, you can aim to improve capability on these measures to foster independence and greater self-confidence. They provide a useful guide to priorities: you can target each in turn, starting with the one that is causing the biggest problems. This is also relevant to dealing with end-of-life care, because particular difficulties that are causing problems for people in their own homes or hospital and hospice care can be targeted in the same way.

### CASE EXAMPLE: JULIE TARGETS ACTIVITIES OF DAILY LIVING WHEN DISCUSSING SELF-DIRECTED CARE

Julie was asked to carry out a self-directed care assessment of Mrs Beaton, who had just been discharged from hospital after treatment for cancer, and interviewed her with her daughter. Mrs Beaton took the view that she managed 'quite well, really', whereas her daughter was worried about how she would manage in her old house, which had several steps between different rooms that Mrs Beaton used regularly. Mrs Beaton was being vague about what she could do, mainly, it seemed to Julie, to avoid having too much interference in her own home, while her daughter was frustrated because she could not get beyond her mother's reassuring stance. So Julie used one of the activities of daily living scales available, defining tasks that Mrs Beaton could do (starting with the positive), could not do and, importantly, would like to do, also looking at what she was previously able to do, but now could not. This made it much clearer what assistive technology and help from carers was required, and what would be most valued by Mrs Beaton.

Many agencies have ADL and IADL scales as part of their assessment and care documentation, and as well as completing the scales in a tick-box way for assessment purposes, discussion around these can help service users and carers be clearer about how best to help, particularly if the assessment does not lead to commissioning of services. If your agency does not use them, they can still give useful practical guidance for older people and carers.

## Strategies for independence

Citizenship social work implies acting in ways that promote independent living for older people in their preferred location, extending the period in which they can do this for as long as possible before more intensive care services lead to a limitation in independence and, consequently, in citizenship. Pursuing such strategies is often termed 'prevention', and they are citizening because they prevent escalation of problems with the activities of daily living which lead people to need hospital, nursing home or residential care. Policy for working in a preventive way includes:

- involving older people, their families and carers in deciding an approach that suits their needs and wishes;
- promoting a positive image of ageing and resisting ageist attitudes;
- developing information services so that people are well informed about their options and can do their own advance care planning;
- building partnerships with services that are not specifically for ageing or dying people, so that you can raise issues and work together with them;
- creating a culture of prevention among interacting services, including a shared sense of purpose and commitment to prevention, belief in empowerment and participation of older people, their families and carers, listening to their preferences, keeping an ear to the ground in community and voluntary service networks, and having a 'can-do' approach, as well as being creative with ideas and resources;
- promoting services so that they are well known and valued and easily found and accessed (Fiedler, 1999).

Falling, for example, is an important factor in maintaining people's independence, particularly since people with a history of falls limit their activity because of a fear of falling again. You can evaluate whether older people are afraid of falling; generally they have a history of falling, do poorly on tests of gait and balance, have poor vision, need assistance with ADLs, and rate their health as poor (Cumming *et al.*, 2000). Thus, an older person talking about their awareness of being in poor health, having poor, and possibly deteriorating, vision and being able to see visible difficulties in walking should lead you to seek medical, physiotherapy or nursing assessment for this important issue.

## Social work's safeguarding role: Security and citizenship

### *Issues of risk and security*

Social work in most societies has a safeguarding role, to protect people whose life circumstances place them at risk of abuse and neglect. Social workers also play a role in protecting older people affected by disasters and emergencies, because they are more at risk, having less resilience to unexpected problems than younger adults. These roles are particularly important to citizenship, because insecurity is de-citizening. But they also present difficulties for citizenship because they lead to risk-based thinking and excessive surveillance and social control which may be just as or more de-citizening. If person-centred care planning aims to enhance freedom of choice, how do we balance that with loss of freedom through insecurity and surveillance?

One of the difficulties of safeguarding work with older people is that we are usually looking at a risk of harm rather than positive risks, and excessive concern with risk also contributes to de-citizening, because we then restrict older people too much. Older citizens often benefit from risks that offer freedom to maintain their preferred lifestyle. Risk is a chance, maybe not a big chance. If risks do not lead to problems, we intervene unnecessarily and perhaps oppressively. Ageing is universal, so should we intervene to prevent or manage risks that might arise through this universal process? What level of risk justifies our intervention with frailty in an older person? Should we intervene if self-neglect leads an older person to poor nutrition? Or should we wait until this leads to more serious disease? What factors might justify forcing them to accept help to prevent later ill-health? Should we persuade them assertively to accept unwillingly a place in a care home where they will be unhappy but safe from falling?

In such situations, practitioners balance possibilities and points of view. Relatives of older people, other professionals or politicians may seek to avoid risk that an older person happily accepts. Anxiety to make things secure leads us to prefer safety over freedom. Consequently, social workers may focus on risk because they fear criticism for things that go wrong. Such criticism is often of people who are socially excluded or whose behaviour is seen as morally wrong. Gilliom (2001) makes the point that, throughout history, welfare services, including social work, have been used to maintain surveillance of the poor and of groups in society that potentially present problems of social order and social disruption. Patterns of social oppression mean that powerful groups and opinion-formers use moral and social failings to justify surveillance. They also exercise power by blaming professionals for failing to prevent risks from materializing as actualities. Such criticism is always made with hindsight: critics know what went wrong, even though there was a low risk of the worst happening. Social workers and other officials dealing with risk develop approaches to protect themselves from criticism; such approaches include formal assessment tools or emphasizing administrative and legal responsibilities for protecting vulnerable people. And we have seen that assessment and care planning in social care focuses on administration rather than accompanying older people through an important phase of life.

The modern state represents a shift from personal forms of social control towards bureaucratic and organizational control (Dandeker, 1990). Social workers and all helping professions play a part in this. Social order benefits many people, including those whose freedoms are limited, and people feel more secure in a socially ordered state. For example, people who live in violent and physically deteriorating neighbourhoods may well be strong supporters of surveillance and risk-avoiding practice. While order is always a balance between advantages and restrictions, it is particularly de-citizening when restrictions are secret or partially concealed. A caring attitude that hides social restrictions that accompany it is de-citizening because it hides loss of autonomy.

Graham and Wood (2003) have suggested that official records are crucial aspects of surveillance in the modern state. People are put into categories by the use of apparently neutral technical devices such as records, for example according to where and how they live, and particularly where inequalities label them as potentially in danger, difficult or in need, and by surveillance. For example, if you go to the information service of your local government offices, you can often select your own information or receive leaflets and advice freely. If, however, you are referred to a social work agency, a record of your identity and assessment of your needs is retained. Some of this may be helpful or desirable, but the use that agencies make of these records may in the future disadvantage you or limit your freedom.

## Elements of safeguarding older people's security

Fallon's (2006) New Zealand study identifies four elements of a safeguarding service:

1. Local services to support older people and respond to difficult or risky situations; this is a positive citizening approach to security.
2. Professional health and social care interventions to help and protect individuals to avoid the de-citizening effect of abuse and neglect.
3. Advisory group support for professionals engaged in this difficult work and local coordinators of services; this is citizening because it helps practitioners manage the complexities of their safeguarding roles.
4. National policy development and coordination; this is potentially citizening because it enhances the effectiveness of safeguarding, but it may be de-citizening if it is excessively risk-averse.

The supportive and preventive roles are often neglected, but thinking about these responsibilities enables us to mitigate the tendency to focus on risk, and instead to think positively about what will achieve, maintain and enhance older people's sense of security (Payne, 2012). That sense is inevitably an important aspect of their quality of life. If they are fearful about other people's treatment of them, older people will lose the self-confidence that they can manage their affairs.

Three important physical and emotional aspects of security for anyone are:

1. physical security – for example, avoiding unwanted change, accidents, violence, or fear of them;
2. legal security – for example, feeling that the law and administrative procedures protect their interests;
3. self-security: being respected and valued by others (Payne, 2010: Chapter 8).

Important social work practice techniques for enhancing security are:

- dialogue and narrative that enables older people and their carers to know that practitioners have built up an understanding of the situation from the clients' and carers' points of view, and are thinking about balancing their conflicting interests;
- the security of knowing that regular checks will be made efficiently – for example, when practitioners maintain regular telephone contacts and check on the work of care staff regularly;
- demonstration of forethought and planning through advance care planning and personalization.

## Safeguarding from abuse

Safeguarding in family and domestic situations requires identifying people at risk of abuse or neglect. It may include responding to and investigating allegations of abuse or neglect and then intervening to protect older people from the abuse or neglect. Thinking about end-of-life care, it is important to see that people cannot die well if they feel insecure or abused.

An international systematic study of prevalence studies (Cooper et al., 2008) found that 6 per cent of the older population, 25 per cent of vulnerable adults and one third of family caregivers report being involved in significant abuse, but only 1 to 2 per cent of this is reported officially. If they are directly asked, however, older people and their caregivers are prepared to report it, so it is important for practitioners to ask. Older people or family members may report abuse when they want services to do something about it. The practitioner therefore needs to pick up passing comments, which may be a prompt to see if we are responsive to problems of abuse and neglect. Many older people and carers are unsure whether any particular professional or service is responsible for responding to abuse and neglect although they may also try to avoid having caring relationships disrupted. For example, the older person may be concerned about abuse, but may also be concerned that their main carer may be angry about accusations, or where pressing an allegation may lead to family conflict.

An example of safeguarding responsibilities is recent changes in the UK legislation through the introduction of the Care Act 2014 which required local government social care authorities to:

- lead a multi-agency local adult safeguarding system aiming to prevent abuse and neglect and stop it quickly when it happens;
- make enquiries, or request others to make them, when they think an adult with care and support needs, including older people, may be at risk of abuse or neglect and they need to find out what action may be required;
- establish Safeguarding Adults Boards, including the local authority, National Health Service and police, which will develop, share and implement a joint safeguarding strategy;
- carry out Safeguarding Adults Reviews when someone with care and support needs dies as a result of neglect or abuse and there is a concern that the local authority or its partners could have done more to protect them;
- arrange for an independent advocate to represent and support a person who is the subject of a safeguarding enquiry or review, if required (Social Care Institute for Excellence, 2015).

The UK official guidance lists types of abuse that older people may experience, and this is set out in Table 7.1. This listing has developed over the years. For example, the category of 'modern slavery' is new, and practitioners may wonder about its utility when working with older people. It does, however, draw attention to the ways in which we may exploit both informal and paid carers.

Self-neglect is an important category of behaviour, which is widespread across the world (Fallon, 2006). There are two main aspects: not carrying out self-care activities in daily living which enable older people to manage their lives satisfactorily; and failing to take actions to prevent conditions or situations from arising that are dangerous for the health and safety of

**TABLE 7.1** Types of abuse of adults at risk

| Type of abuse | Examples | Practice examples |
|---|---|---|
| Physical abuse | Assault, hitting, slapping, pushing, misuse of medication, over-restraint (e.g. in an attempt to prevent falling or inappropriate physical sanctions). | An adult son became frustrated when caring for his elderly mother and hit her. She had a history of alcohol abuse and mental illness. Nurse and social worker interviewed them separately, and negotiated a behaviour contract. |
| Domestic violence | Psychological, physical, sexual, financial, emotional abuse; so-called 'honour'-based violence. | An older woman with dementia was slapped by her husband to get her to take medication. |
| Sexual abuse | Rape, sexual harassment, inappropriate looking or touching, sexual teasing or innuendo, sexual photography, subjection to pornography or witnessing sexual acts, indecent exposure and sexual assault or sexual acts to which the adult has not consented or was pressured into consenting. | Nurses found that the husband of a virtually comatose older woman was continuing to assert his 'marital rights'. The social worker firmly discussed the issue of consent with him. |
| Psychological abuse | Emotional abuse, threats of harm or abandonment, deprivation of contact, humiliation, blaming, controlling, intimidation, coercion, harassment, verbal abuse, cyber bullying, isolation or unreasonable and unjustified withdrawal of services or supportive networks. | The husband of an older woman whose dementia was deteriorating turned off his hearing aid to avoid listening to her repetitive conversation. |
| Financial or material abuse | Theft, fraud, internet scamming, coercion in relation to an adult's financial affairs or arrangements, including in connection with wills, property, inheritance or financial transactions, or the misuse or misappropriation of property, possessions or benefits. | After her husband died, an older woman who did not understand their investments worried that the husband's cousin (the nearest relative who was given lasting powers of attorney because of his financial experience) was taking their money because of his business problems. |
| Modern slavery | Slavery, human trafficking, forced labour and domestic servitude. Traffickers and slave masters use whatever means they have at their disposal to coerce, deceive and force individuals into a life of abuse, servitude and inhumane treatment. | A Middle-Eastern family paid a fee to a Pakistani man to employ his teenage daughter as a carer for an elderly woman family member, keeping her passport 'safe', paying only for her living costs and making her work very long hours. She was terrified and subjected to criticism for her 'failings' as a carer. |
| Discriminatory abuse | Harassment, slurs or similar treatment because of race, gender and gender identity, age, disability, sexual orientation or religion. | An African Caribbean man in a care home felt that he was avoided by the majority of white women and their visitors. |

(continued)

**TABLE 7.1** (continued)

| Type of abuse | Examples | Practice examples |
| --- | --- | --- |
| Organizational abuse | Neglect and poor care practice within an institution or specific care setting such as a hospital or care home, for example, or in relation to care provided in one's own home. This may range from one-off incidents to ongoing ill-treatment. It can be through neglect or poor professional practice as a result of the structure, policies, processes and practices within an organization. | A nursing home resident told her visiting palliative care nurse that she thought several other residents who did not have visitors were treated very poorly by staff. On reporting this to the local coordinator for adult safeguarding, she found that several other professionals had made similar reports, and an inspection found training needs among inexperienced staff. |
| Neglect and acts of omission | Ignoring medical, emotional or physical care needs, failure to provide access to appropriate health, care and support or educational services, the withholding of the necessities of life, such as medication, adequate nutrition and heating. | A cousin looking after an older man's affairs failed to renew broken spectacles and hearing aids, thinking it was not worthwhile because death was so close. The family had a history of poverty and caution in expenditure. The social worker explained quality-of-life issues to him. |
| Self-neglect | Neglecting to care for one's personal hygiene, health or surroundings, including behaviour such as hoarding. | An older woman who had been fond of cats earlier in her life had fed many cats from the neighbourhood, who congregated in her house, causing a health hazard. |

*Source*: Social Care Institute for Excellence (2015)

the older person or others around them (Naik et al., 2008). Dong et al.'s (2009) large Chicago study showed that self-neglect is associated with increased mortality within a year of it being reported to social care services, with increased risk thereafter, as was also the case with elder abuse. Intervening is difficult because older people's autonomy prevents professionals from being engaged, and self-neglect may also isolate the older person, so that the problems are not reported or are reported inappropriately, presenting housing problems or public health hazards. A citizening social work approach to such issues is to try to build a relationship with the older person, identify what is important and not important to them, and try to carry out improvements with them. If practitioners engage cleaning services, it is helpful to be with the older person as cleaners do their work to establish the acceptability of a routine. Cognitive-behaviour therapy to try to reduce the impact of fears may also be helpful if the older person has some insight into the deterioration of their environment and wants change.

Practitioners should also look out for situations in which people are likely to be highly stressed as carers, since this de-citizens carers and eventually the people they care for because it reduces the quality of the care they receive. A cross-European study of family care suggests that some social factors that lead to people experiencing their care for family members as a burden are similar to risk factors in elder abuse. 'Several studies suggest that the risk for both increases in cases of cohabitation, of high amounts of care provided, when the care recipient presents behavioural disturbances, when the carer suffers from depression and low self-esteem, when a negative relationship between carer and elder existed already in the past, and when the carer does not feel supported by formal services' (Lamura et al., 2008).

> ### CASE EXAMPLE: A MENTALLY ILL OLDER WOMAN AND HER SON
>
> An elderly woman with a history of mental illness was becoming increasingly frail, although she managed well at home, but her behaviour was often bizarre and sometimes violent. Her adult son lived with his mother, working on building contracts, and was usually in regular employment. However, advised by their doctor that his mother was becoming increasingly frail, he took a period away from working to look after her. She later complained to her mental health social worker that he had hit her on a number of occasions. The social worker interviewed the son privately about these allegations, which he admitted were true. He felt ambivalent, valuing himself because he was making an effort to care for his mother. However, he had also been feeling isolated and that he was wasting his life caring for a very difficult older woman. The social worker discussed with the son a number of ways in which he could manage his anger and frustration. It was important to recognize both the contribution he was making as well as the difficulties in the relationship. The mother was happy to have his care, although she could not always control the symptoms of her illness.

This case illustrates the mixed feelings common in such situations, and also shows that various protective devices can often be achieved to re-citizen the people affected. Practitioners can often organize an increase in regularity of visiting to check on clients' circumstances by coordinating visits made by different professionals.

The starting point of investigations of allegations of abuse is to contact all the professionals involved, and informal and community caregivers if possible, to see the extent to which concerns are shared. Many professionals may have picked up signs of abuse, and when these are coordinated by a case conference or similar meeting, problems may become clearer. Strategies for protection may then be worked out between agencies. The autonomy of adults means that in many legal systems no direct intervention can be made – for example, to remove an abuser or shift a victim to a safe place. However, much abuse is a criminal offence and the possibility of legal action must be considered because it is a citizen's right. It may be a warning to perpetrators of abuse, may protect the client and justice is their entitlement. Some jurisdictions make legal interventions possible. For example, in Scotland, the Adult Support and Protection (Scotland) Act 2007 requires local social services authorities to promote cooperation between agencies and to make enquiries if allegations come to their attention. It also provides for legal orders to require assessments in situations that are identified to be carried out, to remove someone who is at risk from a particular situation or to ban an abuser from being present in the home of an abused person.

Two potential sources of abuse and neglect exist: some take place within the family and other important personal relationships, whereas some abuse and neglect are perpetrated by strangers. Safeguarding children and disabled adults who are dependent on others for the quality of their life and care often leads us to focus on abuse and neglect in domestic and family situations. Older people, however, are also vulnerable to stranger abuse. Examples are financial abuse by services and individuals helping to manage their money, and purse snatching, street assaults or mugging where the older person may be too frail mentally or physically to protect themselves. Such assaults may also lead to general deterioration in an older person's physical condition unless practitioners focus on security needs afterwards.

The risks raised by a mismatch between an older person's capabilities and needs and the environment may be mediated by their own attitudes and ability to cope, and by changes in the environment and the help they are given. In looking at all these issues, we are again exploring the citizenship balance: how far are we citizening by supporting the capacity of older people and carers to manage: how far are we de-citizening by avoiding the responsibility to take robust action to support security.

## Dementia

Dementia is important both for social work with older people and also for citizenship because:

- Although it is a disease that can affect anyone, people are most strongly affected in later life, so social workers with older people will come across it more than others. A disease associated with later life may be de-citizening if it is assumed to be affecting older people rather than being diagnosed and appropriate care being provided.
- It is progressive, so once people are affected it will worsen, and older people and their families and carers can only look forward to things getting worse; this is very distressing, but may be de-citizening if it immobilizes people and services from enhancing opportunities and freedoms for people with dementia.
- It leads to the loss of 'personhood': people's sense of identity. This is also very distressing for carers, who have a sense of loss of the person whom they knew. It may compound other losses experienced through bereavements and lead to a sense of early bereavement before the person has died (O'Connor and Purves, 2009). Loss on this scale is potentially de-citizening. It is important to find ways of re-citizening through advance care planning, activity and participation in life, family and community. Early reaction to diagnosis and good planning for later stages of care and the end of life help to preserve a citizen's rights and decisions.
- It is terminal, so it will always lead to death, although because some types of the disease (particularly Alzheimer's disease) progress slowly, some older people will die of other conditions first. Consequently, being diagnosed with dementia strongly raises older people's awareness of their mortality; this means that social workers should often consider end-of-life issues when dealing with dementia.
- As it progresses, dementia increasingly seriously affects people's capacity to think and plan for themselves and eventually their physical ability to carry out the main activities needed to manage their daily lives. Social workers often need to develop and manage increasingly complex and expensive care packages, including citizening measures.
- There are often behavioural and psychological symptoms, so both paid and informal carers and social workers have to deal with challenging behaviour and families distressed by behaviour change. It is important not to be de-citizening by being over-controlling or over-watchful.

Table 7.2 sets out information about the main types of dementia affecting older people. The most common and well-known form is Alzheimer's disease, and clients and their families may need to discuss the diagnosis and their expectations if other forms of the disease are identified. Among the less commonly encountered forms of dementia, social workers

**TABLE 7.2** The main types of dementia affecting older people

| Dementia type | Percentage of dementias | Symptoms and progression | Main causes of death |
| --- | --- | --- | --- |
| Alzheimer's disease (AD) | 62% | Worsening memory, initially of recent events, language impairment and deteriorating capacity to plan and organize | Pneumonia because bodily functions and movement are impaired (swallowing, weight loss, loss of muscle strength) |
| Cerebrovascular disease | 17% | Patchy, episodic change in visual and motor skills, slowing mental capacity (e.g. concentration, apathy, depression, emotional lability) | Cardiac or cerebral 'event', such as a stroke |
| Mixed Alzheimer's and cerebrovascular disease | 10% | Features of both conditions | Pneumonia due to immobility or cardiac/cerebral events |
| Lewy bodies Parkinson's disease dementia is similar, but caused by progression from Parkinson's disease | 6% | Cognitive changes, with fairly intact memory, including deficits in visual and spatial skills, fluctuations in attention and consciousness, loss of physical movement and facial expression, rigidity and loss of feeling | Pneumonia due to immobility |
| Frontotemporal dementias | 2% | Personality and behaviour changes, lack of social awareness, impulsiveness, mental rigidity, obsessions, changes in eating habits (liking for sweet foods), self-neglect, eventual loss of speech and muscle movement | Pneumonia due to immobility |
| Others | 3% | | |

*Source*: Theodoulou (2014); de Vries (2014)

may particularly come across Korsakoff's syndrome, a form of dementia arising from chronic alcohol abuse. This is not strictly a dementia, but it does generate short-term memory loss.

## Diagnosis and assessment

Four major areas of the symptoms of dementia have to be assessed:

1. memory, looking at detailed examples of forgetting recent conversations and events;
2. loss of language skills, looking at examples of being unable to find words for common events or things, and loss of ability to use complex words;
3. visuospatial skills, looking at examples where this affects activities of daily living, for example choosing and finding appropriate clothes, finding things or places;
4. judgements and personality, looking at examples of concern for the feelings of others and inappropriate or impulsive social behaviours which lead to behaviour such as shop lifting or sexual coarseness (Coope and Richards, 2014b).

An important issue that many older people and families want to discuss with social workers is whether they should seek medical assessment and diagnosis when they have worries about whether they have dementia. Perhaps they would rather not know, and until the 21st century medical opinion often agreed with this. No longer, and failing to seek diagnosis is de-citizening because it means that possible help is lost in the important early stages. There are several reasons for this change in attitude in healthcare services:

- Medication to control symptoms and slow the progression of the disease only works in the early stages, so early diagnosis gives the best opportunity to slow down people's growing disability.
- Older people can have a good quality of life living with dementia for a long time with good medical treatment, healthcare and support and help from their families and carers, so early diagnosis can help everyone plan.
- Careful assessment can remove anxiety about symptoms that seem like dementia but are something else, and may mean that treatment can reduce the impact of those symptoms, or remove anxiety, low self-esteem and depression that may come from fearing ageing and dementia.
- Diagnosis and assessment can give you access to many helpful services.

Older people or families worried about the possibility of dementia would normally go to their general practitioner or family doctor, who may carry out an assessment or have it done within the resources of their primary healthcare team. Alternatively, they may refer the older person to a specialist, usually either a neurologist, geriatrician or psychiatrist, depending on the symptoms presented to them and the arrangements in their area. Many areas have memory clinics or specific dementia services, with a range of specialist expertise available.

Two issues for many older people, carers and social workers are:

1. deciding that there is a real problem that justifies asking for assessment;
2. advocating for assessment or reassessment in the face of complacency or reassurance from healthcare staff.

Both issues arise because the onset of dementia in the early stages is insidious, and people develop techniques for managing memory loss which hides problems. Because older people may not want to acknowledge difficulties, for various reasons including their fear or avoidance of thinking about approaching death or fear of a loss of independence, they may actively conceal problems from relatives, carers and professionals. They may prefer not to face the certainty of diagnosis. Memory loss in older people is common, particularly if people do not regularly work at building good memory. Healthcare professionals may be inappropriately reassuring, therefore, and this leads to de-citizening delays in diagnosis, assessment and, as a result, getting help.

## Main social work strategies in working with dementia

The main social work strategies in working with dementia are:

- Actively maintain the older person's preferred lifestyle for as long as possible.
- Help people achieve personal and social objectives.
- Help people find practical ways of managing their symptoms.

- Encourage older people, their families and carers to plan ahead for practical care when physical capacity worsens and decision-making when mental capacity becomes more limited.
- Plan to introduce person-centred planning as required, and only as required, as capacity to manage the activities of daily life deteriorates.

These are all citizening because they promote active self-management and participation in meeting personal objectives and good social relationships for as long as possible. They also contribute to end-of-life care in two important ways. The first is that an older person can know at the outset that they are going to be as independent as possible for as long as possible before their death. The second is that people in relationships with that older person can know as they pass through end-of-life care that they are doing as much as possible to preserve and build the quality of life and meet the aims of the person with dementia. And in bereavement, carers can look back and know that they did as much as possible to maintain the continuity of the life course of the person they cared for.

## Practical advice for living with dementia

One citizening way in which social workers help is by facilitating older people and their carers in managing memory loss in the early stages. Helpful pointers might include:

- Keep a diary and events in your life and your plans; this can be written or on the computer; consider a blog (computer weblog) about your activities, your garden, your theatre visits, your church services; carers can do this as well as the older person themselves, and it can be private – it doesn't have to be fully published on the internet.
- Hang a whiteboard or chalkboard in a visible place for a weekly timetable and reminders.
- Invest in modern storage, and label doors, cupboards and storage boxes.
- Keep a list of names and telephone numbers by a landline phone, practise texting and using a mobile phone or tablet, and make sure it is stocked with similarly useful information.
- Invest in regular delivery of provisions, including re-heatable food and maintain freezer and refrigerator storage (also labelled).
- Have a newspaper delivered daily or have a regular download to a tablet or computer to remind you of the date and keep your mind active.
- Keep a television or other entertainment programme open at the current day, or download it to a tablet or computer.
- Put keys and other valuables in the same place every time you use them (but not visible to potential thieves who may come to the front door).
- Tell your family and friends to remind you about visits or important things (expanded and updated from Graham and Warner, 2009).

## The importance of keeping up activities

### CASE EXAMPLE: HEALTH WALKS

The Thistle Foundation in Scotland developed a series of health walks in the neighbourhood. Six walks lasted for about 20 minutes. Then when people became fitter, they offered a series of six one-hour walks. See http://www.thistle.org.uk/publications.

## Conclusion

My aim in this chapter has not been to provide a guide to social work practice with older people. Instead, I have focused on a number of areas of practice that particularly raise the possibilities of citizenship strategies to maintain for as long as possible the capacity of older people to continue with the direction of their earlier life course while continuing with their personal development in new areas. As increased limitations on their lives from the ageing process appear, it is important for their citizenship that older people maintain as much control of their daily living and positive activity as possible. Social workers' roles in managing social care assessment and commissioning and in working with safeguarding and dementia can contribute a great deal to a good quality of life in the small things, making it possible to maintain purposeful and enjoyable personal development in the big things of the person's life. Most important, they can maintain a citizenship balance between security and surveillance or freedom and progress in the lives of the people that they help. Part of that has been facilitating and planning the move, when it comes, towards the end of life.

### ADDITIONAL RESOURCES

#### Personal development, including the arts

Barton, J., Grudzen, M. and Zielske, R. (eds) (2003) *Vital Connections in Long-term Care*. Baltimore: Health Professions Press.

Part of the focus of this interesting collection is spiritual work in long-term care, and it also covers less-commonly discussed issues such as the importance of pleasurable food and eating experiences, and the use of the arts.

Bolton, G. (2007) *Dying, Bereavement and the Healing Arts*. London: Jessica Kingsley.
Buchalter, S. I. (2011) *Art Therapy and Creative Coping Techniques for Older Adults*. London: Jessica Kingsley.
Hartley, N. (2013) *End of Life Care: A Guide for Therapists, Artists and Arts Therapists*. London: Jessica Kingsley.

These three books focus on end-of-life care and working with older adults, and are among a huge range produced by this publisher, concerned with the arts in helping situations.

#### Dementia

Coope, B. and Richards, F. (eds) (2014a) *ABC of Dementia*. Oxford: Wiley/BMJ Books.

This is a useful, understandable guide to dementia healthcare, authoritatively based on research and practice experience, although it contains almost nothing about social work or anything deriving from social work knowledge and research.

For more complex and detailed information, you might try the annual series of World Alzheimer reports, available on the website of Alzheimer's Disease International: http://www.alz.co.uk/research/world-report.

Webb, S. A. (2006) *Social Work in a Risk Society: Social and political perspectives.* Basingstoke: Palgrave Macmillan.
A useful analysis of risk applied to social work in many different situations.

## Websites

### Dementia

The SCIE Dementia gateway contains a range of useful information and training material on dementia for social care practitioners:
   http://www.scie.org.uk/dementia/

Alzheimer's associations have useful information and training resources, much of which translates to other countries:
Alzheimer's Disease International (the global federation): http://www.alz.co.uk/
Alzheimer's Australia: https://fightdementia.org.au/
Alzheimer Association Canada: http://www.alzheimer.ca/en
Alzheimer's Association India: http://www.alz.org/in/dementia-alzheimers-en.asp
Alzheimer's New Zealand: http://www.alzheimers.org.nz/
UK Alzheimer's Society: http://www.alzheimers.org.uk/
US Alzheimer's Association: http://www.alz.org/

### Practice

The Age UK website provides comprehensive and regularly updated information for policy and planning for older people in the UK:
   http://www.ageuk.org.uk/

The Office of the Public Guardian provides useful information about lasting powers of attorney (LPAs) and other mental capacity issues; it also registers LPAs:
   https://www.gov.uk/government/organisations/office-of-the-public-guardian

### Research and guidelines

The Adult Social Care Outcomes Toolkit provides comprehensive guidance using quality of life outcomes relevant to social care:
   http://www.pssru.ac.uk/ascot/references.php

# 8

# AGEING, END-OF-LIFE AND BEREAVEMENT CARE

In this chapter, I move on to examining social work in the end-of-life phase of ageing, and with bereavement care after an older person has died. My aims are to:

- Identify ways in which social work and social care services, interacting with healthcare services, should respond to older people's needs in the end-of-life care phase.
- Examine social work practice in end-of-life care situations.
- Understand appropriate social work responses to bereavement and grief.

Social workers share with healthcare professionals the problem of identifying when someone is entering the end-of-life phase. Healthcare policy defines end-of-life care as increased care provided within the last 12 months of life, but healthcare professionals cannot be certain about the length of time anyone has to live, at least until the last few days.

Social care practitioners face greater difficulties because they are usually more distant than healthcare professionals from the detailed medical assessment and decision-making around the complex of illnesses that many older people experience. Having carried out assessments and arranged person-centred care for an older person, social workers fall out of the information loop about changing healthcare needs. As a result, they may not be made aware of slow deterioration of physical and mental health or of health crises that require healthcare intervention. At some point, an older person's GP in the UK may place them on the end-of-life care register, signifying a judgement that death within a year is to be expected. While national and local policy and procedures stress the importance of keeping the whole multi-professional group involved with an older person informed of such judgements, in practice adult social care staff are often outside the usual network of communication within healthcare. By paying attention, however, to the progression of older people's conditions, talking with carers and the older person themselves about how their condition is changing, they can often make a similar judgement themselves, or be involved with the healthcare assessment, so that they are aware of a progression towards the end of life.

English end-of-life care policy reflects common international assumptions. It adopted a 'care pathway' approach to providing end-of-life care. Six steps or stages in the dying process are identified:

1. open and honest communication when services identify the likelihood that someone will die within the next year;
2. an agreed care plan and assessment of carers' needs;
3. coordination of services to organize integrated individual care;
4. high-quality services provided in a range of settings;
5. identification of a dying phase, the last few days of life, during which people should have a choice about where they die, support for themselves and their carers, and recognition of their wishes about resuscitation and organ donation;
6. care and support in the phase immediately after death and bereavement care (Hayes *et al.*, 2014).

The policy assumes that social care services will be provided throughout this period. More recent developments have emphasized the concept of patient choice, and a review (Choice in End of Life Care Programme Board, 2015) carried out a survey which provides evidence of public opinion on the services that should be available:

- I want to be cared for and die in a place of my choice.
- I want involvement in, and control over, decisions about my care.
- I want the right people to know my wishes at the right time.
- I want access to high-quality care given by well-trained staff.
- I want access to the right services when I need them.
- I want support for my physical, emotional, social and spiritual needs.
- I want the people who are important to me to be supported and involved in my care.
- I want care where and when it's needed.
- I want coordinated care.
- I want the right care of the right quality with the right staff.

While these ideas arose from a public consultation, they were influenced by professional ideas about end-of-life care generated in the exercise. Nevertheless, they reflect public preferences, even though they asked people to express their ideal, rather than take realities into account. It is clear from the review document that Department of Health concerns about the expense of unnecessary admission to hospital for end-of-life care continue to influence policy-making.

Bereavement care has always been an important part of the social work role in hospices and other palliative care settings (Agnew *et al.*, 2011). Emotional, psychological and social reactions to dying and death are equally an important focus of social work intervention in practice with older people, their families and carers. It is a crucial forward-looking aspect of practice with older people because experience of dying and loss throughout life is an important preparation for ageing, and dying well and dealing effectively with experiences of loss in life help to build resilience to losses in family life and in dealing with future deaths and bereavements. Bereavement has also become more important in hospital settings, since failing to deal with the emotional consequences of bereavement led to adverse reactions later on.

This is a shift in practice coming from acceptance that hospitals have wider responsibilities than curative medicine.

## Practice strategies: End-of-life care and bereavement

As in Chapters 6 and 7, I first explore important areas of life as the basis for identifying appropriate practice strategies for this phase of working with older people.

### *Finances*

When increasing frailty or a terminal illness herald imminent death, finances for care costs can be focused on this period. During end-of-life care and bereavement, successive phases are associated with different costs; these costs are balanced, often inadequately, by families' resources (Bechelet *et al.*, 2008; Reith and Payne, 2009: 119). Among the variety of additional costs that practitioners may need help with are:

- Increased costs for older people, arising from the disability, frailty or illness. This may include increased medication and provision for managing it, such as boxes that help people manage complex combinations of medications. Families may also face the need to provide specialized furnishings, such as riser-recliner chairs, which help people to remain mobile, or changed arrangements at home, aids in and adaptation to the home. New or additional clothing is often needed because of extra wear caused by the disability or changed body shape that may come from some medication, such as steroids, or damage to clothing because of incontinence of difficulties in eating. Travel for treatment may also be an issue – for example, to hospitals and for more advanced illnesses (i.e. those that have progressed beyond ordinary medical interventions); this may include more distant specialist hospitals.
- Increased costs for carers, who may have to give up work or reduce working hours.
- Increased costs for both family members and older people themselves in going out, taking part in social activities and meeting up, which may be important in reducing social isolation and maintaining positive attitudes and mood; examples are treats or visits from and shared activities with grandchildren.

These costs may be balanced by special provisions at the end-of-life stage of care. Retirement pensions or other insurance or social security rights may be triggered by older people or carers giving up work because of increasing frailty, diagnosis of a serious condition or a prognosis that a condition is terminal. Many life insurance policies make provision for early claims once a terminal condition has been diagnosed, so that expenses during the dying phase can be met. Even if this is not formally written in, some insurance companies may release funds early on request. Some employers, former employers or industry bodies and trade unions may have special funds. In the UK, application for attendance allowance (for people over 65 years of age) or personal independence payment under the 'special rules' for people identified as having a terminal condition often improves families' financial arrangements.

Older people and carers may not remember or see the relevance of insurance or imagine that applications will be time-consuming or complex for very little gain. Social workers' skill in completing complex application forms and making cases for discretion by social security authorities is citizening, because it enables people to maintain their rights and resources to deal with the problems that they face. Since they normally deal with people in poverty, however, social work practitioners may not be accustomed to checking for private resources such as insurance companies or employers' pension or welfare provisions, and may imagine that for-profit companies may not be free to act with generosity. With your clients' and their carers' knowledge and permission, making clear you are helping someone who is dying (euphemisms such as 'end-of-life care' may not be well-enough understood to be effective) may mean that all sorts of things become possible. Many healthcare staff are accustomed to everything being provided for by healthcare services, and may not look for other sources of finance or feel it to be part of their job to make special cases for discretion (see Chapter 3), so this is a special skill that social workers can offer any end-of-life care situation.

Upon death, further costs emerge:

- Costs of a funeral continue to rise and outpace the insurance and grant aid (in the UK, mainly a discretionary funeral payment from the Department of Work and Pensions' Social Fund) that people use to make provision to cover it (Drakeford, 1998; Woodthorpe et al., 2013). A regular study of funeral costs (SunLife, 2014, is the most recent at the time of writing) identifies three types of cost, which vary regionally across the UK, London being the most expensive:
    - Basic costs averaged UK£3590 in 2014, including fees for the funeral director, the cremation or burial, the doctor, and the minister or celebrant; these are essential for most people.
    - Discretionary costs average UK£1833, including any memorial, death and funeral notices, flowers, sheets showing the order of church or other memorial or celebratory service, limousines, the venue and catering for a wake.
    - Professional costs average UK£3004 – for example, for a solicitor to administer the estate.

As a consequence, many people in poverty use free funerals provided by local authorities for public health reasons (Local Government Association, 2011). Similar issues arise in other countries. It is citizening to help people think through ways of managing funerals in economical but respectful ways. Basic costs and most discretionary costs can be avoided by how you plan your funeral. Emotional commitments may nevertheless lead people to spend more than is strictly necessary or than they can afford. Some people fear that local authority free funerals mean having a common grave and 'pauper funeral'. The local authority's contractors are, however, usually a local funeral director providing an economical but respectable service without luxuries. Costs are reduced by holding the funeral at unpopular times – for example, early in the morning. Since many people are now cremated rather than having a grave, people can think of less formal memorials for the deceased person.

Loss of financial support for carers and a need for additional financial support often affects people at the end of life. Social workers may need to help with financial planning and debt advice.

Financial difficulties also arise during bereavement. Families often need to reconstruct the family finances for the long term, after the death of an important contributor to household costs. They may need to regularize changes in the rights to housing or ownership of property, manage existing household costs if regular income has reduced and find new sources of income to replace pensions or wages earned by the deceased person. The main social work function here is helping people to think through their income and outgoings realistically, make appropriate plans and claim available benefits.

### *Home and housing*

Although in the fourth age an older person may have adapted their home to cope with increasing difficulty in managing the activities of daily living, end-of-life care may require additional changes at home and possibly more extensive and intensive care in a care home, hospital or hospice. I look at this below, under 'Care arrangements'.

### *Activities, including leisure, work and community involvement*

Maintaining activities, including work, is part of our lifelong journey until the moment of death. It is an important citizening practice strategy to help with this for two main reasons. One, because older people face a greater risk of social isolation when they are extremely frail, activities may provide stimulating events in their lives to enable them to maintain conversation and interaction with family members and friends. Activities mean that they have more positive things than their illness and treatments to talk about. The second reason for working on these opportunities is that older people may resist personal involvements because they fear pity from others or anxiety about people's discomfort around a dying person. A useful practice strategy is to rehearse with them how they might present their illness and approaching death to other people, neither minimizing nor emphasizing its consequences, and making clear their wish to do as much as possible to meet their life plans. They may also want to rehearse expressing appreciation and thanks to people for their friendship, love or help.

### *Health and safety*

As older people become increasingly frail, or affected by the symptoms of an illness, practitioners will need to contribute to decisions about services or changes in living arrangements required to maintain their safety. A difficult re-citizening issue arises about allowing people to return home – for example, after treatment or a period of respite care provided to help carers. Sometimes, increased frailty or the symptoms of an illness place the older person at increased risk compared to when they came into hospital, hospice or care home. Then the care team worries about whether to prevent or discourage discharge home, to protect the older person against falling or having to cope with a sudden escalation of their illness.

First, care staff may prevent discharge to avoid safety issues at home, and potential criticism for discharging someone who later has an accident. UK social workers may be more aware than other members of a palliative care or end-of-life care service team of the requirements of the deprivation of liberties safeguards contained in amendments to the Mental Capacity Act 2015. These require an authorization procedure if someone is in a care home or hospital, including a hospice, is subject to continuous supervision or control and is not free to leave, or would not be allowed by staff to leave if they showed signs of doing so. Social workers may need to raise questions about whether authorization is required, since there is some evidence that hospitals and care homes are not gaining the required authorizations.

In end-of-life care, practitioners may need to strike a citizenship balance between the possibility of an accident and the natural course of dying. An older person may have entered a hospital or hospice for treatment when already frail; and, of course, they are safer in the hospital. Then, treatment finished, they are discharged, and the care team fear an increased risk of accident at home. But this risk has only increased compared with the hospital or hospice: they are at much the same risk at home as they were before, and this had been well accepted at the time. The risk has to be balanced with the emotional benefits of being in the home environment, and, from a citizenship perspective, the right of the older person to pursue a preference for being at home, particularly if this means that they can die at home. Carers may need to be helped to think the issue through. A case example may make the point clearer.

> **CASE EXAMPLE: MR PALETHORPE PREFERS TO DIE AT HOME**
>
> Mr Palethorpe lived alone in an old house that had not been adapted to his needs, visited by community primary care staff and occasionally by a daughter who lived two hours away. He was admitted to the local hospice at the request of his GP for pain and symptom management. When pain and symptoms had been stabilized, the daughter and the GP questioned whether he should be returned home because there was a risk of his falling and dying. The hospice care team took the view that this was always a risk in his house, and he had a very strong wish to die at home; he did not want to die in a clinical environment. The social worker was asked to talk the situation through with his daughter, and identified her worry that she would feel guilty if he fell, lay for some time in pain and then died and was not found for some time. While some discussion about her other care responsibilities for her husband and children helped her to accept her father's right to go home, she was also helped by arrangements for a night and morning visit from a volunteer from a local older person's charity to check on his condition, and increased community nursing visits.

## *Holidays and other travel*

Older people who are able to afford holidays may wish to have a final visit to a favourite holiday place, and short holidays or periods of respite may allow relief from the constant grind of long-term care both for the older person and family and paid carers. A particular issue for people at the end of life may be to visit family members in other parts of the country or abroad. Economical package holidays may not be suitable for this purpose, although on occasion they may facilitate to visit to a favourite location. If flights are required, there may be difficulties for people at the end of life, since travel insurance may not be available for people with serious medical conditions, and airlines may refuse to carry people without insurance. Specialist insurers and travel agents exist to help with such difficulties. Practitioners may need to help older people consider the options if they die abroad: whether they want their body returned to their home for burial or cremation or whether they are happy to have their funeral and disposal of the body in their travel destination.

## Care arrangements, including end-of-life care

Most older people use healthcare increasingly during their last few years, particularly in what turns out to be the final year of life. They will probably experience periods of treatment in hospital. As they become increasingly frail, they may become unable to manage the activities of daily living at home, and require social care, or require intermediate care for rehabilitation after hospital treatment, or nursing home care. Social workers may be involved in the care arrangements, either through assessment for social care support, since older people at this stage are likely to meet the most stringent criteria for care, or by arranging for moves of residents in care or nursing homes or admissions and readmissions to or discharges from hospitals. While government policy is for care at home, this policy requirement is contaminated by the financial stringencies in state healthcare provision and people are discharged without planning for their home care. If carers are seriously stressed, older people may shift to preferring residential nursing care. The care arrangements that older people will prefer depends upon the care available. Gomes *et al.*'s (2015) well-conducted study shows that people experience greater peacefulness when dying at home and dealing with grief during the dying phase and in bereavement. This is only so, however, if the whole process is well managed, and success requires a discussion of preferences, GP home visits, and relatives to be given time off work.

## Social work and social care in the end-of-life care phase

How do we decide when the end of life is relevant to social care practice? Palliative care focuses on the point at which there is a diagnosed illness which requires care rather than cure. Larkin *et al.* (2007) studied the transition between curative medicine and palliative medicine across Europe as an important emotional and social turning point for people, because they have to accept that cure is no longer possible and shift their thinking towards the end of life. There was often uncertainty and poor communication, with mixed messages from staff about what is happening. Hayes *et al.* (2014: 27) acknowledge that different professions identify the end of life at different points. In gerontological practice, colleagues refer to a 'final phase' of life, often longer than the dying phase in palliative care, in which there is a worsening of chronic illness in ageing leading towards death. Social care services may focus on an even earlier starting point, where there is increased frailty and family and community social support becomes insufficient, bringing an older person to the point at which their need for paid care becomes critical (National End of Life Care Programme, 2010).

Social workers are most likely to be involved in the care arrangements at the end of life in two different situations. One is where they are already involved with an older person in providing person-centred social care. Second, they may be required to assess an older person for discharge from hospital or hospice as part of a package of care to enable an older person to go home to die. They are unlikely to be involved where a patient is only receiving healthcare services and is transferred into palliative home care. Many older people do not stay in one place, and there may be constant movement between hospital, care home, hospice and home settings, including movements between the older person's own home and family members' homes. An important practice strategy is to minimize these, especially if older people are suffering from dementia or are less mentally alert than previously because medication or their illnesses are likely to be made worse by constant moves. Moving people unnecessarily also contributes to a reduction in the sense of security which is so important to people maintaining their personal development and life course activities.

## Social work practice at the end of life

The main aim of practice at the end of life is to enable people to die well, and their families, carers and the community around them to experience the older person dying well. An older terminology refers to 'a good death'; but some people find this an uncomfortable phrase, implying that death is a good thing, when they want to continue living. Older people and their families balance the benefits of extending life against end-of-life care which makes the process of dying more comfortable. Dying well means:

- Work with the dying older person.
- Work with families, carers and particularly children who are involved with the dying person.

This second area is particularly important because family members may give a higher value to active treatment than dying people, especially in Asian cultures (Malhotra et al., 2015).

The main psychosocial needs of people who are dying are to:

- Maintain their personal and social identity.
- Maintain as much independence as possible and control of the dying process.
- Be supported psychologically, emotionally and spiritually (Dix and Glickman, 1997).

It is quite difficult to conceptualize maintaining personal and social identity, and it helps to have gone through the process of creating an advance care plan (see Chapter 5), or if you are coming new to the situation, to review the plan. The ACP process starts off with people saying what is most important to them, and this can give you clues to their personal identity. Is it their grandchildren, their sports team, their workmates, or perhaps some particular hobbies? Keeping the grandchildren away to prevent them from disturbing (or being distressed by) someone who is very sick stops people from maintaining their personal identity. Likewise, feeling that they can no longer go out to or participate in an event, or are not well enough to complete a project, has a similar effect. It is important to think of creative ways of keeping them in touch, at least with information, or preferably with some degree of participation.

> ### CASE EXAMPLE: THE CHOIR MAINTAINS THE SINGING IDENTITY OF A DYING MEMBER
>
> Carole was dying of cervical cancer in an upstairs bedroom, and was no longer able to go to church, although the church sent flowers and the minister and members of the church visited. She had been an active member of the choir, and had sometimes played the organ for services. Her husband asked if the choir would be prepared to sing for her. It was one of the best-attended choir practices ever. They stood in the hall of her house and, accompanied by the choirmaster with a portable keyboard, sang some favourite hymns and anthems.

The main social work practice strategies are:

- managing the practical and emotional consequences of increasing frailty, a progressive condition or a life-threatening illness;
- responding to the 'bad news' of becoming aware that they are soon to die, and other news about progression of a disability or illness;
- living their life with their family and within a community;
- completing social and relationship tasks;
- preparing for death.

The main emotional difficulties that people face are:

- Their fear of what the dying process may involve for them, and the need to protect others, such as spouses and particularly children, which then leads on to relationship difficulties.
- The emotional consequences of major illness or increasing frailty, including feeling trapped by physical incapacity and becoming isolated from ordinary social interactions. Family and friends may also find it difficult to talk to them about their illness, and avoid them.
- Denial, anger, hopelessness and depression may build up and then challenge older people's communication skills and existing relationships. This may lead to collusion between the older person and their carer to avoid discussing their feelings – 'I don't want to upset her.'

All of these difficulties are potentially de-citizening because they make it more difficult for people to maintain and build active relationships and social supports, and to go through the dying process in a way that helps the people around them live with their grief. It cannot be straightforward living with the knowledge that you are dying, so it is unsurprising that responses to coping with such an emotionally painful situation are varied and complex. Often people seem able to move in and out of facing uncomfortable realities; an important skill for social workers is being able to tune in to where someone is as their feelings vary. Denial is an important defence if someone finds their reality intolerable and should therefore only be challenged where it is obstructing intervention and then with great care. It is only a problem if it gets in the way of someone getting the treatment they need or it prevents open communication to the detriment of someone else. 'Unless there are issues about protecting the welfare of others, the principle of autonomy permits the dying person to choose to remain in ignorance or with a limited explanation' (Sheldon, 1997: 60). If someone is said to be in denial, it is always necessary to ask: whose problem is it? Is what you see an adaptation to the situation rather than denial? Sometimes, it is the family who finds it too painful to acknowledge that their loved one is dying; sometimes they literally cling to the older person in the hope that they will live and not leave them (Jeffreys, 2005: 198). If families are not helped to face the reality of what is happening, a mismatch between end-of-life care and unrealistic expectations can cause even greater distress. 'The personal characteristics and emotional strain of family [carers] may create barriers to placement of patients in appropriate care settings, leading family inappropriately to insist on or reject care in the intensive care unit, long-term care setting, home, or institutional hospice' (Rabow et al., 2004).

A preparedness to be open and to raise what people find difficult to talk about is the main citizening practice strategy in dealing with these emotional reactions. The language of planning and thinking about arrangements may help – for example, in thinking through alternative courses of action depending on how things turn out: plan A and plan B.

> **CASE EXAMPLE: NOT WANTING TO GO TO A NURSING HOME**
>
> Mr Simpson was finding it difficult to talk to his wife, who was in hospital recovering from injuries after a fall, about moving to a nursing home, which the ward team advised was the best option. The social worker led a family meeting with the Simpsons' son and daughter, and a niece who also supported them. Mrs Simpson was increasingly frail and used her poor hearing to avoid discussing difficulties, managing her hearing aid to ignore conversation about difficult topics. The discussion in the meeting started from listing positive things about returning home and about the care home, with information from the ward team. It moved on to barriers to returning home, to make these available for discussion, and to help the son and daughter be clear about what problems might get in the way. The meeting then looked at the problems with the care home, and this revealed that the perceived difficulties were Mrs Simpson losing contact with her niece, and reduced opportunities for Mr Simpson to be involved in caring for his wife, which was thought to be unsafe in many respects. An alternative care home was identified nearer to the Simpsons' home, and it was agreed (plan A) there would be a weekend at home, to see how the couple managed, and (plan B) a week's stay at the nearer care home, with an agreement with the home that Mr Simpson could be involved in various activities to support his wife. After this experience, Mrs Simpson accepted many of the difficulties of returning home, and agreed to stay at the care home, hoping that her condition would improve. After some time visiting the home every day to help with Mrs Simpson's care, Mr Simpson decided to move in with his wife when a double room became available. When she died, he returned home for a period, but eventually moved into the home for what turned out to be the last few months of his life.

## Quality and length of life and assisted dying

Assisted dying has become increasingly significant in concerns about end-of-life care. This is an area in which citizenship issues may be raised, because some people argue that it is a human right to be able to choose to die, and to receive professional help to do so. The implication is that it is de-citizening to deny this freedom. I discuss towards the end of this section the pros and cons of this debate. Citizenship is also engaged because Parliament has decided in the UK (but not in other countries) that it is not legal to assist people to die, and it is de-citizening to fail to comply with legal requirements. The interpersonal practice of social workers is focused on the human conflicts and consequences of this issue. I argue, therefore, that it is citizening to help people work through this issue openly, rather than closing it down. The social worker's role is to facilitate people in making open and personally and interpersonally appropriate decisions; doing so is a citizening practice strategy.

Assisted dying is bound up with the quality of life that older people are experiencing or expect to experience as they go through the dying phase of their lives. Anyone working in end-of-life care experiences older people and carers concerned that treatment may hasten their death. Supporting feelings of hope is an important part of end-of-life care practice, balancing this with realism in thinking about how much time people have left and what it is possible to do with it (Reith and Payne, 2009). Many people seek any and all forms of treatment for their condition. Studies of terminally ill people's attitudes suggest that a desire for death has been found, but it is often transient and may be linked to depression (Brown et al., 1986, 1995; Emanuel et al., 2000), which can often be treated. Pacheco et al.'s (2003) study of 30 people with incurable cancers found that they might welcome death when it came but rejected hastening it, building their resilience with emotional, social and spiritual support, in which social work can play a part.

Older people who experience unpleasant symptoms or pain, and fear that this will reduce their quality of life, are the most likely to consider assisted dying. Often a factor in this is whether they or relatives fear that their symptoms will worsen, and whether they see their suffering as unusually extreme. Someone experiencing breathing difficulties, for example, common with lung cancer and motor neurone disease, may fear desperately trying to catch their breath as they are dying. A detailed discussion about such fears may ease them, because most symptoms have less impact as people approach death and appropriate care and treatment will manage most problems; however, this is not always true with motor neurone disease. It is important to give people the opportunity to discuss this, if they are thinking about it, and they may raise it with anyone who is working with them. Social workers therefore need to respond to paid and informal carers who are anxious when an older person raises the possibility of hastening death either because they fear or because they want this. There may be a tendency to try to avoid or downplay the issue, but as with all end-of-life issues, openness is usually more helpful. Asking directly and openly what they are thinking about usually works well, and you can then ensure that the right medical or nursing colleague can discuss options and realities with them. Social workers being alongside healthcare colleagues can help because, while medical and nursing colleagues are often comfortable with and experienced in assessing and discussing physical symptoms, they are sometimes less at ease discussing family relationships or social consequences, because they feel it intrudes into areas outside their role.

The illegality and moral unacceptability of assisted dying is the 'established' position in many societies, and this is so in the UK (Payne, 2015), although the Supreme Court of Canada (2015) has determined that requesting professional help to die in some circumstances is a human right; an increasing number of countries are making some provision for it. For a long period, this position has been challenged by 'right to die' groups and individual campaigners, leading to public controversy. In many countries there have been legal judgements over difficult cases, including judgements made at the European Court of Human Rights. A number of different terms are in use, which refer to slightly different issues and I set these out in Table 8.1 for ease of reference.

Table 8.1 identifies the similarity between the terms 'assisted dying' and 'assisted suicide'. Many older people prefer to use the former term: they may see suicide as associated with mental disturbance. The two main areas of argument are moral and practical. The moral argument in favour of physician-assisted suicide (PAS) is the assertion of an individual's rights to self-determination and control in their various aspects. Battin (1995) argues that there are three such rights: to liberty, non-interference and assistance in securing the individual's welfare. Against PAS, ethical, moral and religious arguments about the sanctity of life are asserted. The practical arguments in favour are that PAS offers relief from suffering, particularly where

**TABLE 8.1** Euthanasia, assisted dying and related terms

| Term | Meaning | Comments |
|---|---|---|
| *Euthanasia* | Mercy killing, 'deliberately ending a person's life to relieve suffering' (NHS Choices, 2014) | Active euthanasia is an intervention to end life.<br>Passive euthanasia is withholding or withdrawing treatment necessary to maintain life. |
| *Suicide* | Taking one's own life | |
| *Assisted suicide* | Helping a person to commit suicide or attempt to commit suicide | |
| *Physician-assisted suicide* (PAS) | A physician or medical practitioner helps a person to commit suicide or attempt to commit suicide | The physician may prescribe the necessary drugs, to be injected or otherwise |
| *Assisted dying* | Helping someone commit suicide who is close to death or who suffers from a permanent disability or illness likely to lead to death | 'Assisted dying' and 'physician-assisted dying' are sometimes used interchangeably with assisted suicide; using these terms perhaps implies less disapproval. |

this becomes unbearable, and the main argument against is various aspects of the 'slippery slope' argument.

One option for the relief of suffering is the practice of continuous deep sedation until death. This provides for patients who are not yet experiencing major organ failure, which will lead rapidly to death, but who are in severe pain or have other distressing symptoms. International comparisons are available which suggest, for example, that continuous deep sedation until death is given in about 15 per cent of all deaths in Flanders, Belgium; 8 per cent in the Netherlands; and 17 per cent in the UK. Variations in who is given sedation and the settings in which this occurs suggest that there are cultural and organizational differences in different countries which lead to different medical practices (Anquinet *et al.*, 2012). Doctors will discuss the possibility of continuous deep sedation where this is a possibility, but older people may want a chance of further discussion or involvement by their family. One of the issues is that most people want to retain symptom-free alertness, and dislike the idea of becoming drowsy through medication. Well-managed palliative medication can usually avoid this, and this is another common fear that social workers may need to call on doctors and nurses to discuss.

Unlike medical and nursing colleagues, social workers cannot prescribe medication and so may feel absolved from engagement with assisted dying. But social workers do become involved in it, for a variety of reasons. If colleagues are asked for assistance with dying or questioned about whether they are hastening death, the wider team will become involved. This provides professional support for those directly involved and for everyone to agree how to respond to questions. Social workers may be asked to offer opportunities for open discussion and family involvement, even though this is finally a decision for the older person themselves. Older people or their carers may ask social workers to discuss the issue as part of advance care planning or person-centred care planning, or may ask for assistance in putting a case for assisted dying to medical or nursing professionals. Help may be requested to organize travel to legal jurisdictions where assistance with dying is permitted. This includes several European countries, and various American states. In Europe, the particular legal requirements of other countries means that travel to the Dignitas Clinic in Switzerland is a commonly discussed option.

Another issue that arises is differences of view between older people, family members and medical and nursing professionals about what constitutes suffering. A study of patients who requested but were not granted euthanasia in the Netherlands in 2005 found that patients and physicians agreed that not all patients who requested euthanasia thought their suffering was unbearable, although some had a lasting wish to die. Patients 'put more emphasis on psychosocial suffering, such as dependence, deterioration, and not being able to participate in life anymore, whereas the physicians refer more often to physical suffering. Moreover, some physicians compare the situation of a patient who requests euthanasia with that of other patients in similar situations' (Pasman et al., 2009). Older people may compare their present position with past experience or remember the experiences of family members.

Approaching death may be frightening; but nursing, social and psychological support can assist people to experience this successfully. In particular, although there is a high incidence of depression and other emotional reactions among people approaching the end of life, this is often treatable (Robinson and Scott, 2012). Others feel that dying with dignity comes through the endurance of suffering, and that this is ennobling or has redemptive value for the sufferer.

Because assisted dying is a current hot issue for many service users and their carers, practitioners will need to have thought it through, be clear about the arguments on either side and prepared to present and defend their position. A useful practice strategy is to make sure that the agency's policy is clear and well defined. Practitioners need to be prepared to discuss the issue at length and repeatedly with service users, because its import is so serious that they will want to go over it several times, and to support other colleagues faced with such issues. Agency policy will vary; but in my view it is not unreasonable to direct service users and carers to resources available on the internet, making them aware that much of the public debate is by campaigning groups, who have a particular point of view.

Seeing older people as citizens suggests that social workers should be sympathetic to older people being free to retain control of their lives and make the decision to die at a time and in circumstances of their choosing. If they thought this, they are in tune with public opinion in the UK, as the regular surveys of opinion by the British Social Attitudes survey shows:

> The view that life is a sacred gift means that religious institutions often oppose euthanasia as well as abortion. This is a topic where the traditional religious view has long lacked widespread public support. Even 30 years ago (in 1983) only 23 per cent of the public agreed that if a patient has 'a painful incurable disease' a doctor should not be allowed 'by law to end the patient's life, if the patient requests it'. The proportion now stands even lower, at just 16 per cent. But, in contrast to both abortion and same-sex relationships, this is one topic on which the country's legislators have so far proved reluctant to align the law with majority public opinion.
>
> *(Park* et al.*, 2013: ix)*

Since legislation does not permit assisted dying in the UK, however, whatever their personal views, social workers and their agencies have to comply with the law. Many people regard assisting people to die as an important moral issue (Payne, 2015), so family members are likely to be uncertain about it. Much of the public debate about right to die assumes that there is agreement within the family, or that the patient's right to decide should be paramount.

## CASE EXAMPLE: MR AND MRS MOORE DISAGREE ABOUT ASSISTED DYING

Mr Moore was discharged after treatment for lung cancer, and advised that no further treatment was possible; a home palliative care service was provided. Mr Moore decided that he would like to travel to the Dignitas Clinic in Switzerland to die before his symptoms incapacitated him, and wanted his wife to travel with him and take part in the procedure. She approached the hospital social worker, anxious because she did not want him to do this. Their son supported her in this view, but Mr Moore was adamant. The social worker, with the aim of allowing all the people involved to understand each other's point of view, convened a family meeting, which included a doctor to explain how pain and symptom control would be effective at the end of life. Mrs Moore continued to be very distressed, but felt she must assist her husband, and with great trepidation started to make the arrangements. The social worker, following hospital policy, was unable to assist in the practical arrangements. In the event, Mr Moore's symptoms worsened rapidly, and he was unable to travel, dying in reasonable comfort at home. Mrs Moore, later sought bereavement help about feeling guilty in being unwilling to pursue his wishes and perhaps delaying travel, making it impossible for him to achieve what he wanted.

As in this case, family disagreement and conflict may be irreconcilable, and this may particularly be so where one party is accustomed to having their way within family relationships. An appropriate practice strategy is to facilitate family debate and personal consideration of the issues in each case. Currently, in the UK, as in other jurisdictions where assisted dying is not legal, practitioners may be required to avoid expressing a view or assisting in carrying out a decision to help a service user commit suicide. One of the issues that may arise is the effect on children, and it may be necessary to make sure that this is included in family considerations.

## CASE EXAMPLE: KATHERINE DECIDES NOT TO HELP HER HUSBAND DIE

Katherine rang the social worker to say she had collected the morphine necessary to help her husband to fulfil his expressed wish to die. He was very distressed by the disability caused by a progressive illness. She loved him very much and wanted to help him. The social worker sat in the grounds of the hospital to review what she was thinking and feeling. The couple were very close to their grandchildren, aged four and six, whom they had cared for frequently. Eventually, Katherine decided not to help her husband die, and he died naturally some weeks later. Afterwards, the social worker helped with her bereavement, which included her guilt about not helping the man she loved in this way. An important factor, which she had not realized at the time, was her grandchildren's reaction; they asked things like: 'Can we build a ladder to heaven to see him?' She realized that in later years explaining that she had helped him die would have been very difficult.

Guidance is issued in the UK by the Director of Public Prosecutions (2010) to indicate the circumstances in which people who assist others to die will be prosecuted. This makes it clear that professionals involved with helping a person to die are more likely to be prosecuted than a relative who acts with compassion. The relevant paragraph (43.14) is as follows:

> A prosecution is more likely to be required if ... the suspect was acting in his or her capacity as a medical doctor, nurse, other healthcare professional, a professional carer [whether for payment or not], or as a person in authority, such as a prison officer, *and the victim was in his or her care* [emphasis in original].

Much of the public debate on assisted dying focuses on the issue of whether it is a human right to be able to decide to end your life in a way and at a time of your choosing. In a careful assessment of the rights arguments, Lewis (2007) concludes that competing and irreconcilable differences in rights-based arguments mean no final agreed view could achieve widespread public support for legislation or policy in either direction.

Seven rights-based arguments for assisted dying are that:

- Since rights to liberty are basic to human rights, individuals should be free to do as they wish, unrestricted by the prohibition on assisted dying.
- Rights to autonomy and self-determination permit individuals to define their own conceptions of good, leaving them free to make quality-of-life decisions.
- Rights to privacy mean that the state, professionals and other individuals should not intervene in important private decisions such as suicide.
- Rights to dignity allow us to decide on our own definition of what is a dignified death.
- Rights to equality argue that, since suicide is legal in most jurisdictions, people who, because of disability, cannot secure their own suicide are treated unequally by the law and the state because they are denied a legal choice available to others. Since people have the right to refuse life-sustaining medical treatment, it is illogical that they are not permitted to take their lives, which amounts to the same thing.
- Rights to freedom of conscience and religion argue that states are imposing a moral prohibition deriving from public opinion or religious belief.
- The individual has rights to ownership of their body and life; this point is often used to rebut religious or moral arguments about the sanctity of life (Lewis, 2007).

Rights-based arguments can similarly argue against assisted dying:

- Rights to life are inalienable and therefore mandatory.
- Rights to equality and equal protection, arguing that legalization may particularly affect already marginalized groups such as physical and learning disabled people and older people, who may be most subject to other pressures in life, and also to mental disturbance arising from those pressures, or might be more likely to be pressurized, subtly or otherwise, to take up a right to life. Legalization of assisted suicide is often proposed only for terminally ill people and people with severe physical disability, and this could be seen as prejudicial treatment favouring people who would not then have equal protection with other citizens.

- Rights to property, arguing that our bodies are entrusted to us by God, and that legalization merely substitutes the state for God as the holder of our bodies as property; for example, it may be said that the state has an interest in the preservation of citizens' lives.
- Rights to autonomy, arguing that legalization poses a threat to autonomy by establishing the social, cultural and political context of people's personal choices, including, for example, financial barriers to palliative and community-based care and a culture saturated by media images of trivialized and apparently justified killings (Lewis, 2007: 35–42).

If rights-based arguments do not resolve debates about assisted dying, are practice issues more helpful? Some of the practical arguments about assisted dying are as follows:

- There is a gradation of situations and it is hard to decide between situations where people might agree that assisted dying was desirable and situations where it would be harder to get agreement.
- If assisted dying is permitted by law, agencies such as hospitals or hospices would have to investigate cases thoroughly and bureaucratize decision-making in order to avoid public criticism of their decisions in particular cases.
- Physicians would have the right, as with abortion, to opt out of performing assisted suicides: physicians who agreed to do so might become a focus of demand and conflict if campaigning groups opposed their work, in the way that has happened in some countries around abortion.
- Professional practice in health and social care relies on trust; the possibility that a professional might later be involved in decisions about assisted dying might inhibit trust.
- Patients and families may experience conflicts and may fear financial losses to their capital if long-term care is required; this may apply pressure to them and to patients to agree to assisted suicide.
- People may change their minds; there is evidence that many thoughts about hastening death are fleeting.
- Good care will reduce the impact of feared symptoms, but it may be hard to accept this before the symptoms are relieved; people may not understand what will happen at their death.
- The prognosis that death is imminent may be wrong, and some decisions to hasten death would be premature.
- Anxiety and depression affect many people approaching the end of life, and may lead to a wish to hasten death, but treatment would remove or reduce the impact of the wish (Reith and Payne, 2009: Chapter 8).

## Bereavement care

### *What are bereavement and bereavement care?*

Bereavement is the state of mind that people experience over a period after they have lost someone who is important to them through death. It is de-citizening because it is often a disturbing and difficult experience that cuts people off from social relations and support in their community and family. Bereavement care is therefore an important re-citizening element of end-of-life care, aiming to help people manage their lives during the period in which they experience that state of mind and find a renewed way of life in new social relationships. Stroebe *et al.* (2007) in a systematic review of research identify a number of de-citizening health consequences of bereavement, including the following:

- psychological reactions, usually mild and short-lived, but in some people extreme and longer-lasting; where people experience intense feelings of grief, they sometimes fail to seek help;
- an increased risk of death, including death by suicide;
- increased rates of consultation with doctors, disability, hospitalization and use of medication;
- other medical and social consequences such as impaired memory, eating and nutritional problems, work and relationship difficulties and difficulties that arise from a reduction in participation in social life.

Among older people, bereavement may lead to health difficulties, including higher mortality rates, possibly from existing health conditions, reduced physical activity and higher rates of depression, which suggests that informal contacts to check on people's condition may be important. Bereaved older people are more likely to suffer from loneliness, have difficulty in establishing appropriate continuing bonds with the lost person, and in adjusting to changed social identities – for example, in taking part in social life without a partner and going on holidays (Stephen, 2012).

To understand and work with bereavement, practitioners need to disentangle different aspects of what is going on for people, which are expressed in a range of concepts. Bereavement is a state of mind, coming from grief, which is the sorrow that we feel when we experience a loss. In bereavement care, we are dealing with people's states of mind and the social consequences of them, since they very often seek help with the social consequences in work and relationships that their state of mind generates. Common states of mind include:

- Disbelief: 'I cannot believe she has actually died.'
- Denial: 'I'm constantly expecting him to walk through the door again.'
- Preoccupation with the deceased person: 'I'm spending hours each day just thinking about the happy times we had.'
- A sense of the deceased person's presence: 'I caught sight of him waiting at the check-out', or 'I can hear him telling me how to mend this.'
- Poor concentration, poor memory and little sense of purpose.
- Restlessness and searching for the deceased person.

One of the important initial social work responses is to build the relationships that will enable practitioners to be trusted when they reassure people that experiences of seeing, hearing or talking to the deceased person are common in many people; they are not going mad. People also commonly experience physical problems similar to those that go with anxiety, such as a lack of energy, hollowness in the stomach, tightness in the chest and throat, sensitivity to noise, muscle weakness, sleep disturbance and eating disturbances – either eating too much or too little.

Feelings of grief are another useful aspect of bereavement that practitioners can focus on, encouraging them to express and think through their feelings. Signs of the emotional reactions that people experience include:

- Profound sadness, constant weeping, tearfulness.
- Yearning: 'I wish she could be with me.'
- A sense of shock and numbness: 'I'm not sad or worried, I just can't feel anything.'
- Anger – directed at incompetent medical staff, uncaring nurses and social workers, thoughtless bureaucrats, God, the deceased person, family friends and the unfairness of the world in general. This often leads to complaints, and these may sometimes develop into formal complaints. To help bereaved people, it is useful to respond to these fully and as quickly as possible. Otherwise, it is useful to help people deal with this anger more rationally. Practitioners can ask: 'What happened that makes you feel angry about the nurse?' and this may help, if appropriate, to formulate a clear complaint. Alternatively, it may be helpful to move people towards more balanced views: 'Are there some ways in which the medication helped her?' Where the anger is more symbolic, thinking it through may help. For example, practitioners might avoid accepting 'I'm never going to church again', hoping that the bereaved person will change their present determination after a cooling-off period. This might deprive someone of social and spiritual support, so engaging them with a more detailed thinking through of their reaction may help them: 'What is it about what happened that makes your God punish you in this way?'
- Guilt, self-blame and regret: 'I didn't do enough to help her'; 'I should have noticed she was getting worse.' Sometimes people feel a sense of freedom, release from a caring burden, and this becomes associated with guilt: 'I shouldn't be feeling like this.' Again, it may help people to explore and try to balance things that went wrong with more positive contributions that they made to the life of the deceased person.
- Anxiety about the strength of feelings and inability to cope: 'It seems never-ending.'
- Helplessness and disorganization: 'I can't seem to get anything done.'

In working with feelings of grief, practitioners need to allow the bereaved person to express their feelings, and accept the strength of the feelings that they are expressing, because this may shock them or make them fear that you will reject them because of their emotions, particularly anger and guilt. Balancing this, though, it is important to avoid allowing an incapacitating circle of emotion. The dual process model of bereavement (Stroebe and Schut, 2001) suggests that most people switch between looking backwards at what they have lost, and looking forwards at the changes they need to make to restore their life to a new pattern. As people express their feelings of loss, therefore, it can help them to pick up an area of life that they are talking about and shift towards planning for the future. For example, you can respond to regrets such as: 'Now he'll never see our grandchildren growing up' with 'I wonder if there's a way in which you can keep the memories of his love for them, so that they can see it as they grow up', and introduce the idea of a memory box or photo album, containing mementos or photos of time the deceased person spent with his grandchildren.

Bereavement and grief arise from loss, the experience of being deprived of something or someone that is important to us. An important issue for practitioners to explore is what deprivations a bereaved person is experiencing. Is it companionship, practical support, security in housing and financial support, opportunities or plans for the future? Again, the dual process of looking back at the deprivations can be balanced with a restoration focus on planning new ways of dealing with the deprivation.

Mourning is social behaviour that expresses our loss. It is concerned with expectations of behaviour when someone is bereaved, and with the rituals that people follow to help them to deal with their grief. Traditionally, people wore sombre colours, closed the curtains of their house or apartment and did not take part in light-hearted social events. Different religious groups follow particular customs.

> **CASE EXAMPLE: JOSEPH SITTING SHIVA IN HIS JEWISH RELIGION**
>
> Joseph, in his 30s, was not very orthodox in following the Jewish religion, although he was committed to it. When his father died, he felt that 'sitting shiva' was not a useful activity. As a visitor to shiva in other families, he felt it was like a prolonged 'wake', a social event in which people visited the family and had to be entertained. His mother explained that the tradition was that the family stayed together in their home, to be visited by friends and relatives of Joseph's father, who would bring refreshments, rather than being entertained by the family. The purpose was to enable memories to be rehearsed and stories about his father to be told. Experiencing it, he found it was a positive experience, remembering his father and his life, and being together with his family.

### Sources of bereavement care

There are four main sources of bereavement care:

1. *Hospital bereavement services*. These are fairly universal, but are often basic, dealing with administrative issues such as notifying death to relatives, patients' property and the immediate needs of family members. More complex needs are passed to community bereavement services. This approach fails to see bereavement as integral to the experience of end-of-life care. But seen in a more limited way, it is a reasonable response to bereavement situations faced by hospitals. Because most people manage bereavement themselves with the support of family and friends and only have immediate practical needs, it is only later that more complex bereavement issues emerge.
2. *Hospice bereavement services*. These usually provide comprehensive bereavement services for the families of their own patients, and sometimes more widely as a community service. Many of the services use volunteer bereavement support workers, supplemented by their own social workers or counsellors to respond to more complex needs and more occasionally psychiatric help.
3. *Community bereavement services*. These have grown up since the 1980s, provided either by local community organizations or by local groups of national organizations. For example, in the UK, Cruse has become a major player in this field, developing from being a more general organization serving widows. Many of these organizations provide group work and counselling or social work support, and some also provide support in schools and workplaces affected by a major incident or by individual bereavements. Some organizations are specialized. In particular, there has been an important development of services for bereaved children.
4. *Help with bereavement provided by individual professionals* as part of broader services. The most common source of this form of help is counselling provided through primary

healthcare teams, with GPs employing a counsellor or social worker to serve their patients. Inevitably, though, as we saw in Chapter 6, a thoughtful preventive approach in ageing and end-of-life care includes helping people through experiences of bereavement, so that they are able to become more resilient when facing grief and loss later in life.

## Bereavement interventions

How should social workers intervene in bereavement issues? Research has found that most bereaved people do not need or benefit from bereavement services (Schut et al., 2001; Schut and Stroebe, 2005). The exceptions are children, older people and people with symptoms of psychiatric disorder. Generally, the more complicated the person's bereavement process the more likely it is that interventions will be helpful (Parkes and Prigerson, 2010: Chapter 13). It is important to avoid an assumption that (and talking as though) people have to 'work through' stages or tasks in bereavement, in order to come out the other end coping well with their grief. Many bereaved people say that they don't want to forget the deceased person, and set about memorializing them in various ways. Social workers' involvement with older people is likely to cease around death, and you will not be the obvious person to go to for help with bereavement, which typically does not become an issue for some months.

A systematic review of research into bereavement interventions identifies three levels of intervention:

1. Primary interventions available to everyone experiencing bereavement; only people who request help have been shown to benefit from intervention.
2. Secondary interventions designed for people who have been identified as at risk and who want help; careful assessment and strict criteria for offering help are necessary to effective intervention.
3. Tertiary interventions for people with complex grief or post-traumatic stress disorder; psychological and psychiatric interventions including pharmacological interventions have been found effective (Stroebe et al., 2007).

Research shows that people are most helped in the following ways:

- By being able to prepare for bereavement by discussing impending death with the dying person and others in their family (Parkes and Prigerson, 2010), particularly children, or other vulnerable family members. Professional commentary suggests that people may also need to complete life tasks during the dying process, including exchanges with the dying person of messages such as 'goodbye', 'thank you', 'sorry' and 'I love and value you' and may have difficulties during bereavement if they are not able to do so (Reith and Payne, 2009: Chapter 6). Help with dealing with financial problems of serious illness or disability and obtaining financial and practical assistance is valued.
- Around the time of death, people may be helped with legal and practical problems such as assistance with registration and funeral arrangements, informing other people (particularly children) about the death, immediate financial problems, deciding about viewing the dead, rituals of mourning and similar issues.

- In the immediate period after the funeral, listening and discussion may be helpful, including helping the bereaved person to understand that an unaccustomed and possibly frightening intensity of emotion is normal.
- In later bereavement, people may be helped to establish their autonomy, making a balance between grieving and building a new life, and identifying 'turning points' in which major changes of feelings, attitudes and behaviour have become settled (Parkes and Prigerson, 2010: 197–219). Planning for new financial circumstances and longer-term needs may also be necessary (Bechelet et al., 2008).

A valid practice strategy, therefore, is to provide basic information about bereavement as you work on end-of-life issues. This might include information about contacting local bereavement services, with advice that it is appropriate to do so months or even a year or more after the death. People often experience a strong reaction on the anniversary of the death. It may also be useful for a leaflet to explain common manifestations of grief that may be unfamiliar to many people, such as the tendency to hear or see the deceased person. If greater help with bereavement seems justified in a particular case, the main practice strategy is to offer opportunities to discuss the deceased person and the way in which the bereaved person and their family is responding to the loss. Groupwork can be helpful, and many bereavement services train volunteers to do this listening task (Reith and Payne, 2009: Chapter 6).

Where bereavement is uncomplicated, referral for counselling may be counterproductive because:

- Interventions interfere with the support of family and friends.
- Treating people with uncomplicated bereavements as fragile, sick or damaged victims encourages them and their families to accord them a 'sick' identity, enabling them to retreat from responsibilities and challenges.
- Anger, a common aspect of bereavement, may be inappropriately channelled by sympathetic support into revenge-seeking.
- Counselling may, inadvertently, favour either the grief or restoration elements of the dual process rather than helping people balance the two.
- Interventions developed for one culture may be inappropriate when applied to others (Parkes and Prigerson, 2010: Chapter 13).

Special problems are most likely to arise in three circumstances, which may overlap:

- traumatic loss (accidents, criminal acts such as murder, disasters, refugee and asylum seeking, suicide, terrorism, war);
- vulnerable people (children, people with learning disabilities, people experiencing mental illness);
- lack of social and family support (older people and others with family living at a distance, or who have lost through death many people in their previously existing support networks; otherwise isolated people) (Parkes and Prigerson, 2010: Chapter 14).

*Complicated (or pathological or traumatic) grief* is a deviation from the cultural expectation in the time course or intensity of specific or general symptoms; there is debate about whether it can be considered a clinical disorder, or whether it is an extreme form of a normal reaction (Stroebe *et al.*, 2013). Three important sub-types of pathological grief are chronic, absent and delayed grief. Complicated grief may lead to reactions of depression or anxiety that are severe and over an extended period (Stroebe *et al.*, 2013). Psychiatric assessment is often required.

A useful practice strategy for identifying this is by asking people whether the bereavement has gone as they expected. Does their personal reaction fit with what they expected, and what is expected within their cultural and social backgrounds? Most bereaved people say they feel as they would have expected given the circumstances. Bereaved people who are depressed are more likely to see themselves as being different. While hearing or seeing the deceased person is normal, other delusions or hallucinations or active suicidal thoughts may indicate depression. Common normal feelings are of guilt focused on things done or not done for the person who died, and feeling that without the person they would be better off dead. Wider guilt is of greater concern or wider thoughts of death, a preoccupation with worthlessness, and prolonged and marked inability to get on with the daily tasks of life are of greater concern. Younger people may be more restless, lonely, fatigued and weepy, and experience what they describe as severe symptoms of sleep, appetite and memory disturbances initially. Regular daily routines and structure may act as a protective factor that helps counter depression.

Corr (1999) suggests that the concept of disenfranchised grief enables a more complex understanding of feelings and social reactions to bereavement, grief and mourning. Disenfranchised grief occurs if the death cannot be openly or publicly mourned, and can lead to difficulties in bereavement (Doka, 1989, 2002). Disenfranchised grief arises where the death is either stigmatized or hidden. It may be difficult to mourn an ex-partner, or stepparent, stepchild, an in-law or caregiver. Death arising from stillbirth and abortion is often hidden and in the case of the latter may also be stigmatized. Other stigmatized deaths include suicide and homicide. Hidden grief may arise following the death of a partner in a same-sex relationship, or an extra-marital affair, for example. Glackin and Higgins (2008) in a study of Irish same-sex couples, one of whom died, found that where the couple is 'out' – that is, people around them are aware of the relationship – it may not be disenfranchised. In many instances, however, they were unable to acknowledge fully their grief.

## Children's bereavement

Because death is hidden and medicalized, many adults feel awkward talking about death, especially to children, partly also because they have not addressed their own fears about death. Family members are dealing with their own grief, and find it difficult to respond to children's needs. A useful practice strategy, therefore, is supporting bereaved adults to reach out to their children and this can help with their own grief.

Children are resilient and able to accept an honest attempt to explain death. Honest, open communication with bereaved children is very important, and Christ's (2000) significant qualitative study of American children shows that most successfully adapt to the death of a parent, but that the grief processes are different at different ages. Children under the age of two will not have an understanding of death, but they will be aware that things are different and that the person to whom they are attached has disappeared (Dyregrov, 2008). They will react to this loss as separation even though their limited language skills make it impossible for them to talk about their distress. They may become withdrawn, unhappy or distraught and will need extra reassurance and comforting from an adult that they know well. Children up to the age of five years may see death as potentially reversible or fear that they have caused the death by their behaviour. As young children develop language, therefore, they need to be given information and explanations about the person who has died so as to enable them to integrate this history into their own life story. Letters from the deceased person, photographs and life stories may be helpful. Children may neglect them and pick them up again in later years, reintegrating them into their lives in different ways. Older children are increasingly aware of the permanence of death, but unreasonably still blame others or themselves for the death.

If the adults around them are displaying their own distress, this will affect children. It is natural to be sad and to cry; sharing this expression of grief can help children by giving them permission to express rather than hide feelings. They also value adults' attempts at openness. While protecting children from sadness and pain following someone's death is not possible, adults can do a lot to help children cope. As Silverman says: 'If we exclude children or protect them from death and bereavement, what we are really doing is not preparing them to deal with life. We are not teaching them anything. We are not helping them to grow and develop' (Silverman, 2000: 73). A helpful strategy is to work on helping people to see that their support to their children does not have to be perfect.

## Conclusion: The end of life and bereavement

This book argues that end-of-life and bereavement care should be an integral part of social work with older people because it is integral to the experience of later life in the ageing journey. To neglect it is therefore de-citizening, because it cuts people off from opportunities to make the most of life during their leaving of it. While much end-of-life care will be provided by specialist services, social workers may become involved in the provision, and need to coordinate their work with end-of-life healthcare. Particularly, where there is already an existing relationship through provision of social care and social work, perhaps especially where families are coping with a long-term condition, social workers may also need to make contributions (see Chapter 3). In particular, social workers may be able to maintain a grasp on help for families and carers, when end-of-life healthcare focuses more strongly on the needs of the dying person themselves. In this way, re-citizening by the incorporation of the family into health and social care in an important phase of older people's lives.

### ADDITIONAL RESOURCES

### Books

In addition to the books recommended in the Introduction about social work with older people and in palliative care, the following articles provide practical guidance for social workers dealing with end-of-life care situations:

Hayes, A., Henry, C., Holloway, M., Lindsay, K., Sherwen, E. and Smith, T. (2014) *Pathways through Care at the End of Life: A guide to person-centred care.* London: Jessica Kingsley.

Monroe, B. (2004) *Social work in palliative medicine*. In Hanks, G., Cherny, N. I., Christakis, N. A., Fallon, M., Kaasa, S. and Portenoy, R. K. (eds) *Oxford Textbook of Palliative Medicine*, 4th ed. Oxford: Oxford University Press: 184–196.

Monroe, B. and Sheldon, F. (2004) *Psychosocial dimensions of care*. In Sykes, N., Edmonds, P. and Wiles, J. (eds) *Management of Advanced Disease*. London: Arnold: 405–437.

This book brings together guidance for practitioners on the approach to end-of-life care generated by the National End of Life Care Programme during the period of the Labour administration in power until 2010.

There is very extensive literature on bereavement. The best general guide is:

Murray Parkes, C. and Prigerson, H. (2009) *Bereavement: Studies of grief in adult life*, 4th ed. London: Routledge.

A useful practical guide is:

Gross, R. (2016) *Understanding Grief: An introduction*. London: Routledge.

## Official documents

National End of Life Care Programme (2010) *Supporting People to Live and Die Well: A framework for social care at the end of life*. Report of the Social Care Advisory Group of the National End of Life Care Programme. London: Department of Health.

This UK report, although produced during the Labour administration ending in 2010, provides a good overview of policy initiatives to integrate social care into end-of-life care.

Choice in End of Life Care Programme Board (2015) *What's Important to Me: A review of choice in end of life care*. London: Department of Health.

This document is a review of the latest iteration of the English policy of patient choice in end-of-life care, and includes an important survey of patient wishes to inform end-of-life care policy:

https://www.gov.uk/government/publications/choice-in-end-of-life-care

### *Assisted suicide*

R (on the application of Nicklinson and another) (AP) (Appellants) versus Ministry of Justice (Respondent). Retrieved 12 October 2015 from https://www.supremecourt.uk/cases/uksc-2013-0235.html.

This judgement contains a very full, well-written account of the British law, European and international judgements on assisted dying, understandable to the layperson, which is well worth reading to gain a full appreciation of the legal issues and to be able to explain legal problems to service users. The Canadian Supreme Court decision supporting assisted dying as a human right is available on the internet and is cited in this chapter.

Director of Public Prosecutions (2010) *Policy for Prosecutors in Respect of Cases of Encouraging or Assisting Suicide*. London: Crown Prosecution Service. Retrieved 21 November 2013 from http://www.cps.gov.uk/publications/prosecution/assisted_suicide_ policy.html.

UK practitioners in this field also need to be familiar with this policy so that they can explain this to service users and ensure that their own assistance to service users does not lead to the risk of prosecution; readers in other jurisdictions may find the approach taken in the UK of interest.

Demos (2012) *The Commission on Assisted Dying*. London: Demos. Retrieved 21 November 2013 from http://www.demos.co.uk/publications/thecommissiononassisteddying. This report is a recent UK publication about assisted dying in the UK.

The Canadian government (prior to the Supreme Court decision mentioned in this chapter) looked at assisted dying internationally, and a number of documents are available on the internet, including a literature review about policy and practice in different countries:

Nichol, J., Teiderman, M. and Valiquet, D. (2013) *Euthanasia and Assisted Suicide: International experiences*. Ottawa: Library of Parliament. Retrieved 30 October 2015 from http://www.parl.gc.ca/content/lop/researchpublications/2011-67-e.htm.

## Websites

This is a link to the annual reports on the average costs of and grants for funerals:
http://www.sunlifedirect.co.uk/press-office/?utm_source=About-Sun-Life-Direct%2FPress-Office%2FResearch%2FSocial-Fund-Funeral-Payments%2F%26utm_medium=redirect%26utm_campaign=redirect

Winston's Wish is a UK charity concerned with children's bereavement. There are a wide range of services and publications, including free resources:
http://www.winstonswish.org.uk/

The NHS Inform site is a good resource for older people in the UK, and is part of a wider 'bereavement zone':
http://www.nhsinform.co.uk/bereavement/grief/olderpeople/

Independent Age is a voluntary organization which produces a useful guide on bereavement in old age, downloadable from the internet and part of a larger publication:
http://www.independentage.org/advice/factsheets/wise-guides/healthy-happy-connected/8-coping-with-loss/

This is a useful and practical regularly updated SCIE guide to 'deprivation of liberties' safeguards under the Mental Capacity Act 2005:
http://www.scie.org.uk/publications/ataglance/ataglance43.asp

# 9
# CONCLUSION
## Practice strategies for older people's citizenship

The main aims of this chapter are to:

- Bring together its arguments about citizenship social work; these points are made in various contexts throughout the book, they are here summarized in a single stream of argument.
- Summarize methods of citizening throughout the life course, avoiding de-citizening and promoting re-citizening in later life.
- Identify practice strategies for social work with older people at the end of life.

## Citizenship social work with older people

The starting point of a citizenship social work is an understanding of citizenship. We saw in Chapter 2 that this is a complex idea. Citizenship is about belonging both to a nation as a legal entity and also to its cultural, economic, political and social ways of life. Social citizenship is citizens' rights and duties to take up and pursue those social aspects of citizenship.

Citizenship is not only a status, something unchanging that we either possess or do not. It is also a process, in which belonging is lost and built up in social interactions and relationships. For example, children become citizens through a process of education and socialization and migrants lose aspects of their previous citizenship and build a new citizenship over time. The process of citizenship is two-way: it does not only involve people in taking up rights and responsibilities, but in others accepting their citizenship, behaving towards them and interacting with them as co-citizens. Citizenship involves building both rights and duties, but the extent and meaning of those rights and duties is contested. How far are they conditional, so if you don't or can't accept the duties to participate in social relations, you don't get the rights? This is clear for offenders, for example: in prison, you lose many of your rights to participate in formal matters such as elections, as well as to participate in family life. It is also clear for migrants, who in Britain need formal recognition of 'unconditional leave to remain' in the country, and who must take a course and pass an examination to receive formal recognition as a citizen. Less clearly, the position of socially excluded people is complex. Women, people from ethnic minorities, disabled people may not share the same opportunities as fit men from the ethnic majority, and even if they have the same opportunities may not benefit from the same outcomes in employment, recognition and participation. How far, then, are they non-citizens or part-citizens?

Citizenship social work seeks to address as part of its practice those exclusions and complexities. It is humanistic because it puts recognition of the humanity and human rights of all the people that social work serves at the centre of practice. It asks practitioners to hold in mind throughout social work practice that the people we work with share a common human heritage with us. I called this citizenship thinking. A focus on citizenship requires a rights-based, quality-of-life focus: how is the quality of life of this person, this family, this community enhanced if we make sure they receive their rights in the same way as other human beings around them? Citizenship is maintained by promoting good relationships in families and communities and helping people remain in control of their life experience. It is enhanced by careful planning and the clarity and certainty of a focus on people's security in their personal and social lives. This means not only safeguarding their well-being in formal ways, such as investigating and responding to abuse of all kinds, but thinking: 'What will help this person lead a more secure life, on which they can then build their future self-actualization?'

The citizenship of older people and people at the end of life is at risk, because they face serious losses. These include the possibility of losing their most important personal relationships – for example, as life partners die and children move away – and social connections (e.g. in their work and earning capacity). Older people know they are moving to the point at which their own lives will end. They may be less socially valued because retirement cuts them off from valued social roles. Illness and increasing disability may isolate them from past relationships and activities. They face substantial social change as technological and globalizing change takes place without their involvement and understanding.

Focusing on the citizenship of older people means valuing their continuing lives, their contributions and rights, and their opportunities to do new things and create new activities, just like every child and adult. It means valuing their end-of-life experiences, too. Valuing their citizenship means enabling them to live well and to die well. Loss of any kind, including the loss of capacity, does not mean the loss of the right to age in the place that you want to be and to make the most of the social environment in which an older person lives. Continuity of experience across the life course is an important part of maintaining citizenship because it helps us to build our identity and common human experience with others. End-of-life care for older people is needed because it is important that they should experience their loved ones' deaths as part of the continuity of their lives, and know that their own end-of-life experience will be worthwhile. These services, therefore, need to be equally available to the whole population, to older people whose capacity fails over time as well as people dying with diagnosed illnesses, perhaps at a younger age. Planning is crucial for citizenship social work with older people as with younger people: it creates involvement between services, practitioners, older people and carers. As a result, clarity and certainty bring the security that helps older people and their carers gain influence over how services respond to their needs and enables older people to have influence over decisions that may be personally important to them.

## Citizening, de-citizening and re-citizening

To explore some ways to implement citizenship social work, Chapter 2 introduced the ideas of citizening, de-citizening and re-citizening, and I have referred to them throughout the book. These ideas refer to citizenship as a process in which rights and opportunities may be gained or lost and built up or destroyed by what happens in our lives. A citizenship social work, therefore, does not involve just a concern for thinking about the citizenship of older people but a practice that aims to:

1. Citizen by facilitating successful ageing in a positive pattern of social relations and in people's communities.
2. Oppose the de-citizening of older people that takes away their human rights.
3. Re-citizen their lives by building on their human rights to a successful later life leading to dying well.

Citizening is maintaining and building social rights and participation in community and family. It is the process of gaining aspects of citizenship that facilitate people's rights in later life and at the end of life. Services for older people emerge from valuing them as participants in their communities; and therefore citizening involves participation of service users and their carers in providing services but also in participating in a full life within their communities. Citizening involves educating co-citizens to appreciate and value others' citizenship. It is citizening to recognize the importance of health to older people, as well as valuing their human involvement in relationships and community.

Citizening is consonant with an ethics of care view of human life. It sees care as an integral part of all human existence, not a rational, calculating approach to our relationships as an exchange of contributions to a family or society, but based on shared humanity, shared experiences and mutual interdependence in relationships. Citizening aims to help build family and community relationships and facilitate connections between people at times of difficulty so that we can pursue that ideal of citizen caring. Connectedness in relationships, families and communities is essential in caring. Caring must be included in preparation for citizenship: young people and adults all need to gain experience and validation as successful carers in their lives. This means that their rights to being cared for and if necessary dependent in later life and at the end of life is accepted by their families, communities and the older people themselves.

Caring and dependence is citizening because it creates ties and relationships in people's lives. Dependence is not a mark of decline but a signal that the community must take responsibility for enabling older people to continue in active citizenship. Many cultural traditions value interdependence. Rather than denigrating dependence, we should value it as a relationship of great worth. Young people should learn about and value ageing and dying as phases of life, and fear and avoidance should be reduced through experiencing contact with people in these phases of life.

Adults should think and plan for ageing and the end of life by engagement with an older generation in their families and communities. Extending advance care planning into planning for the whole care career is crucial to citizening for older people at the end of life, because it creates continuity in their experience of later life towards the end of life. Planning for social relationships in later life and end of life care enhances choice, opportunity and well-being; it is citizening because it increases the possibility of maintaining control over what is important to older people and people at the end of life. Citizening means involving the family and community in discussing issues about treatment and thinking through what is happening so that they can be supportive or raise their concerns and opposition clearly. An example is involving family members in understanding medical decisions about food and drink.

To social work practitioners, citizening means having a focus on the citizen and carer and community needs, not on the services or the management of them. It requires us to overcome conflicts that get in the way of interpersonal connections between older people at the end of their lives and the carers, families and communities. Part of that involves an understanding of and respect for the continuities in older people's needs and wishes, rather than a focus on what care services can most conveniently or cheaply provide.

De-citizening is the process by which older people lose elements of their citizenship through ageing. The loss of opportunity when illness and disability cuts people off from community social relations is particularly important. Devaluing ageing and older people ('the little old lady') is de-citizening because takes away citizenship. At present, dependence often means that older people increasingly lose the physical and mental capacity to exercise their citizenship, and they and others begin to question their contribution to society in exchange for citizenship. Getting out of touch with technology is also de-citizening, is because it also reduces older people's access to options.

De-citizening places older people into a care ghetto, in which we only think about care needs instead of human needs. It is de-citizening to neglect both the value of the social and the importance of good healthcare in older people's lives, as complementing each other and requiring a concern for both. Not knowing about the range of care available de-citizens, because you cannot use what you are not confident about, and you cannot be confident unless you know what you want. Neglecting older people's end-of-life care de-citizens them of their right to the best possible care. Focusing social work on providing care services may become de-citizening if it emphasizes official confirmation that independent management of everyday life has been lost. It may be de-citizening to emphasize structural coordination as part of developing service partnership because it can exclude older people and carers if they do not participate in planning or policy-making meetings. Emphasizing the economic burden of care on the state and on co-citizens such as carers creates personal uncertainty for individuals and wider social insecurity, because it raises the prospect that care is conditional and may not be provided. It is de-citizening to assume that older people are waiting for death, rather than co-producing services to make the most of their life. It is de-citizening to focus on healthcare end-of-life care pathways that see social work and social care as required only in a healthcare-led dying phase, rather than incorporating end-of-life care into social work with all older people. Barriers to advance care planning are de-citizening because they prevent people either from knowing that planning is possible or from being fully involved in it. Avoiding planning or accepting lack of planning in older people and their families is also, as a result, de-citizening, because it takes choices out of people's own hands.

Re-citizening is the process of building lost elements of citizenship that enable successful later life and end of life. It involves the positive maintenance and promotion both of personal independence and also of interdependence between people in a local community. An important re-citizening focus is on integrating formal and informal services to provide effective support for freedom and advance care planning, facilitating advance care planning, finding ways of managing and transcending disability. Re-citizening enables older people and people at the end of life to take part in generalized rather than specialized services and to take part in creative activities and personal development opportunities to enhance their social engagement with society and ultimately their human self-actualization.

## Practice strategies with older people at the end of life

In the second part of this book, I have focused on putting citizening, de-citizening and re-citizening at the heart of practice for older people as they approach the end of life. I argued in Chapter 1 that incorporating the end of life into practice with older people throughout their childhood and adult life, and throughout their involvement in care services, is crucial to the citizenship social work. This is because it accepts the whole of their life, its continuity and its ending, and includes the role of caring and connectedness in family, community and life experience. Human continuity demands a concern for integrating end-of-life care into care for older people as part of the experience of ageing and later life. This does not always require new assessment schemes or legal requirements, but rather insists on carrying out our present practice in ways that represent the whole of the human life and human person we are working with in what we are doing. Throughout the book I have explored some practice strategies that may help in this, and in Table 9.1, I have summarized them in order to provide a brief guide to where you can find them in the book.

**TABLE 9.1** Practice strategies summary

| Definition | A practice strategy is a focus on your service responsibilities that shifts how you take on those responsibilities. | Chapter 1 |
|---|---|---|
| Practice strategies | 1. Promote and do not hinder participation in worthwhile activities with co-citizens.<br>2. Maintain and enhance people's lifelong personal identity and developing social identities, expressed in their social relationships.<br>3. Facilitate people in using the civil and political rights that go with their citizenship.<br>4. Enable people to use their rights to receive services from the state.<br>5. Enhance older people's participation; respect and value informal care and community contributions.<br>6. Connect participation and co-production with social class and health inequalities, power relations and the role of the state. | Chapter 2 |
| | 1. Build and maintain connections in families and communities to promote long-term caring relationships.<br>2. Aim to generate community support as a natural part of professional social work tasks.<br>3. Shift people towards maintaining healthy lifestyles, balancing adverse health impacts with positives in their lives.<br>4. Be clear and provide feedback to colleagues about the aspects of the social that you are concerned with.<br>5. Clarify safeguarding strategies and their achievements to colleagues.<br>6. Be aware of and prepared to explore spiritual issues.<br>7. Identify and explore expectations of caring among different people involved with an older person.<br>8. Identify where the social is a barrier to good healthcare and how social work can help.<br>9. Build skill in talking about the end of life or dying phase of care, while maintaining hope. | Chapter 3 |

(continued)

**TABLE 9.1** (continued)

| | | |
|---|---|---|
| *Definition* | *A practice strategy is a focus on your service responsibilities that shifts how you take on those responsibilities.* | *Chapter 1* |
| Practice strategies (continued) | 1. Take particular responsibility for linkages with non-healthcare services and in the wider community.<br>2. Pick up situations where working with external agencies and advocacy will meet the needs of clients.<br>3. Facilitate relatives in discussing nursing and medical decisions.<br>4. Combine both continuity and innovation in the best quality of life in care arrangements.<br>5. Enable users and carers to understand service coordination, to aid participation.<br>6. Help paid care staff work more interactively, avoiding working through checklists of tasks.<br>7. Consider who to involve in service structures.<br>8. Become involved in staff development and training for paid care staff.<br>9. Focus on interpersonal aspects of cooperation as you work with end-of-life specialist teams. | Chapter 4 |
| | 1. Initiate ACP as early as possible in an older person's care career.<br>2. Review and encourage interactions about family members' understandings of healthcare decisions.<br>3. Help people to communicate in advance about their wishes to family members. | Chapter 5 |
| | 1. Build up personal, career and team strategies to promote adult preparation for later life.<br>2. Help people to maintain interpersonal links across the life course.<br>3. Work on social action benefiting older people's citizenship.<br>4. Support the role of carers, in general, and with older people and as they approach the end of life. | Chapter 6 |
| | 1. Focus on users' priorities in maintaining their quality of life.<br>2. Plan ahead for potential changes in finances.<br>3. Plan interventions around activities of daily living and instrumental activities of daily living.<br>4. Extend the period of independent living for as long as possible.<br>5. Plan with other agencies potential supports to safeguard older people from abuse where direct interventions are not possible.<br>6. Promote active self-management and participation for as long as possible with people affected by dementia. | Chapter 7 |
| | 1. Focus help with finances on the three phases of changes in the end-of-life and bereavement period.<br>2. Focus help with housing on short-term adaptations and care arrangements.<br>3. Maintain activities to avoid social isolation and help with others' reactions to the end of life.<br>4. Rehearse how clients might present their illness and death to others.<br>5. Minimize moves between services and changes in living arrangements.<br>6. Provide basic information on bereavement as part of end-of-life care.<br>7. After bereavement offer opportunities to discuss the deceased person and responding to loss.<br>8. Ask bereaved people about how their experience of bereavement has fitted with their expectations.<br>9. Support bereaved adults to reach out to their children.<br>10. Help people to see that help to children and others does not have to be perfect. | Chapter 8 |

## And in the end

We all age; most of us will live through a phase of 'later life' and we will all die. It is natural to human beings. Caring, coming about because of our connectedness with other human beings, in social groups, social organizations and personal relationships, is woven through our life experience. Providing care services is one particular aspect of caring where social workers have a professional role in other people's human lives. Social work in later life and at the end of life has the potential to make a distinctive and strong contribution to caring in human lives through its professional role in social and health services. Understanding citizenship social work as a process of contributing to citizening, combating de-citizening and promoting re-citizening can help you to develop practice strategies to fulfil that professional role in ways that respect the rights and choices of people in later life and at the end of life. All of these ideas offer you ways of renewing practice and contributing to people's opportunities to live and to die well.

Finally, developing practice strategies, and citizening, de-citizening and re-citizening have the strong potential to contribute to other forms of social work too.

# BIBLIOGRAPHY

Abrahams, C. (2016) It is wrong and unfair to denigrate older people because of the EU Referendum result. *Age UK Blog*. Retrieved 12 July 2016 from: https://ageukblog.org.uk/2016/06/27/it-is-wrong-and-unfair-to-denigrate-older-people-because-of-the-eu-referendum-result/.

Adam, S., Browne, J. and Johnson, P. (2012) *Pensioners and the Tax and Benefit System* (IFS Briefing Note BN130). London: Institute for Fiscal Studies.

Agnew, A., Manktelow, R., Haynes, T. and Jones, L. (2011) Bereavement assessment practice in hospice settings: Challenges for palliative care social workers. *British Journal of Social Work*. 41(1): 111–130.

Altilio, T. and Otis-Green, S. (eds) (2011) *Oxford Textbook of Palliative Social Work*. Oxford: Oxford University Press.

Anquinet, L., Rietjens, J. A. C., Seale, C., Seymour, J., Deliens, L. and van der Heide, A. (2012) The practice of continuous deep sedation until death in Flanders (Belgium), the Netherlands, and the UK: A comparative study. *Journal of Pain and Symptom Management*. 44(1): 33–43.

Ariès, P. (1974) *Western Attitudes towards Death: From the Middle Ages to the present*. Baltimore, MD: Johns Hopkins University Press.

Arup (2015) *Shaping Ageing Cities: 10 European case studies*. London: Helpage International.

Audit Commission (2004) *Older People: A changing approach 1*. London: Audit Commission.

Badger, F. J., Shaw, K. L., Hewison, A., Clifford, C. and Thomas, K. (2010) Gold Standards Framework in care homes and advance care planning. *Palliative Medicine*. 24(4): 447–448.

Ball, M. S. (nd) *Aging in Place: A toolkit for governments*. Atlanta, GA: Atlanta Regional Commission/ Community Housing Resource Center.

Balloch, S. and Hill, M. (eds) (2007) *Care, Community and Citizenship: Research and practice in a changing policy context*. Bristol: Policy Press.

Baltes, M. M. (1998) The psychology of the oldest-old: the fourth age. *Current Opinion in Psychiatry*. 11: 411–415.

Barlow, J., Singh, D., Bayer, S. and Curry, R. (2007) A systematic review of the benefits of home telecare for frail elderly people and those with long-term conditions. *Journal of Telemedicine and Telecare*. 13: 172–179.

Barnes, H., Green, L. and Hopton, J. (2007) Social work theory, research, policy and practice – challenges and opportunities in health and social care integration in the UK. *Health and Social Care in the Community* 15(3): 191–194.

Barnes, K., Jones, L., Tookman, A. and King, M. (2007) Acceptability of an advance care planning interview schedule: a focus group study. *Palliative Medicine* 21: 23–28.

Barnes, M. (2006) *Caring and Social Justice*. Basingstoke: Palgrave Macmillan.

Barnes, M. (2012) *Care in Everyday Life: An ethic of care in practice*. Bristol: Policy Press.

Bartlett, R. and O'Connor, D. (2010) *Broadening the Dementia Debate: Towards social citizenship*. Bristol: Policy Press.

Barton, J., Grudzen, M. and Zielske, R. (eds) (2003) *Vital Connections in Long-term Care*. Baltimore, MD: Health Professions Press.

Battin, M. P. (1995) *Ethical Issues in Suicide*. Englewood Cliffs, NJ: Prentice-Hall.

Bechelet, L., Heal, R., Leam, C. and Payne, M. (2008) Empowering carers to reconstruct their finances. *Practice* 20(4): 223–234.

Ben-Galim, D. and Silim, A. (2013) *The Sandwich Generation: Older women balancing work and care*. London: Institute for Public Policy Research.

Biggs, S. (1993) User participation and interprofessional collaboration in community care. *Interprofessional Care.* 7(2): 151–160.

Black, K. (2007) Advance care planning throughout the end-of-life: Focusing the lens for social work practice. *Journal of Social Work in End-of-Life and Palliative Care.* 3(2): 39–58.

Blaikie, A. (2008) *Ageing and Popular Culture*. Cambridge: Cambridge University Press.

Bolton, G. (2007) *Dying, Bereavement and the Healing Arts*. London: Jessica Kingsley.

Bonnie, R. J. and Wallace, R. B. (eds) (2003) *Elder Mistreatment: Abuse, neglect and exploitation in an aging America*. Washington, DC: National Academies Press.

Bristow, J. (2015) *Baby Boomers and Intergenerational Conflict*. Basingstoke: Palgrave Macmillan.

Brittain, K., Corner, L., Robinson, L. and Bond, J. (2010) Ageing in place and technologies of place: The lived experience of people with dementia in changing social, physical and technological environments. *Sociology of Health and Illness.* 32(2): 272–287.

Brown, J. H., Henteleff, P., Barakat, S. and Rowe, C. J. (1986) Is it normal for terminally ill patients to desire death? *American Journal of Psychiatry.* 143: 208–211.

Buchalter, S. I. (2011) *Art Therapy and Creative Coping Techniques for Older Adults*. London: Jessica Kingsley.

Bullock, K. (2006) Promoting advance directives among African Americans: A faith-based model. *Journal of Palliative Medicine*, 9(1): 183–195.

Butchers, A. (2008) Craft work. In Hartley, N. and Payne, M. (eds) *The Creative Arts in Palliative Care*. London: Jessica Kingsley: 98–112.

Butler, A. and Tinker, A. (1983) Integration or segregation: Housing in later life. In Department of Health and Social Security (ed.) *Research Contributions to the Development of Policy and Practice*. London: HMSO.

Canda, E. R. (1998) Afterword: Linking spirituality and social work – five themes for innovation. In Canda, E. R. (ed.) *Spirituality in Social Work: New directions*. New York: Haworth Press: 97–106.

Care and Support Planning Working Group/Coalition for Collaborative Care (2016) *Personalised Care and Support Planning Handbook: The journey to person-centred care: Core information*. London: NHS England.

Challis, D., Dunleavy, J., Philp, I. and Roberts, H. (1994) Social functioning and the elderly. In Philp, I. (ed.) *Assessing Elderly People in Hospital and Community Care*. London: Farrand Press: 65–97.

Charnley, H. (2001) Promoting independence: a partnership approach to supporting older people in the community. In Balloch, S. and Taylor, S. (eds) *Partnership Working: Policy and practice*. Bristol: Policy Press.

Choice in End of Life Care Programme Board (2015) *What's Important to Me: A review of choice in end of life care*. London: Department of Health.

Christ, G. C. (2000) *Healing Children's Grief: Surviving a parent's death from cancer*. New York: Oxford University Press.

Clark, D., Small, N., Wright, M., Winslow, M. and Hughes, N. (2005) *A Little Bit of Heaven for the Few? An oral history of the modern hospice movement in the United Kingdom*. Lancaster: Observatory Publications.

Clarkson, P. (2012) What research tells social workers about their work with older people. In Davies, M. (ed.) *Social Work with Adults*. Basingstoke: Palgrave Macmillan: 300–314.

Clifton, J. (2009) *Ageing and Well-Being in an International Context*, Politics of Ageing Working Paper 3. London: Institute for Public Policy Research.

Commission on Funding of Care and Support Fairer Care Funding (2011) *Fairer Care Funding: The report of the commission on funding of care and support*. London: Department of Health.

Commission on Social Determinants of Health (2008) *Closing the Gap in a Generation: Health equity through action on the social determinants of health: Final report of the commission on social determinants of health*. Geneva: World Health Organization.

Cook, A. and Miller, E. (2012) *Talking Points: Personal outcomes approach: Practical guide*. Edinburgh: Joint Improvement Team. Retrieved 24 June 2015 from: http://www.jitscotland.org.uk/resource/talking-points-personal-outcomes-approach-practical-guide/.

Cooke, B. and Kothari, U. (eds) (2001) *Participation: The new tyranny?* London: Zed.

Coope, B. and Richards, F. (eds) (2014a) *ABC of Dementia*. Oxford: Wiley/BMJ Books.

Coope, B. and Richards, F. A. (2014b) Assessment. In Coope, B. and Richards, F. (eds) *ABC of Dementia*. Oxford: Wiley/BMJ Books: 10–13.

Cooper, C., Selwood, A. and Livingston, G. (2008) The prevalence of elder abuse and neglect: A systematic review. *Age and Ageing*. 37: 151–160.

Corr, C. (1999) Enhancing the concept of disenfranchised grief. *Omega*. 38(1): 1–20.

Craig, G. C. (ed) (2004) *No Water – No Life: Hydration in the dying*. Alsager: Fairway Folio.

Craig, G. (2008) Palliative care in overdrive: Patients in danger. *American Journal of Hospice and Palliative Care*. 25(2): 155–160.

Crawford, K. and Walker, J. (2008) *Social Work with Older People*, 2nd edn. Exeter: Learning Matters.

Csikai, E. L. and Chaitin, E. (2006) *Ethics in End-of-Life Decisions in Social Work Practice*. Chicago, IL: Lyceum.

Cumming, R. G., Salkeld, G., Thomas, M. and Szonyi, G. (2000) Prospective study of the impact of fear of falling on activities of daily living, SF-36 scores, and nursing home admission. *Journal of Gerontology, Biological Sciences and Medical Sciences*. 55(5): M299–M305.

Daly, M. and Lewis, J. (2000) The concept of social care and the analysis of contemporary welfare states. *British Journal of Sociology*. 51(2): 281–298.

Dandeker, C. (1990). *Surveillance, Power and Modernity: Bureaucracy and discipline from 1700 to the present day*. Cambridge: Polity Press.

Dane, B. and Moore, R. (2006) Social workers' use of spiritual practices in palliative care. *Journal of Social Work in End of life and Palliative Care*. 1(4): 63–82.

Davey, J., Nana, G., de Joux, V. and Arcus, M. (2004). *Accommodation Options for Older People in Aotearoa/New Zealand*. Wellington, New Zealand: NZ Institute for Research on Ageing/Business and Economic Research Ltd, for Centre for Housing Research Aotearoa/New Zealand.

de Smidt, G. A. and Gorey, K. M. (1997) Unpublished social work research: systematic replication of a recent meta-analysis of published intervention efficacy research. *Social Work Research*. 21: 58–62.

de Vos, P., de Ceukelaire, W., Malaise, G., Pérez, D. Lefèvre, P. and van der Stuyft, P. (2009) Health through people's empowerment: A rights-based approach to participation. *Health and Human Rights*. 11(1): 23–35.

de Vries, K. (2014) End-of-life care in dementia. In Coope, B. and Richard, F. (eds) *ABC of Dementia*. Oxford: Wiley/BMJ Books.

Delanty, G. (2002) Communitarianism and citizenship. In Isin, E. F. and Turner, B. S. (eds) *Handbook of Citizenship Studies*. London: Sage: 159–174.

Demos (2012) *The Commission on Assisted Dying*. London: Demos. Retrieved 21 November 2013 from http://www.demos.co.uk/publications/thecommissiononassisteddying.

Department of Constitutional Affairs (2007) *Mental Capacity Act 2005: Code of practice*. London: TSO.

Department of Health (2008) *End of Life Care Strategy: Promoting high quality care for all adults at the end of life*. London: Department of Health.

Department of Health (2016) *Care and Support Statutory Guidance*. London: Department of Health. Retrieved 16 June 2016 from: https://www.gov.uk/guidance/care-and-support-statutory-guidance.

Detering, K. M., Hancock, A. D., Reade, M. C. and Silvester, W. (2010) The impact of advance care planning on end of life care in elderly patients: Randomised controlled trial. *British Medical Journal*. 340: c1345.

Director of Public Prosecutions (2010) *Policy for Prosecutors in Respect of Cases of Encouraging or Assisting Suicide*. London: Crown Prosecution Service. Retrieved 21 November 2013 from http://www.cps.gov.uk/publications/prosecution/assisted_suicide_policy.html.

Dix, O. and Glickman, M. (1997) *Feeling Better: Psychosocial care in specialist palliative care*. London: National Council for Hospice and Specialist Palliative Care Services.

Dizon, D. S., Schutzer, M. E., Politi, M. C., Linkletter, C. D., Miller, S. C. and Clark, M. A. (2009) Advance care planning decisions of women with cancer: Provider recognition and stability of choices. *Journal of Psychosocial Oncology*. 27(4): 383–395.

Doka, K. (1989) *Disenfranchised Grief: Recognizing hidden sorrow*. New York: Lexington.

Doka, K. (2002) *Disenfranchised Grief: New directions, challenges and strategies for practice*. Champaign, IL: Research Press.

Dong, X., Simon, M., de Leon, C. M., Fulmer, T., Beck, T., Hebert, L., Dyer, C., Paveza, G. and Evans, D. (2009) Elder self-neglect and abuse and mortality risk in a community-dwelling population. *Journal of the American Medical Association*: 302(5): 517–526.

Drakeford, M. (1998) Last rights? Funerals, poverty and social exclusion. *Journal of Social Policy*. 27(4): 507–524.

Dwyer, P. 2004. *Understanding Social Citizenship: Themes and perspectives for policy and practice*. Bristol: Policy Press.

Dyregrov, A. (2008) *Grief in Children: A handbook for adults*, 2nd edn. London: Jessica Kingsley.

Ebell, M. H., Becker, L. A., Barry, M. C. and Hagen, M. (1998) Survival after in-hospital cardiopulmonary resuscitation: A meta-analysis. *Journal of General Internal Medicine*. 13(12): 805–816.

Ellershaw, J. and Wilkinson, S. (eds) (2010) *Care of the Dying: A pathway to excellence*, 2nd edn. Oxford: Oxford University Press.

Emanuel, E. J., Fairclough, D. L., and Emanuel, L. L. (2000) Attitudes and desires related to euthanasia and physician-assisted suicide among terminally-ill patients and their caregivers. *Journal of the American Medical Association*. 284: 2460–2468.

European Commission (DG ECFIN) and Economic Policy Committee (AWG) (2009) *The 2009 Ageing Report: Economic and budgetary projections for the EU-27 Member States (2008–2060)*. Brussels: European Commission, Directorate-General for Economic and Financial Affairs.

European Union (2016) *Active ageing*. Retrieved 10 May 2016 from: http://ec.europa.eu/social/main.jsp?catId=1062.

Evers, A. and Guillemard, A.-M. (2012) Introduction: Marshall's concept of citizenship and contemporary welfare reconfiguration. In Evers, A. and Guillemard, A. M. (eds) *Social Policy and citizenship: The changing landscape*. Oxford: Oxford University Press: 3–34.

Fallon, P. (2006) *Elder abuse and/or neglect*. Wellington: Ministry of Social Development. Retrieved 11 June 2016 from: http://www.msd.govt.nz/about-msd-and-our-work/publications-resources/literature-reviews/elder-abuse-neglect/index.html.

Faulks, K. (2000) *Citizenship*. London: Routledge.

Featherstone, M. and Wernick, A. (eds) (1995) *Images of Aging: Cultural Representations of Later Life*. London: Routledge.

Fiedler, B. (1999) *Promoting Independence: Preventative strategies and support for older people – report of the SSI study*. London: Department of Health.

Fink, J. (ed.) (2004) *Care: Personal Lives and Social Policy*. Bristol: Policy Press.

Formiga, F., Chivite, D., Ortega, C., Casas, S., Ramos, J. M. and Pujol, R. (2004) End-of-life preferences in elderly patients admitted for heart failure. *Quarterly Journal of Medicine*. 97: 803–808.

Foti, M. E., Bartels, S. J., Merriman, M. P., Fletcher, K. E. and van Citters, A. D. (2005) Medical advance care planning for persons with serious mental illness. *Psychiatric Services*. 56(5): 576–584.

Fried, T. R., and O'Leary, J. R. (2008) Using the Experiences of Bereaved Caregivers to Inform Patient- and Caregiver-centered Advance Care Planning. *Journal of General and Internal Medicine* 23(10):1602–7.

Fried, T. R., Bullock, K., Iannone, L. and O'Leary, J. R. (2009) Understanding advance care planning as a process of health behavior change. *Journal of the American Geriatric Society*. 57(9): 1547–1555.

Froggatt, K., Vaughan, S., Bernard, C. and Wild, D. (2009) Advance care planning in care homes for older people: An English perspective. *Palliative Medicine*. 23: 332–338.

Fromme, E. K., Zive, D., Schmidt, T. A., Olszewski, E. and Tolle, S. W. (2012) POLST registry do-not-resuscitate orders and other patient treatment preferences. *Journal of the American Medical Association.* 307(1): 34–35.

Furman, L. D., Benson, P. W., Grimwood, C. and Canda, E. (2004) Religion and spirituality in social work education and direct practice at the millennium: A survey of UK social workers. *British Journal of Social Work.* 34(6): 767–792.

Gallagher, M. & Ireland, E. (2008) *Evaluation of the Nairn Anticipatory Care Project: Final Report.* Stirling: Cancer Care Research Centre. Retrieved 28th September 2010: http://www.cancercare.stir.ac.uk/documents/NairnFinalReport.pdf.

Gest, J. and Gray, S. W. D. (2015) Silent citizenship: The politics of marginality in unequal democracies. *Citizenship Studies.* 19(5): 465–473.

Gilbert, N. (2012) Citizenship in the enabling state: The changing balance of rights and obligations. In Evers, A. and Guillemard, A. M. (eds) *Social Policy and Citizenship: The changing landscape.* Oxford: Oxford University Press: 80–96.

Gilleard, C. and Higgs, P. (2000) *Cultures of Ageing: Self, citizen and the body.* London: Routledge.

Gilleard, C. and Higgs, P. (2002) The third age: class, cohort or generation? *Ageing and Society.* 22(3): 369–82.

Gilleard, C. and Higgs, P. (2013) The fourth age and the concept of a 'social imaginary': A theoretical excursus. *Journal of Aging Studies.* 27(4):368–76.

Gillick, M. R. (2006) The use of advance care planning to guide decisions about artificial nutrition and hydration. *Nutrition in Clinical Practice.* 21(2): 126–134.

Gilligan, C. (1993) *In a Different Voice: Psychological theory and women's development,* Cambridge, MA: Harvard University Press.

Gilliom, J. (2001). *Overseers of the Poor: Surveillance, resistance and the limits of privacy.* Chicago, IL: University of Chicago Press.

Glackin, M. and Higgins, A. (2008) The grief experience of same-sex couples within an Irish context: Tacit acknowledgement. *International Journal of Palliative Nursing.* 14(6): 297–302.

Glasby, J. and Sanderson, H. (2014) *Partnership Working in Health and Social Care: What is integrated care and how can we deliver it?* 2nd edn. Bristol: Policy Press.

Glendinning, C., Clarke, S., Hare, P., Kitchetkova, I., Maddison, J. and Newbronner, L. (2006). *Outcomes Focussed Services for Older People.* Bristol: Policy Press.

Gomes, B. Calanzani, N., Koffman, J. and Higginson, I. J. (2015) Is dying in hospital better than home in incurable cancer and what factors influence this? A population-based study. *BMC Medicine.* 13: 235. Retrieved 14 October 2015 from: http://www.biomedcentral.com/1741-7015/13/235.

Gorer, G. (1867) *Death, Grief and Mourning in Contemporary Britain.* Garden City, NY: Doubleday.

Gorey, K. M. (1996) Social work effectiveness research: Comparison of the findings from internal versus external evaluations. *Social Work Research.* 20: 119–128.

Gott, M., Gardiner, C., Small, N., Payne, S., Seamark, D., Barnes, S., Halpin, D. and Ruse, C. (2009) Barriers to advance care planning in chronic obstructive pulmonary disease. *Palliative Medicine.* 23: 642–648.

Graham, C. (2014) Eight reasons to care about old people's rights. In *HelpAge International: a glocal movement for old people's rights.* Retrieved 7 January 2015 from http://www.helpage.org/blogs/caroline-graham-17/8-reasons-to-care-about-older-peoples-rights.

Graham, N. and Warner, J. (2009) *Understanding Alzheimer's Disease and Other Dementias.* Poole: Family Doctor Books.

Graham, S. and Wood, D. (2003). Digitizing surveillance: Categorization, space, inequality. *Critical Social Policy.* 23: 227–248.

Greene, R. R. (2008) *Social Work with the Aged and Their Families.* New York: Aldine.

Greene, R. R., Cohen, H. L. and Galambus, C. M. (2007) *Foundations of Social Work in the Field of Aging: A competency-based approach.* Washington, DC: NASW Press.

Gremier, A. M. and Gorey, K. M. (1998) The effectiveness of social work with older people and their families: A meta-analysis of conference proceedings. *Social Work Research.* 22(1): 60–63.

Gross, R. (2016) *Understanding Grief: An introduction*. London: Routledge.
Habermas, J. (1996) *Between Facts and Norms: Contributions to a discourse theory of law and democracy*. Cambridge: Polity Press.
Hall, D. and Scragg, T. (2012) *Social Work with Older People: Approaches to person-centred practice*. Maidenhead: Open University Press.
Hamann, J., Cohen, R., Leucht, S., Busch, R. and Kissling, W. (2007) Shared decision making and long-term outcome in schizophrenia treatment. *Journal of Clinical Psychiatry*. 68(7): 992–997.
Hanks, G., Cherny, N. I., Christakis, N. A., Fallon, M., Kaasa, S. and Portenoy, R. K. (eds) (2010) *Oxford Textbook of Palliative Medicine*, 4th edn. Oxford: Oxford University Press.
HAPPI (2009) *Housing our Ageing Population: Panel for Innovation 1*. London: Homes and Communities Agency.
Harding, R. (2008) Palliative care in resource-poor settings: Fallacies and misrepresentations. *Journal of Pain and Symptom Management*. 36(5): 515–517.
Harris, J. (2006) Incorporating the social model into outcomes focussed social care practice with disabled people. In Barnes, C. and Mercer, G. (eds) (2004) *Disability, Policy and Practice: Applying the social model*. Leeds: Disability Press.
Harris, J. and Tanner, D. (2007) *Working with Older People*. London: Routledge.
Hartley, N. (2013) *End of Life Care: A guide for therapists, artists and arts therapists*. London: Jessica Kingsley.
Hayes, A., Henry, C., Holloway, M., Lindsay, K., Sherwen, E. and Smith, T. (2014) *Pathways through Care at the End of Life: A guide to person-centred care*. London: Jessica Kingsley.
Henry, C. and Seymour, J. (2011) *Advance Care Planning: A guide for health and social care staff*. London: Department of Health.
Hirschman, K. B., Kapo, J. M. and Karlawish, J. H. T. (2006) Why doesn't a family member of a person with advanced dementia use a substituted judgment when making a decision for that person? *American Journal of Geriatric Psychiatry*. 14(8): 659–667.
Hochschild, A. (1995) The culture of politics: Traditional, postmodern, cold-modern and warm-modern ideals of care. *Social Politics*. 2(3): 331–346.
Hodge, D. (2001) Spiritual assessment: A review of major qualitative methods and a new framework for assessing spirituality. *Social Work*. 46: 203–214.
Hodgson, J. (2005) Working together – a multidisciplinary concern. In Parker, J. (ed.) *Aspects of Social Work and Palliative Care*. London: Quay: 51–66.
Holloway, M. (2007) *Negotiating Death in Contemporary Health and Social Care*. Bristol: Policy Press.
Holloway, M. and Moss, B. H. (2010) *Spirituality and Social Work*. Basingstoke: Palgrave Macmillan.
Holloway, M., Adamson, S., Argyrou, V., Draper, P. and Mariau, D. (2010) *Spirituality in Contemporary Funerals: Final report*. Hull: University of Hull. Retrieved 20 June 2016 from: http://www2.hull.ac.uk/fass/pdf/final.pdf.
Holloway, M., Adamson, S., McSherry, W. and Swinton, J. (2011) *Spiritual Care at the End of Life: A systematic review of the literature*. London: Department of Health.
Hudson, P. and Payne, S. (2009) *Family Carers in Palliative Care: A guide for health and social care professionals*. Oxford: Oxford University Press.
Hudson, P., Quinn, K., O'Hanlon, B. and Aranda, S. (2008) Family meetings in palliative care: Multi-disciplinary clinical practice guidelines. *BMC Palliative Care*. 7: 12. Retrieved 24 October 2014 from: http://www.biomedcentral.com/1472-684X/7/12/.
Independent Review of the Liverpool Care Pathway (2013) *More Care, Less Pathway: A review of the Liverpool Care Pathway*. London: Independent Review of the Liverpool Care Pathway.
Ingleton, C. and Froggatt, K. (2009) Commentary on Hewison A., Badger F., Clifford C. and Thomas K. (2009) Delivering 'Gold Standards' in end-of-life care in care homes: a question of teamwork? *Journal of Clinical Nursing*. 18: 1812–1815.
International Longevity Centre – UK (2015) *At a Cross-roads: The future likelihood of low incomes in old age*. London: Centre for Later Life Funding, ILC-UK.
Ismail, S., Thorlby, R. and Holder, H. (2014) *Focus on Social Care for Older People: Reductions in adult social services for older people in England*. London: The Health Foundation/Nuffield Trust.

Janoski, T. and Gran, B. (2002) Political citizenship: Foundations of rights. In Isin, E. F. and Turner, B. S. (eds) *Handbook of Citizenship Studies*. London: Sage: 13–52.

Jeffreys, J. S. (2005) *Helping Grieving People When Tears Are not Enough: A handbook for care providers*. New York: Brunner-Routledge.

JIT (2015) *Improving Lives Across Scotland: A collection of inspiring digital stories on one DVD*. Edinburgh: NHS Scotland.

Johnson, Y. M. and Stadel, V. L. (2007) Completion of advance directives: Do social work preadmission interviews make a difference? *Research on Social Work Practice* 17(6): 686–696.

Kaplan, D. and Berkman, B. (eds) (2015) *Oxford Handbook of Social Work in Health and Aging*, 2nd edn. New York: Oxford University Press.

Katz, J., Holland, C., Peace, S. and Taylor, E. (2011) *A Better Life: What older people with high support needs value*. York: Joseph Rowntree Memorial Trust. Retrieved 26 October 2014 from: https://www.jrf.org.uk/report/better-life-what-older-people-high-support-needs-value.

Kellehear, A. (2005) *Compassionate Cities: Public health and end-of-life care*. London: Routledge.

Kernohan, W. G., Waldron, M., McAfee, C., Cochrane, B. and Hasson, F. (2007) An evidence base for a palliative care chaplaincy service in Northern Ireland. *Palliative Medicine*. 21: 519–525.

Kharicha, K., Levin, E. and Iliffe, S. (2004) Social work, general practice and evidence-based policy in the collaborative care of older people: Current problems and future possibilities. *Health and Social Care in the Community*. 12(2): 134–141.

Kielmann, T., Huby, G., Powell, A., Sheikh, A., Price, D., Williams, S. and Pinnock, H. (2010) From support to boundary: A qualitative study of the border between self-care and professional care. *Patient Education and Counseling*. 79(1): 55–61.

King, M., Speck, P. and Thomas, A. (1995) The Royal Free interview for religious and spiritual beliefs. *Psychological Medicine*. 25: 1125–1134.

Kissane, D. W. and Bloch, S. (2002) *Family Focused Grief Therapy: A model of family-centred care during palliative care and bereavement*. Maidenhead: Open University Press.

Klein, R. and Kwiatkowska, A. (1999) Representations of intimate male violence in the United States and Poland. Paper given to a Council of Europe Seminar on men and violence towards women. Strasbourg, 7–8 October 1999, http://www.eurowrc.org/13.institutions/3.coe/en-violence-coe/04.en-coe-oct99.htm

Lamura, G., Mnich, E., Nolan, M., Wojszel, B., Krevers, B., Mestheneos, L., and Döhner, H. (2008) Family carers' experiences using support services in Europe: Empirical evidence from the EUROFAMCARE study. *The Gerontologist*. 48(6): 752–771.

Larkin, P. J., de Casterlé, B. D. and Schotsmans, P. (2007) Transition towards end of life in palliative care: An exploration of its meaning for advanced cancer patients in Europe. *Journal of Palliative Care*. 23(2): 69–79.

Laslett, P. (1996) *A Fresh Map of Life: The emergence of the third age*, 2nd edn. Basingstoke: Palgrave Macmillan.

Leadership Alliance for the Care of Dying People (2014) *One Chance to Get it Right: Improving people's experience of care in the last few days and hours of life*. London: LACDP.

Le Bihan, B. and Martin, C. (2006) A Comparative Case Study of Care Systems for Frail Elderly People: Germany, Spain, France, Italy, United Kingdom and Sweden. *Social Policy and Administration*. 40(1): 26–46.

Lethin, C., Hallberg, I. R., Karlsson, S. and Janlöv, A-C. (2015) Family caregivers experiences of formal care when caring for persons with dementia through the process of the disease. *Scandinavian Journal of Caring Sciences*. Published online: 8 September 2015. Retrieved on 10 September 2015 from: http://onlinelibrary.wiley.com/doi/10.1111/scs.12275/abstract?campaign=wolearlyview.

Levinas, E. (1985) *Ethics and Infinity*. Pittsburgh, PA: Duquesne University Press.

Lewis, P. (2007) *Assisted Dying and Legal Change*. Oxford: Oxford University Press.

Lister, R. (2003) *Citizenship: Feminist perspectives*, 2nd edn. Basingstoke: Palgrave Macmillan.

Littlechild, B. and Smith, R. (eds) (2012) *A Handbook for Interprofessional Practice in the Human Services: Learning to work together*. London: Routledge.

Lloyd, L., Calnan, M., Cameron, A., Seymour, J. and Smith, R. (2014) Identity in the fourth age: perseverance, adaptation and maintaining dignity. *Ageing and Society*. 34(1): 1–19.

Lloyd, M. (1997) Dying and bereavement, spirituality and social work in a market economy of welfare. *British Journal of Social Work*. 27(2): 175–190.

Local Government Association (2011) *Public Health Funerals: Final report*. London: Local Government Group.

Lorenz, K. A., Lynn, J., Dy, S. A., Shugarman, L. R., Wilkinson, A., Mularski, R. A., Morton, S. C., Hughes, R. G., Hilton, L. K., Maglione, M., Rhodes, S. L., Rolon, C., Sun, V. C. and Shekelle, P. G. (2008) Evidence for Improving Palliative Care at the End of Life: A Systematic Review. *Annals of Internal Medicine*. 148(2): 147–159.

LTCC-JIT (2009) *Long Term Conditions Collaborative: Improving complex care*. Edinburgh: Scottish Government.

Luptak, M. (2004) Social work and end-of-life care for older people: A historical perspective. *Health and Social Work*. 29(1): 7–15.

Lymbery, M. (2005) *Social Work with Older People: Context, policy and practice*. London: Sage.

Lymbery, M. and Postle, K. (2015) *Social Work and the Transformation of Adult Social Care: Perpetuating a distorted vision?* Bristol: Policy Press.

Lynch, R. (2014) *Social Work Practice with Older People: A positive person-centred approach*. London: Sage.

McDonald, A. (2010) *Social Work with Older People*. Cambridge: Polity Press.

McInniss-Dittrich, K. (2013) *Social Work with Older Adults*, 4th edn. New York: Pearson.

Malhotra, C., Farooqui, M. A., Kanesvaran, R., Bilger, M. and Finkelstein, E. (2015) Comparison of preferences for end-of-life care among patients with advanced cancer and their caregivers: A discrete choice experiment. *Palliative Medicine*. 29(9): 842–850.

Manthorpe, J. and Moriarty, J. (2014) Examining day centre provision for older people in the UK using the Equality Act 2010: Findings of a scoping review. *Health and Social Care in the Community*. 22(4): 352–360.

Marmot Review Team (2010) *Fair Society, Healthy Lives: A Strategic review of health inequalities in England post-2010* (The Marmot Review). London: Marmot Review.

Marshall, M. and Tibbs, M-A. (2006). *Social work and People with Dementia: Partnerships, practice and persistence*. Bristol: Policy Press.

Marshall, T. H. and Bottomore, T. B. (1992) *Citizenship and Social Class*. London: Pluto.

Martinson, M. and Minckler, M. (2006) Civic Engagement and Older Adults: A critical perspective. *The Gerontologist*. 46(3): 318–324.

Monroe, B. (2004) Social work in palliative medicine. In Hanks, G., Cherny, N. I., Christakis, N. A., Fallon, M., Kaasa, S. and Portenoy, R. K. (eds) *Oxford Textbook of Palliative Medicine*, 4th ed. Oxford: Oxford University Press: 184–196.

Monroe, B. and Sheldon, F. (2004) Psychosocial dimensions of care. In Sykes, N., Edmonds, P. and Wiles, J. (eds) *Management of Advanced Disease*. London: Arnold: 405–437.

Morales-Asencio, J. M., Martin-Santos, F. J., Kaknani, S., Morilla-Herrera, J. C., Fernández-Gallego, M., García-Mayor, S., León-Campos, Á. and Morales-Gil, I. M. (2014) Living with chronicity and complexity: Lessons for redesigning case management from patients' life stories – A qualitative study. *Journal of Evaluation in Clinical Practice*. doi: 10.1111/jep.12300.

Morrison, R. S., Chichin, E., Carter, J., Burack, O., Lantz, M. and Meier, D. E. (2006) The Effect of a Social Work Intervention to Enhance Advance Care Planning Documentation in the Nursing Home. *Journal of the American Geriatric Society*. 53: 290–5.

Mowat, H. and O'Neill, M. (2013) *Spirituality and Ageing: Implications for the care and support of older people*. Glasgow: Institute for Research and Innovation in Social Services. Retrieved 30 October 2015 from http://www.iriss.org.uk/resources/spirituality-and-ageing-implications-care-and-support-older-people.

Mullick, A., Martin, J. and Sallnow, L. (2013) An introduction to advance care planning in practice. *British Medical Journal*. 347: 16074. Retrieved 16 June 2016 from: http://www.goldstandardsframework.org.uk/cd-content/uploads/files/ACP/An%20intro%20to%20advance%20care%20planning%20in%20practice.pdf.

Naik, A. D., Burnett, J., Pickens-Pace, S. and Dyer, C. B. (2008) Impairment in instrumental activities of daily living and the geriatric syndrome of self-neglect. *The Gerontologist.* 48(3): 388–393.

Naleppa, M. J. and Reid, W. J. (2003) *Gerontological Social Work: A task-centered approach.* New York: Columbia University Press.

Narayanaswamy, A. (2006) Reflections and conclusion. In Narayanaswamy, A. (ed.) *Spiritual Care and Transcultural Care Research.* London: Quay: 176–198.

National End of Life Care Programme (2010) *Supporting People to Live and Die Well: A framework for social care at the end of life* (Report of the Social Care Advisory Group of the National End of Life Care Programme). London: Department of Health.

National End of Life Care Programme (2012) *The Route to Success in End of Life Care – Achieving quality for social work.* London: National End of Life Care Programme.

National Institute for Clinical Excellence (2004) *Improving Supportive and Palliative Care for Adults with Cancer: The manual.* London: National Institute for Clinical Excellence. Retrieved 23 October 2015 from https://www.nice.org.uk/guidance/csgsp.

National Institute for Health and Care Excellence (2011) *End of Life Care for Adults: Quality standard 13.* London: NICE. Retrieved 23 October 2015 from https://www.nice.org.uk/guidance/qs13.

National Institute for Health and Care Excellence (2015) *Older People with Social Care Needs and Multiple Long-term Conditions.* London: NICE.

NCEPOD (National Confidential Enquiry into Patient Outcome and Death) (2009) *Caring to the End? A review of the care of patients who died in hospital within four days of admission.* London: National Confidential Enquiry into Patient Outcome and Death.

Netten, A., Burge, P., Malley, J., Potoglou, D., Towers, A.-M., Brazier, J., Flynn, T., Forder, J. and Wall, B. (2012) Outcomes of social care for adults: Developing a preference weighted measure. *Health Technology Assessment.* 16(16). Retrieved 30 October 2015 from http://www.journalslibrary.nihr.ac.uk/hta/volume-16/issue-16#hometab0.

Neugarten, B. L. (1974) Age groups in American society and the rise of the young-old. *Annals of the American Academy of Political and Social Science.* 415(1):187–198.

NHS Choices (2014) *Euthanasia and Assisted Suicide.* Retrieved 21 June 2016 from: http://www.nhs.uk/conditions/euthanasiaandassistedsuicide/pages/introduction.aspx.

NHS Improving Quality (2014) *Planning for Your Future Care: A guide.* London: NHSIQ.

Nichol, J., Teiderman, M. and Valiquet, D. (2013) *Euthanasia and Assisted Suicide: International experiences.* Ottawa: Library of Parliament.

Noddings, N. (1984) *Caring: A feminine approach to ethics and moral education,* Berkeley, CA: University of California Press.

O'Connor, D. and Purves, B. (eds) (2009) *Decision-making, Personhood and Dementia: Exploring the interface.* London: Jessica Kingsley.

Office for National Statistics (2015) *National Life Tables, United Kingdom, 2012–2014.* London: ONS. Retrieved 22 October 2015 from: http://www.ons.gov.uk/ons/rel/lifetables/national-life-tables/2012-2014/stb-life-tables-2012-2014.html.

Ota, S. (2015) *Housing an Ageing Population (England)* (Briefing Paper 07423). London: House of Commons Library.

Pacheco, J., Hirschberger, P. J., Markert, R. J. and Kumar, G. (2003) A longitudinal study of attitudes toward physician-assisted suicide and euthanasia among patients with non-curable malignancy. *American Journal of Hospice and Palliative Medicine.* 20(2): 99–104.

Park, A.-L. (2014) Do intergenerational activities do any good for older adults' well-being? A brief review. *Gerontology and Geriatric Research.* 3(5): 1–3.

Park, A., Bryson, C., Clery, E., Curtice, J. and Phillips, M. (eds.) (2013) *British Social Attitudes: The 30th report.* London: NatCen Social Research.

Parker, R. (1981) Tending and social policy. In Goldberg, E. M. and Hatch, S. (eds) *A New Look at the Personal Social Services.* London: Policy Studies Institute: 17–32.

Parker, G. and Lawton, D. (1994) *Different Types of Care, Different Types of Carer.* London: HMSO.

Parkes, C. M. and Prigerson, H. G. (2010) *Bereavement: Studies of grief in adult life*. London: Routledge.

Parry, R., Land, V., Faull, C. Feathers, L. and Seymour, J. (2016) Engaging terminally ill patients in end of life talk: How experienced palliative medicine doctors navigate the dilemma of promoting discussions about dying. *PLoS ONE*. 11(5): e0156174.

Partington, L. (2006) The challenges of adopting care pathways for the dying for use in care homes. *International Journal of Older People Nursing* 1: 51–55.

Partridge, R. and Campbell, C. (2007) *Artificial Nutrition and Hydration – Guidance in end of life care for adults*. London: National Council for Palliative Care/Association of Palliat Med.

Pasman, H. R. W., Rurup, M. L., Willems, D. L. and Onwuteaka-Philipsen, B. D. (2009) Concept of unbearable suffering in context of ungranted requests for euthanasia: Qualitative interviews with patients and physicians. *British Medical Journal*. 339: b4362.

Payne, M. (1995) *Social Work and Community care*. Basingstoke: Macmillan.

Payne, M. (2000) *Teamwork in Multiprofessional Care*. Basingstoke: Macmillan.

Payne, M. (2006) Teambuilding: How, why and where? In Speck, P. (ed.) *Teamwork in Palliative Care: Fulfilling or frustrating?* Oxford: Oxford University Press: 117–136.

Payne, M. (2009) *Social Care Practice in Context*. Basingstoke: Palgrave Macmillan.

Payne, M. (2010) Advance care planning in participative social work practice. *Revista Portugueasa de Pedagogia/Psychologica*. Numero Conjunto Comemorativo 30 Anos, 2010: 105–119.

Payne, M. (2011) *Humanistic Social Work: Core principles in practice*. Basingstoke: Palgrave Macmillan.

Payne, M. (2012) *Citizenship Social Work with Older People*. Bristol: Policy Press.

Payne, M. (2014) Exploring meaning in end-of-life care practice. *European Journal of Palliative Care*. 21(5): 240–244.

Payne, M. (2015) Assisted dying: Moral panic or moral issue? In Smith, M. (ed.) *Moral Regulation*. Bristol: Policy Press: 57–68.

Payne, M. and Askeland, G. A. (2008) *Globalization and International Social Work: Postmodern change and challenge*. Aldershot: Ashgate.

Payne, M. and Oliviere, D. (2008) The interdisciplinary team. In Walsh, D. (ed.) *Palliative Medicine*. New York: Saunders Elsevier: 253–259.

Payne, S. and EAPC Task Force on Family Carers (2010) White Paper on improving support for family carers in palliative care: Part 2. *European Journal of Palliative Care*. 17(6): 286–290.

Piaggesi, D. (2003) The knowledge economy: Creating conditions for caring communities of the 21st century in the Latin American region. In: *The Age of Digital Opportunity: Connecting the generations*. New York: United Nations Information and Communication Technologies Task Force, International Council For Caring Communities, Inter-American Development Bank, United Nations Programme On Ageing, United Nation Programme For Human Settlements: 16–18.

Pickard, L. (2015) A growing care gap? The supply of unpaid care for older people by their adult children in England to 2032. *Ageing and Society*. 35(1): 96–123.

Pierret, C. R. (2006) The 'sandwich generation': Women caring for parents and children. *Monthly Labor Review*. September 2006: 2–9.

Pifer, A. and Bronte, D. L. (1986) Introduction: squaring the pyramid. *Daedalus*. 115(1): 1–12.

Pino, M., Parry, R., Land, V., Faull, C., Feathers, L. and Seymour, J. (2016) Engaging terminally ill patients in end of life talk: How experienced palliative medicine doctors navigate the dilemma of promoting discussions about dying. *PLoS ONE* 11(5): e0156174. doi:10.1371/journal.pone.0156174

Rabow, M., Hauser, J. and Adams, J. (2004) Supporting family caregivers at the end of life. *Journal of the American Medical Association*. 291(4): 483–491.

Ratner, E., Norlander, L. and McSteen, K. (2001) Death at home following a targeted advance-care planning process at home: The kitchen table discussion. *Journal of the American Geriatric Society*. 49(6): 778–781.

Ray, M. and Phillips, J. (2012) *Social Work with Older People*, 5th edn. Basingstoke: Palgrave Macmillan.

Ray, M., Bernard, M. and Phillips, J. (2009) *Critical Issues in Social Work with Older People*. Basingstoke: Palgrave Macmillan.

Reed, J., Cook, G., Childs, S. and McCormack, B. (2005) A literature review to explore integrated care for older people. *International Journal of Integrated Care.* 5: e17. Retrieved 31 July 2015 from: http://www.ncbi.nlm.nih.gov/pmc/articles/PMC1395528/.

Reese, D. J. and Sontag, M-A. (2001) Successful interprofessional collaboration on the hospice team. *Health and Social Work.* 26(2): 167–175.

Reid, W. J. and Hanrahan, P. (1982) Recent evaluations of social work: Grounds for optimism. *Social Work.* 27: 328–340.

Reith, M. and Payne, M. (2009) *Social Work in End-of-Life and Palliative Care.* Bristol: Policy Press.

Richardson, V. E. and Barusch, A. S. (2010) *Gerontological Practice for the Twenty-first Century: A social work perspective.* New York: Columbia University Press.

Riley, G. F. and Lubitz, J. D. (2010) Long-term trends in medicare payments in the last year of life. *Health Services Research* 45(2): 565–576.

Robertson, G. K. (2014) Transitions in later life: A review of the challenge and opportunities for policy development. *Working with Older People.* 18(4): 186–196.

Robinson, V. and Scott, H. (2012) Why assisted suicide must remain illegal in the UK. *Nursing Standard* 26(18): 40–48.

Royal College of Physicians (2009) *Advance Care Planning: National guidelines.* London: Royal College of Physicians.

Rubin, A. (1985) Practice effectiveness: More grounds for optimism. *Social Work.* 30: 469–476.

Samanta, A. and Samanta, J. (2006) Advance directives, best interests and clinical judgement: shifting sands at the end of life. *Clinical Medicine.* 6(3): 274–278.

Samsi, K. and Manthorpe, J. (2011) 'I live for today': A qualitative study investigating older people's attitudes to advance planning. *Health and Social Care in the Community.* 19(1): 52–59.

Scharf, T. and Keating, N. C. (eds) (2012) *From Exclusion to Inclusion in Old Age: A global challenge.* Bristol: Policy Press.

Schut, H. and Stoebe, M. W. (2005) Interventions to enhance adaptation to bereavement. *Journal of Palliative Medicine.* 8(s1): S-140–147.

Schut, H., Stroebe, M. S., van den Bout, J. and Terhaggen, M. (2001) The efficacy of bereavement interventions: Determining who benefits. In Stroebe, M. S., Hansson, R. O., Stroebe, W. and Schut, H. (2001) *Handbook of Bereavement Research: Consequences, coping and care.* Washington, DC: American Psychological Association: 705–737.

Sennett, R. (2003) *Respect: The formation of character in an age of inequality.* London: Penguin.

Sevenhuijsen, S. (1998) *Citizenship and the Ethics of Care: Feminist considerations of justice, morality and politics.* London: Routledge.

Shanley, C., Whitmore, E., Khoo, A., Cartwright, C., Walker, A. and Cumming, R. G. (2009) Understanding how advance care planning is approached in the residential aged care setting: A continuum model of practice as an explanatory device. *Australasian Journal on Ageing.* 28(4): 211–215.

Sheldon, F. (1997) *Psychosocial Palliative Care: Good practice in the care of the dying and bereaved.* Cheltenham: Thornes.

Silverman, P. (2000) *Never Too Young to Know: Death in children's lives.* New York: Oxford University Press.

Social Care Institute for Excellence (2015) *The Care Act: Safeguarding Adults.* Retrieved 8 July 2015 from: http://www.scie.org.uk/care-act-2014/safeguarding-adults/.

Speck, P. (2004) Spiritual concerns. In Sykes, N., Edmonds, P. and Wiles, J. (eds) *Management of Advanced Disease.* London: Arnold: 471–481.

Speck, P. (ed.) (2006) *Teamwork in Palliative Care: Fulfilling or frustrating?* Oxford: Oxford University Press.

Spector, W. D., Katz, S., Murphy, J. B. and Fulton, J. P. (1987) The hierarchical relationship between activities of daily living and instrumental activities of daily living. *Journal of Chronic Diseases.* 40(6): 481–489.

SPRU (2000) *Introducing an Outcome Focus into Care Management and User Surveys.* York: Social Policy Research Unit.

Stephen, A. (2012) Bereavement and older people. In Wimpenny, P. and Costello, J. (eds) *Grief, Loss and Bereavement: Evidence and practice for health and social care professionals.* Hove: Routledge.

Stirrat, R. (1997) The new orthodoxy and old truths: Participation, empowerment and other buzzwords. In Bastian, S., Bastian, N. and Niviran, D. (eds) *Assessing Participation: A debate from South Asia.* Delhi: Konark: 67–92.

Stroebe, M. S. and Schut, H. (2001) Models of coping with bereavement: A review. In Stroebe, M. S., Hansson, R. O., Stroebe, W. and Schut, H. (2001) *Handbook of Bereavement Research: Consequences, coping and care.* Washington, DC: American Psychological Association: 375–403.

Stroebe, M. S., Hansson, R. O., Stroebe, W. and Schut, H. (2001) Introduction: Concepts and issues in contemporary research on bereavement. In: Stroebe, M. S., Hansson, R. O., Stroebe, W. and Schut, H. (2001) *Handbook of Bereavement Research: Consequences, coping and care.* Washington DC: American Psychological Association: 3–22.

Stroebe, M., Schut, H. and Stroebe, W. (2007) Health outcomes of bereavement. *Lancet.* 370: 1960–1973.

Stroebe, M., Schut, H. and van den Bout, J. (eds) (2013) *Complicated Grief: Scientific foundations for health care professionals.* Abingdon: Routledge.

Sudore, R. L. and Fried, T. R. (2010) Redefining the 'planning' in advance care planning: Preparing for end-of-life decision making. *Annals of Internal Medicine.* 153(4): 256–261.

SunLife (2014) *Cost of Dying, 2014: The 8th annual report.* London: AXA Wealth Services.

Supreme Court of Canada (2015) *Carter v. Canada (Attorney General)* 2015SCC 5 File No.: 35591. Retrieved 21 June 2016 from: http://scc-csc.lexum.com/scc-csc/scc-csc/en/14637/1/document.do.

Sutherland Commission (1999) *With Respect to Old Age: Long term care – rights and responsibilities.* Report of the Royal Commission on Long-term Care (Cm 4192-I). London: TSO.

Sutherland, S. (2008) *The Independent Review of Free Personal and Nursing Care in Scotland.* Edinburgh: Scottish Government.

Theodoulou, G. (2014) Causes of dementia. In Coope, B. and Richard, F. (eds) *ABC of Dementia.* Oxford: Wiley/BMJ Books.

Thomlison, R. J. (1984) Something works: Evidence from practice effectiveness studies. *Social Work.* 29: 51–57.

Thornicroft, G. (2006) *Shunned: Discrimination against people with mental illness.* New York: Oxford University Press.

Tonkiss, K. and Bloom, T. (2016) Theorising noncitizenship: Concepts, debates and challenges. *Citizenship Studies.* 19(8): 837–852.

Tronto, J. C. (1993) *Moral Boundaries: A political argument for an ethic of care.* New York: Routledge.

Tsiris, G., Tasker, M., Lawson, V., Prince, G., Dives, T., Sands, M. and Ridley, A. (2011) Music and arts in health promotion and death education: The St Christopher's Schools Project. *Music and Arts in Action.* 3(2): 96–119.

Tunstall-Pedoe, H., Bailey, L., Chamberlain, D. A., Marsden, A. K., Ward, M. E. and Zideman, D. A. (1992) Survey of 3765 cardiopulmonary resuscitations in British hospitals (the BRESUS study): Methods and overall results. *British Medical Journal.* 1992(304): 1347–1351.

van Ewijk, H. (2009) *European Social Policy and Social Work: Citizenship-based social work.* London: Routledge.

van Oorschot, W., Balvers, M., Schols, M. and Lodewijks, I. (2009). *European Comparative Data on the Situation of Disabled People: An annotated review.* Leeds: University of Leeds. Retrieved 20 January 2013 from: http://www.disability-europe.net/content/aned/media/ANED%20report%20European%20Comparative%20Data%20on%20the%20Situation%20of%20Disabled%20People%20%28corrected%29.pdf.

Verleye, K. and Gemmel, P. (2009) *Innovation in the Elderly Care Sector: At the edge of chaos.* Leuven: Flanders District of Creativity.

Victor, C. R. (2010) *Ageing, Health and Care.* Bristol: Policy Press.

Victor, C., Scambler, S. and Bond, J. (2009) *The Social World of Older People.* Maidenhead: Open University Press.

Videka-Sherman, L. (1988) Meta-analysis of research on social work practice in mental health. *Social Work*. 33: 325–328.

Volandes, A. E., Paasche-Orlow, M. K., Barry, M. J., Gillick, M. R., Minaker, M. L., Chang, Y., Cook, E. F., Abbo, E. D., El-Jawahri, A. and Mitchell, S. L. (2009) Video decision support tool for advance care planning in dementia: Randomised controlled trial. *British Medical Journal*. 338: b1964. Retrieved 28 September 2010 from: http://www.bmj.com/content/338/bmj.b2159.full.pdf.

Walter, T. (1992) Modern death: Taboo or not taboo. *Sociology*. 25(2): 293–310.

Wanless, D., Forder, J., Fernandez, J.-L., Poole, T., Beesley, L., Henwood, M. and Moscone, F. (2006) *Wanless Social Care Review: Securing good care for older people*. London: The King's Fund.

Warburton, R. (1999) *Improving Management Information for the Effective Commissioning of Social Care Services for Older People: Handbook for middle managers and operational staff*. London: Department of Health.

Watson, M., Lucas, C., Hoy, A. and Wells, J. (2009) *Oxford Handbook of Palliative Care*, 2nd edn. Oxford: Oxford University Press.

Weissbrodt, D. and Divine, M. (2016) Unequal access to human rights: The categories of noncitizenship. *Citizenship Studies*: 19(8): 870–891.

Whittington, C. (2003) Collaboration and partnership in context. In Weinstein, J., Whittington, C. and Leiba, T. (eds) *Collaboration in Social Work Practice*. London: Jessica Kingsley: 13–38.

Wiles, J. L., Leibing, A., Guberman, N., Reeve, J. and Allen, R. E. S. (2011) The meaning of 'Aging in Place' to older people. *The Gerontologist*. 52(3): 357–366.

Woodthorpe, K., Rumble, H. and Valentine, C. (2013) Putting 'the grave' into social policy: State support for funerals in contemporary UK society. *Journal of Social Policy*. 42(3): 605–622.

World Health Organization (1998) *WHO Definition of Palliative Care*. Retrieved 3 September 2015 from http://www.who.int/cancer/palliative/definition/en/.

World Health Organization (2002) *Active Ageing: A policy framework*. Geneva: World Health Organization.

World Health Organization (2007) *Global Age-Friendly Cities: A Guide*. Geneva: World Health Organization.

Ylänne, V. (ed) (2012) *Representing Ageing: Images and identities*. Basingstoke: Palgrave Macmillan.

Youdin, R. (2014) *Clinical Gerontological Social Work Practice*. New York: Springer.

# INDEX

abuse 29–30, 33, 39, 50, 57, 98, 127–9, 130–4, 166, 170
active ageing 21, 110, 115
active citizens 20, 27, 167
active intervention 121–2
activities in later life 103–5, 118–9, 137, 144, 146, 170
activities of daily living 31–2, 34, 118, 125–7, 130, 135
adult social care 7, 12–13, 74, 85, 139
advance decisions/directives 81–3, 86, 88; *see also* advance care planning
advance care planning (acp) 13, 24, 37–8, 79–82, 86–94; *see also* care planning, person-centred care planning
advocacy 65, 108–10, 122, 170
age-friendly cities, environments 110–1, 115
ageing 1–4, 11–13, 112, 115, 127–8, 159, 167–8
ageing in place 123
ageing journey 13–18, 19–20, 162
Alzheimer's disease 134–5; *see also* dementia
assisted dying 1, 34, 149–55
assistive technology 38, 106
autonomy 64, 102, 128, 133, 148, 154–5, 160

bereavement 5, 13, 16–18, 21–3, 34, 58, 60, 107, 118, 134, 137, 140, 141–2, 155–62

cardio-pulmonary resuscitation (CPR) 66, 68, 81, 89
care 13, 15, 54–7, 105–6; costs 100–1, 106–7; deficit 3–4, 124; homes 68, 73–5, 77, 84, 87–9, 91, 102, 106–7, 113, 144–6; management 79–80, 84–6, 122–4
Care Act 2014 85–6, 88, 98, 130

care planning 47–9, 60, 79–80, 84–6, 88; *see also* advance care planning, person-centred care planning, planning for ageing
carers 3, 23, 43, 52–3, 63–6, 69, 72, 79, 85–6, 97–8, 112–4, 121, 137, 142, 145–6, 166–7, 169–70; assessments 85, 141
children and dying 58–9, 83, 107–8, 113–4, 153, 158–60, 161–2
choice 13, 37, 85, 92, 100, 111, 121, 128, 141, 154–5, 167
citizening 2, 5–6, 13, 17–18, 30–1, 41, 45, 49, 53, 56, 59, 63, 65, 66, 69, 97, 99, 117–20, 122, 127, 129, 132, 134, 137, 143, 144, 149, 165–9; definition 28
citizenship 4, 18, 26–8, 36–7, 40, 69–70, 100, 165–6; and older people 13, 20, 29–32; as process 2, 28–9, 165–6; cognitive 30; social work 2–3, 18–21, 33–41, 80, 91–2, 97, 117–8, 127, 138, 165–6, 169
class 17, 39, 46, 98, 169
co-citizens 26, 35, 165, 167–9
communication 23, 30–1, 35, 67–70, 80, 83, 89, 108, 110, 120–1, 140–1, 146, 148, 161, 170
communitarianism 20, 29, 40
community 3–6, 13, 16, 18, 22–3, 31, 34–5, 37, 40, 43–4, 46, 50–1, 57, 60, 63–4, 74–5, 83, 100, 103, 107–8, 110–1, 114–5, 118–9, 144, 125, 127, 144, 148, 167–70
confidentiality 64, 65, 76,
connectedness in care 56–7, 103, 167, 169, 171
continuing bonds in bereavement 156
continuity: in the life course 13–14, 32, 38, 43, 50, 57–9, 69, 97, 119, 122–3, 137–8, 166–9; of care 57–9, 63–4, 69–70, 76, 86, 89
continuous deep sedation 151
control 37, 117

coordination, policy and structural 71–3, 129, 141, 168

death 1, 12–14, 16, 18, 21–3, 31–6, 58–9, 67, 82–4, 107, 140–4, 152, 155, 159–162
de-citizening 2, 13, 18, 20–1, 30–1, 35–6, 40–1, 46–9, 52, 54, 72, 91–2, 100, 106, 111, 114, 118, 120, 122, 124, 127–9, 134, 136, 148, 155–6, 162, 165–9; definition 28; *see also* citizening, re-citizening
deprivation of liberties safeguards 144, 164
direct payments 86, 106, 112, 123; *see also* person-centred care planning
disenfranchised grief 161
diversity, spiritual 52–3
dementia 30–1, 84, 87, 88, 93, 105, 113, 134–7, 139; *see also* mental capacity
dependence/-y 15–17, 19, 20–2, 27–8, 31–22, 40, 80, 152, 167–8; ratio 11–12
dignity 5, 37, 56, 98, 108–9, 118, 152, 154
discretion 65, 71, 142–3; *see also* advocacy
dying 2–5, 13–19, 22, 31–3, 40, 43, 58–9, 68, 72, 74, 98, 107, 127, 141, 144–9, 167
Dying Matters consortium 116
dying well 2–4, 13–18, 34, 62, 107, 147–9

emotional labour 5, 56
end-of-life care 2, 4, 16, 18, 21–4, 32, 43, 120, 80, 121–2, 141–9, 162, 163; settings for 5, 32, 43 55, 70, 73–5, 86, 92, 102, 141
ethics of care approach 20, 31, 45, 56, 113, 167
European Association for Palliative Care 87
exclusion 26, 29–32, 37, 40–1, 65, 72, 77, 83, 107, 121, 128, 162, 164, 166, 168

families, social work role with 23, 34–5, 37, 40, 43, 49–50, 55–7, 60, 63–5, 82–3, 86–7, 107–8, 113–4, 141–4, 147–55, 158–62
finances in later life 100–1, 118, 142–4
fourth age 15–18, 115, 117–8
frailty 4, 33, 44, 47, 54, 60, 69, 83, 84, 87–8, 114, 121, 128, 142, 145–8
funerals 32, 88, 100, 120, 143–4, 146, 159–60, 164

Gold Standards Framework (GSF) 67, 75, 78
grief 5, 18, 32, 140, 146, 156–64

healthcare system 2, 50, 64, 65, 114
health in later life 104, 119, 144
high support needs 3, 15, 18, 47
holidays in later life 104–5, 120, 145
holistic practice 22, 23–4, 43, 47, 50–1, 63–4, 86, 90, 97
housing in later life 101–3, 106, 110, 118–9, 144; *see also* supported housing
humanistic social work 2, 18–19, 104, 119, 166

human rights 2, 22, 33, 36, 92, 119, 154, 166–7; *see also* rights
hydration 66, 68–9, 82

independent budgeting 85–6; *see also* person-centred care planning
inequalities 1–2, 29, 39–40, 46, 75, 128, 169
innovation strategies 108–9
integration: in family/community 22, 64, 102; in health & social care 2, 37, 63–4, 70–1, 86, 106, 108
interdependence 15, 31, 167–8

Leadership Alliance for the Care of Dying People 67, 69–70
learning disabilities 22, 83, 160
linkages 64, 65, 170
Liverpool Care Pathway 67–9
local authority/government 36, 43–4, 51, 85–6, 102–3, 130, 143, 145
long-term care 81, 84, 87, 91–2, 138
long-term conditions 78, 80, 83–4, 87, 90–2, 105, 107, 114, 121–2, 162

meaning 32, 52–3
medical model 49
mental capacity 31, 81, 84, 89, 93, 120, 135, 137, 139, 144, 164
multiprofessional 6, 13, 23–4, 43, 63–4, 70–1, 73, 75, 77

neo-liberal policy 14, 19, 21, 31
National Council for Palliative Care 93
National End of Life Care Programme 2, 4, 18, 67–8, 93, 146, 163
National Institute for Care and Health Excellence/for Clinical Excellence (NICE) 18, 50, 87
neglect 3, 33, 50, 98, 127, 129, 130, 132; *see also* self-neglect
negotiation 64, 85, 113, 122
networks, service/support 22, 30, 34–5, 64, 83, 98, 103, 115, 122–3, 127, 131, 160; *see also* linkages
new technology 3, 30, 41, 109, 111, 168; *see also* assistive technology, telecare
nutrition 66–9, 82, 128, 132, 156

ordinary living movement 85
other, older person as 18–19
outcomes approaches 124–5, 139

palliative care 16, 33, 42–4, 47–50, 54–6, 59–61, 65–8, 73, 76, 79–81, 84, 85, 87–8, 105, 114, 141, 146; registers 72, 109
participation 2, 13, 18, 22, 27, 33, 35, 39–40, 83, 87, 91, 98, 110, 118, 119, 123–5, 167, 169–70

partnership 63, 69–71, 86, 110, 122, 127; barriers to 71–2
pathway for end-of-life care 5, 18, 21, 71–3, 141; *see also* Liverpool Care Pathway
personal assistants 85–6, 112
personalization *see* person-centred care planning
person-centred care planning 2, 4, 45, 47, 69, 77, 86, 112, 122–4, 128, 137, 150, 163; *see also* advance care planning, care planning
Physician Orders for Life-Sustaining Treatment (POLST) 89
planning for ageing 5, 99–100, 118, 120
poverty 4, 51, 98, 101, 106–7, 119, 143
practice strategy 5, 19, 98–9, 165, 169–71; definition 5, 169–70
Preferred Priorities for Care 66, 80
proxy decision-making 84–5, 120
public choice policy 85

quality of life 3, 5, 38, 45–7, 57, 60, 70, 90, 103, 108–12, 119, 121, 125, 137, 139, 149, 166, 170

re-citizening 2, 13, 28, 32, 41, 46, 49, 50–2, 92, 97, 114, 117, 133–4, 144, 155, 162, 165–9; definition 28; *see also* citizening, de-citizening
resuscitation 67–9, 89–90, 141; *see also* cardio-pulmonary resuscitation
rights: for patients 65–6; to end-of-life care 33–4; *see also* human rights
risk 29–30, 39, 82, 103–4, 109, 125, 127–34, 144–5, 159

safeguarding 3–4, 60, 117, 127–34, 166, 169–70
sandwich care 113–4

schools 107–8, 112, 116, 158
security 3–4, 31, 100, 104, 118, 127–9, 133–4, 138, 147, 157, 166
self-determination 47, 53–4, 60, 150, 154
self-directed support *see* person-centred care planning
self-neglect 132, 135
social, the 22, 42–6, 50, 60, 64
social action 99, 108–12, 170
social citizenship 26–9, 165–6; *see also* citizenship
social work: and healthcare 42–6, 57–9; in end-of-life care 4, 21–3, 54–7, 60, 75–6, 147–9; valuation 44–5; with older people 2, 4, 7, 19, 21, 52, 110, 125–6, 134, 162
spirituality 51–4, 60, 61, 83
supported housing 101–2, 106
surprise question 88
surveillance 57, 128
Sutherland Commission on long-term care 107
symptom management 47–9, 60

teamwork, interpersonal 64, 70–1, 76–7, 99
telecare 38; *see also* new technology
third age 15–18, 98–9, 101
transcendence 52–3
transition: between curative and palliative care 58; in later life 14–15
transport 30, 36, 110

Wanless review of social care 107
well-being 34, 44–7, 97–8
World Health Organization (WHO) 2, 6, 21, 58, 61, 110–1

# Taylor & Francis eBooks

## Helping you to choose the right eBooks for your Library

Add Routledge titles to your library's digital collection today. Taylor and Francis ebooks contains over 50,000 titles in the Humanities, Social Sciences, Behavioural Sciences, Built Environment and Law.

Choose from a range of subject packages or create your own!

**Benefits for you**
- Free MARC records
- COUNTER-compliant usage statistics
- Flexible purchase and pricing options
- All titles DRM-free.

**Benefits for your user**
- Off-site, anytime access via Athens or referring URL
- Print or copy pages or chapters
- Full content search
- Bookmark, highlight and annotate text
- Access to thousands of pages of quality research at the click of a button.

REQUEST YOUR **FREE** INSTITUTIONAL TRIAL TODAY

**Free Trials Available**
We offer free trials to qualifying academic, corporate and government customers.

## eCollections – Choose from over 30 subject eCollections, including:

| | |
|---|---|
| Archaeology | Language Learning |
| Architecture | Law |
| Asian Studies | Literature |
| Business & Management | Media & Communication |
| Classical Studies | Middle East Studies |
| Construction | Music |
| Creative & Media Arts | Philosophy |
| Criminology & Criminal Justice | Planning |
| Economics | Politics |
| Education | Psychology & Mental Health |
| Energy | Religion |
| Engineering | Security |
| English Language & Linguistics | Social Work |
| Environment & Sustainability | Sociology |
| Geography | Sport |
| Health Studies | Theatre & Performance |
| History | Tourism, Hospitality & Events |

For more information, pricing enquiries or to order a free trial, please contact your local sales team:
www.tandfebooks.com/page/sales

 Routledge
Taylor & Francis Group

The home of
Routledge books

www.tandfebooks.com

Printed in Great Britain
by Amazon

82750416R00113